Ritual, Personhood and the New Animism.

Ritual, Personhood and the New Animism

Essays in Honour of Graham Harvey

Edited by
David G. Robertson and Paul-François Tremlett

SHEFFIELD UK   BRISTOL CT

Published by Equinox Publishing Ltd.

UK Office 415, The Workstation, 15 Paternoster Row, Sheffield,
    South Yorkshire S1 2BX
USA ISD, 70 Enterprise Drive, Bristol, CT 06010

www.equinoxpub.com

First published 2025

© David G. Robertson, Paul-François Tremlett and contributors 2025

All rights reserved. No part of this publication may be reproduced or transmitted in any form or by any means, electronic or mechanical, including photocopying, recording or any information storage or retrieval system, without prior permission in writing from the publishers.

British Library Cataloguing-in-Publication Data

A catalogue record for this book is available from the British Library.

ISBN-13		
	978 1 80050 580 3	(hardback)
	978 1 80050 581 0	(paperback)
	978 1 80050 582 7	(ePDF)
	978 1 80050 669 5	(ePub)

Library of Congress Cataloging-in-Publication Data

Names: Robertson, David G. (David George) editor | Tremlett, Paul-François editor | Harvey, Graham, 1959- honoree
Title: Ritual, personhood and the new animism : essays in honour of Graham Harvey / edited by David G. Robertson and Paul-François Tremlett.
Description: Sheffield, South Yorkshire ; Bristol, CT : Equinox Publishing Ltd, 2025. | Includes bibliographical references and index. | Summary: "Graham Harvey's work has had an impact on fields as diverse as environmentalism, ritual, indigenous religion, folklore, and beyond academia. Yet there is a clear through-line, as this volume suggests, a concern with personhood, communication and community which bridges the lived religion approach with emerging network- and rhizome-based theoretical models"-- Provided by publisher.
Identifiers: LCCN 2025020331 (print) | LCCN 2025020332 (ebook) | ISBN 9781800505803 hardback | ISBN 9781800505810 paperback | ISBN 9781800505827 pdf | ISBN 9781800506695 epub
Subjects: LCSH: Indigenous peoples--Religion | Animism | Ritual | Rites and ceremonies | Material culture
Classification: LCC BL380 .R58 2025 (print) | LCC BL380 (ebook) | DDC 202/.1--dc23/eng/20250617
LC record available at https://lccn.loc.gov/2025020331
LC ebook record available at https://lccn.loc.gov/2025020332

Typeset by Sparks – www.sparkspublishing.com

Contents

1 Introduction: Live in Fragments No Longer   1
  Paul-François Tremlett and David G. Robertson

2 In Search of Ceremony: Dialogues with Indigeneity and Graham
  Harvey at the ORIGINS Festival   15
  Michael Walling

3 Indigenous Tourism: A Perfect Site for "Guesthood" Research?   33
  Helen Jennings

4 "Guesthood" as a Scientific Method: Principles Supporting
  Relational Research   55
  James L. Cox

5 Harebrained?   73
  Michael Houseman

6 Spirit Possession and Trance as Humpty Dumpty Words:
  Reflection on Adjusted Styles of Communication   91
  Bettina E. Schmidt

7 Plants and People/Plants as People: Plants and Their Medicinal
  and Ritual Uses in Mesoamerica and South America and
  Religions in the Caribbean   106
  Christina Welch

8 The Animacy of Fire and Personhood of Plants in Indigenous-
  led Land Restoration   130
  Sarah M. Pike

9 Gaian Animism: Ritual Innovation and Nature Spirituality in
  Radical Environmentalism and the Global Environmental Milieu   147
  Bron Taylor

10 Rituals, Wood, Bone, and Stone: Material Approaches to
    Indigenous Religions   169
    Amy R. Whitehead

Index   189

1 Introduction: Live in Fragments No Longer

Paul-François Tremlett and David G. Robertson

Introduction

> Only connect! That was the whole of her sermon. Only connect the prose and the passion, and both will be exalted, and human love will be seen at its height. Live in fragments no longer. (Forster, 1910)

Graham Harvey's career has been defined by connection. Connections with academic communities, pagan and indigenous communities and also non-human communities. Graham's work – from his early publications on British Pagans, his pioneering work on the New Animism to more recently the everyday relational model of religion presented in *Food, Sex and Strangers* – has had an impact on fields as diverse as environmentalism, ritual, indigenous religion, folklore and beyond academia. Yet there is a clear through-line, as this volume will suggest, a concern with personhood, communication, ethics and materiality which bridges the lived religion approach with emerging network- and rhizome-based theoretical models. He pursued work that connected Religious Studies and other disciplines – environmentalism, anthropology, politics and social theory. In doing so, he established a network of colleagues and students who have been inspired by his work, or benefitted from working with him – and some of them are contributors to this volume. And as Graham is a well-known raconteur, let us begin with his story.

Graham gained his PhD at the University of Newcastle under the supervision of Professor John F. A. Sawyer in 1991, on the rhetorics of group identity in ancient Jewish literatures (including the Qumran scrolls, apocryphal and apocalyptic texts, as well as early Christian and formative Rabbinic writings). A version of this thesis later was published as his first monograph, *The True Israel: Uses of the Names Jew, Hebrew and Israel in Ancient Jewish and Early Christian Literature*, by Brill in 1996. He taught part-time at Newcastle during this period, but in 1996 he took up a job as Reader/Principal Lecturer in Religious Studies at King Alfred's College, Winchester (now the University of Winchester).

But, having grown up near Stonehenge and having participated in the free festivals at the site during the 1970s and early 1980s, he had also begun conducting fieldwork among Pagans. Combining his interests in religion, place and ecology, this research resulted in a second monograph a year later, entitled *Listening People, Speaking Earth: Contemporary Paganism* (1997). Those interests would in time shift to include indigenous cultures and field research in Aotearoa, Australia, Hawaii, Newfoundland, Nigeria, and Ojibwe and Sápmi traditional territories, centred around the contested concept of "animism". Graham Harvey joined the Open University in 2003, shortly before *Animism: Respecting the Living World* was published. Paul-François Tremlett became his colleague at the Open University in 2010. He writes:

> When I joined the Religious Studies department, I was very much looking forward to the challenges and opportunities of the post. What I did not anticipate was a significant re-orientation of my theoretical and methodological interests and priorities, largely as a result of working with Graham. We worked together writing new modules, co-supervising PhD students (Owen Coggins, Alison Robertson and Hilde Capparella) and co-editing a book together (with Liam T. Sutherland) on the contemporary resonances of E.B. Tylor (Tremlett, Sutherland and Harvey, 2017) to the field of religious studies, and we also worked together as the UK researchers on the REDO project which ran from 2014–2017 (*Reassembling Democracy: Ritual as Culture Resource*).[1] We already shared a strong feeling of disenchantment with the standard model of religious studies with its preference for institutions, elites and official beliefs over ordinary, embodied life with its unpredictable flows and cominglings, as well as an affinity for eco-politics. But Graham became a kind of intellectual mentor to me introducing me to books, articles, theories and methodologies which steadily shifted my learned predilection for textualism, turning it towards what I will call here "animist materialism".
>
> Central to my training as a PhD student at the School of Oriental and African Studies was the "linguistic turn", which was in keeping with the spirit of a university department with a reputation for rigorous training in languages and the careful translation and interpretation of religious texts, although my supervisor's background was in theology and social anthropology, and he directed me to follow his interests in philosophical hermeneutics, dialogism and Antonio Gramsci. Coupled with my anthropological background in Clifford Geertz's textualism and French structuralism, semiotics and deconstruction, this meant that I acquired an excellent foundation in theories and practices of translation and interpretation, particularly as metaphors for the work of ethnography. But I did not properly investigate the implication of that foundation,

---

1   Reassembling Democracy: Ritual as Cultural Resource (REDO) (completed). University of Oslo, Faculty of Theology, www.tf.uio.no/english/research/projects/redo/.

as an ontology, in a certain manner of writing about and representing non-Western religions and cultures or indeed as a particular face of the colonial encounter, and nor did I sufficiently explore the alternatives.

When it came to my doctoral fieldwork in the Philippines at the extinct volcano Mount Banahaw, I was fascinated by the churches constructed by the religious groups that had established themselves there, the numerous amulets that the mountain was famous for and that could generate a range of effects from invisibility to invulnerability, as well as the shrines that had been established in its manifold caves, tunnels and special spots along its various pilgrim paths and trails. I saw myself interpreting these things and parsing their multiple, palimpsestic layers, as if materials, objects and things were simply passive vehicles for meaning that could be made accessible through the painstakingly learned practice of reading and interpretation. Meeting Graham, reading his work and talking with him about the intellectual labour of colleagues including Eduardo Viveiros de Castro, John Law and Ron Grimes among others, introduced me to an alternative that took as its point of departure materials, things and objects not as inert or as tractable vehicles for meaning but as elements that when combined with human and other non-human actants including animals and plants, formed assemblages with their own agentive capacities and affordances. This alternative took shape in particular through our shared interest in Bruno Latour's work and his pithy and provocative remarks such as "no society of humans exists without the non-humans to hold it together" (Latour, 1990: 73) and the sociologist needed to accept "a certain dose of fetishism" (Latour, 1996: 230).

Importantly, this alternative approach entailed a completely different orientation to religious and social worlds. Textualism relied on a constellation of metaphors which were implicated in generating forms of epistemic authority reminiscent of Enlightenment conceptions of reason and rationality. It combined theatrical metaphors of front and backstage, architectural metaphors of foundations and superstructures and a linguistic metaphor of a deep, organising grammar, ordinarily hidden from view, implying that beneath the surface of everyday interactions and transactions were deep structures and fundamental relationships orchestrating social and religious life and experience. Meaning was everywhere, it just needed decoding by the qualified specialist. Or, effects were everywhere but their causes needed to be identified by the appropriate expert.

One of the compelling attractions of these different iterations of the "hermeneutics of suspicion" was their potential for attentiveness to matters of power and justice. However, addressing such matters while maintaining an arguably positivist approach to epistemic authority was problematic, as Michel Foucault's account of his theoretical shift from archaeology to genealogy made clear (Dreyfus and Rabinow, 1983). As such, the materialism that Graham gently pointed me towards approached religious and social worlds as flat planes of interactions that entangled or magnetised not just people but monuments, spectres, germs, butterflies, trees and indeed a multiplicity of non-humans suggestive of a radical de-centring of the human not to be replaced by some other *archon* but instead to be embedded in a "Parliament of Things" (Latour, 1993: 144) where the purism of modernity could be jettisoned along with its anthropocentric hubris. Importantly, this Latourian "ontological turn" connected with social practices central to Graham's way of doing religious studies and which encompass "animism" and "guesthood", two terms which have been central to his work for some time.

The late nineteenth century Western fascination with religion was conducted with a self-styled sense of restrained bodily comportment and logical reasoning in contrast to the allegedly transgressive character of non-Western cognition and action, particularly in relation to religion. For E.B. Tylor and his contemporaries, animism was a belief, a doctrine, an idea and a theory that attributed to a range of materials, things and objects – some made, some not – "souls or spirits… which to us are not merely soulless but lifeless" (Tylor in Harvey, 2017a: 31). If Tylor's animism was enmeshed in the ontological assumptions of Victorian anthropology and its conviction in the universal scope and reach of its science, Graham's animism, inspired in part by Irving Hallowell's fieldwork among the Ojibwa, evoked interactions not between animate humans and inanimate rocks or differently animate fish and trees, but rather a series of relational encounters "within which humans are one kind of person among many" (Harvey, 2017a: 42). Animism, then, was less a belief as Tylor had insisted, but more a protocol for interacting with the world. Graham's work on guesthood spoke to the same concern, namely that the "negotiation of relationships between locals and strangers that transform the former into hosts and the latter into guests" constituted a way to "learn to deal with imbalanced power dynamics" (Harvey, 2017b: 87) with implications for thinking through the ontological politics of ethnographic research and of indigenous knowledge and religion more widely (Smith, 1999). This was of a piece with Graham's embracing of a process metaphysics that began not with monolithic and static categories such as "Christianity" but rather with the turbulent and contingent flows that recalled Malory Nye's notion of "religioning" and Paul Johnson's of "indigenising" (see Harvey, 2017b: 81).

Graham's theoretical work did not get in the way of him supporting his colleagues, his students and many early-career academics, in multiple ways. David Robertson met Graham as a doctoral student at the 2011 conference of the British Association for the Study of Religions (BASR). He writes:

My colleague Chris Cotter and I had come up with the idea of recording some podcasts and decided to do a trial run at BASR 2011 in Durham. I'd met Graham previously and knew he was approachable, and he readily became our second interviewee. A few months later, this interview became one of the first to be released as an episode of the Religious Studies Project (RSP).² During the interview I suggested a definition of animism as "the attribution of a soul of some kind to non-human beings", paraphrasing E.B. Tylor from his much-cited 1871 book, *Primitive Culture*. Graham's response was to offer an alternative: animism is (at least in the formulation that has become known as *new animism*) rather the relationship between persons (including obligations, etiquette and rituals), not all of whom are human.

You can hear my moment of realisation in the recording as this subtle distinction gave me a new way to think about *belief*. I was unsatisfied by the way that my lecturers seemed to assume that belief was something extraordinary – be that in the form of some special kind of belief (faith?) that typified so-called World Religions, or alternatively belief as naïve knowledge which divides the world into primitive Indigenous cultures and the "developed world". This was later cemented when, as a result of Graham's frequent references, I began to read Latour. I was particularly struck by his neat summary of this fallacy, which I have cited many times since – "We believe that we know. We know that the others believe" (Latour, 2013, 173).

We Moderns are indeed deep in networks of relationships with visible and invisible persons, from the dead husband we still ask for advice from, the bastard printer that just will not connect to the computer, to Mother Earth we seek to dominate or act as stewards for. Graham's Latourian New Animism gave me a new way to think about how it is that we can treat dogs as persons who go to heaven and deserve treats, but not the cow or fish whose body parts sit on our dinner plates. These networks of relationships are encoded in language and enacted in multiple, often mundane ways.

Religious Studies has arguably never reconciled itself to the fact that more people believe in ghosts than in a creator god in the UK, or indeed with the often implicit assumption that religious belief is somehow distinct from other ways of knowing.³ Indeed, I suspect feel that if it were it to do so, it would result in the undermining of its very *raison d'etre*, at least as its purpose and value to society has been traditionally conceived. But those of us who feel that there is still a useful and distinct perspective to be offered by Religious Studies are seeking new ways of formulating the many different ways that relationships with the unseen continue to be a feature of human lives. That is exactly what Graham attempted to do in *Food, Sex and Strangers* (2014). Indeed, this shift from thinking about "beliefs" as things that some people hold, somehow separate from other aspects of human life, to thinking about networks of relationships predicated on shared ontological and epistemological assumptions, was the start of the shift in my thinking towards the epistemic aspects of social life. I think that, in most cases, we don't choose the networks of relationships

---

2   The interview was released on 17 February 2012, and can be heard at www.religiousstudiesproject.com/2012/02/13/podcast-graham-harvey-on-animism/.
3   https://yougov.co.uk/topics/politics/articles-reports/2016/03/26/o-we-of-little-faith.

we exist in any more than we choose to accept dress codes, food norms, the value of money or which sounds vowels are supposed to make.

Soon after this inerview, Graham became President of the BASR, and the organisation began to financially support the RSP. I was invited to join the Committee, initially to help manage their online presence, but I was involved in all the Committee's discussions and decisions from the off. It seems remarkable today that our proposal to set up social media accounts was seen as controversial by some members, but nevertheless the initiative was positively encouraged by Graham and the rest of the committee. That this level of trust was extended to someone still in the middle of a PhD (in an unconventional and controversial subject to boot) struck me as unusual, but Graham has a history of embracing innovation and creating the space for people to get on with making new things and forming new connections. Graham's disdain for empty formality and unnecessary bureaucracy, though without the negativity that disdain might suggest, came through in many ways, from the emails beginning with the familiar salutation "Dear comrades", to a penchant for Che Guevara and Big Lebowski T-shirts.

I saw a good example of this at a later BASR conference, where Graham had organised an open discussion on "Religion and the Senses". There were no speakers scheduled other than Graham himself, and no programme or formal structure. He'd been speaking to a publisher about a book series, and wanted to share the idea and see if anyone had any suggestions. He walked out of that ninety-minute session with enough material for the entire series. I learned that it was fine to move quickly, to try things out, let them develop and to not be afraid to improvise.

But one shouldn't mistake Graham's informality for a lack of connection, depth or interest; rather, it is a deep involvement in only the parts that are worth doing – understanding human societies, making things from the insights, and helping others to do the same. This is an attitude that seems unusual to me in the academy today, where getting lost in the weeds of minutiae academic or bureaucratic, or emphasising process over outcome, seems a more natural fit with many of my colleagues. I didn't learn such an attitude from Graham, but he gave me a template for how to reconcile it with the life of an academic. I was able to put this into practice when I joined Graham and Paul-François at the Open University in 2017.

Harvey's Legacy in the Study of Religion

For both of us, perhaps most importantly of all, these theoretical and methodological shifts, turns and moves constituted a gentle but firm decolonial politics committed to transforming Religious Studies not simply by expanding the curriculum or the research strategy to include non-Western, Indigenous religions or animism, but more fundamentally by changing how

Religious Studies has been done. At the end of the first quarter of the twenty-first century, Religious Studies in the UK sits precariously, an unfashionable research field squeezed by dwindling student numbers in a sector increasingly hawkish on small Arts and Humanities departments in schools, colleges and universities. At a national level, Religious Studies remains marginalised, with government usually considering the subject irrelevant in a rapidly secularising state, but reaching out to insiders or confessional scholars when they do (such as the recent Bloom Report), and outnumbered in organisations such as the British Academy or TRS-UK by confessional scholars. Religious Studies is similarly balanced theoretically, although there where the outlook is rather better. As in other social sciences, the deconstruction of post-structuralist and postmodern critique is giving way to new methodologies and models, many based instead on connection – Actor-Network Theory, Deleuze and Guattari's rhizomes, the Global History movement (see Conrad, 2016), and so on. At the same time, there is a need to decolonise the subject, but again, the process is balanced between, on the one hand, a desire to look at human religious lives in all their variety and complexity, without prioritising one over any other, and on the other that the *idea* of religion, as a unique aspect of human lives distinct from the secular or mundane, is itself a product of Christianity. To do one undermines the other, and vice versa. Graham's approach, which marries the deep engagement of anthropology and ethnography with the insights of post-structural theory that religion is not a thing-out-there but a category we use to think about relationships between people, some of whom may not be human, may offer a theoretical and methodological path through these issues.

At least, many of the contributors to this volume think so. When Graham announced his retirement, a *Festschrift* to honour his contribution to our thinking and our lives seemed only fitting. Needless to say, it did not take us long to find willing friends and colleagues to contribute. Unsurprisingly, Graham continues to work away at various projects (including an event for 2023's summer solstice at the Crawick Multiverse), but his attention turns ever more towards his relationship with the beings in his allotment. In the remainder of this "Introduction" we provide an overview of the chapters and an indicative bibliography of Graham's most important books and articles.

Outline of Chapters

First up is Michael Walling, Director of the biennial ORIGINS Festival, which brings Indigenous artists and activists to the UK. Since its inaugural edition in 2009, the Festival has had a strong relationship with Graham, particularly in relation to the use of ceremony. In his contribution "In Search of Ceremony: Dialogues with Indigeneity and Graham Harvey at the ORIGINS Festival", Michael takes three key moments of interaction with Graham as starting points for a wider discussion of ceremony as practised within the Festival. As well as looking at its meaning and function in the context of post-colonial justice, Walling discusses the distinction between spectacle and participation, and the tension between appropriate learning and cultural appropriation, and the potential for politicised ceremony the context of the Climate Crisis and the Covid-19 pandemic.

Next is Helen Jennings's chapter "Indigenous Tourism: A Perfect Site for 'Guesthood' Research?", which explores Indigenous Tourism in British Columbia, Canada, which in part has been set in train by Indigenous communities themselves in order to establish sites and occasions for education and dialogue. Jennings explores her transition from tourist to guest-researcher and constitutes a careful meditation on the ethics of pursuing research with Indigenous communities through the lens of guesthood. James L. Cox (University of Edinburgh) takes the idea of guesthood further in his "'Guesthood' as a Scientific Method: Principles Supporting Relational Research". Drawing on the physicist Carlo Rovelli, Graham's 2003 *Numen* article and others, Cox presents an approach he calls "relational research" which combines guesthood, phenomenology and action research.

Next comes "Harebrained?", in which Michael Houseman (École Pratique des Hautes Études, Paris) begins with an anecdote of time spent with Graham at Druid Camp, and their encounter with a woman "taken with hares". Thus begins an extended folkloric meditation on hares, rabbits, witches and creativity that begins and ends with Graham's insistence on "an etiquette of interspecies relationality" (2013: 215). Bettina E. Schmidt's (University of Wales, Trinity St. David) "Spirit Possession and Trance as Humpty Dumpty Words: Reflection on Adjusted Styles of Communication", which picks up on a comment in Graham's contribution to the edited volume *Spirit Possession and Trance* (2010), continues the conversation about non-humans. Graham proposed taking the abbreviation ASC to mean not "Altered States of Consciousness" but "Adjusted Styles of Communication". This highlights what Schmidt sees as an important critique of the standard academic approach to spirit possession and trance – the centrality of Western ideas about spirits. She instead offers a relational model, building on Graham's work, which places centrally the relationships between persons of different species, humans and otherwise. The concern with non-humans gathers pace in Christina Welch's (Winchester University) chapter "Plants and People/Plants as People: Plants and their Medicinal and Ritual Uses in Mesoamerica and South America and Religions in the Caribbean" explores the notion of "plants as people" and their roles in ritual and as medicine among indigenous and enslaved people in the Caribbean historically and the present day.

In "The Animacy of Fire and Personhood of Plants in Indigenous-led Land Restoration", Sarah M. Pike (California State University, Chico) draws on fieldwork with an Indigenous-led land restoration project in northern California to explore how they are decolonising the landscape by ritualising relationships with fire and plants. Catastrophic wildfires have led to calls for a revival of Indigenous relationships with fire that include giving fire agency and treating plants as relatives.

Next is Bron Taylor's (University of Florida) "Gaian Animism: Ritual Innovation and Nature Spirituality in Radical Environmentalism and the Global Environmental Milieu", where Bron looks at the Council of All Beings to examine the rise since the 1980s of what, drawing from Graham's work, he calls Gaian Animism – a milieu involving "entangled" spiritualist animism (involving communication with spiritual beings of whatever kind) and naturalistic Animism based on a deeply-felt reverence for the natural world. If we use this broader understanding of animism, as Harvey suggests, Taylor concludes, then it becomes clear that this form of spirituality is increasing steadily in popularity in the West today, with significant implications for cultural and political influence in the future.

Finally, in "Rituals, Wood, Bone and Stone: Material Approaches to Indigenous Religions", Amy Whitehead (Massey University, New Zealand) explores how Graham's work has inspired material approaches to Indigenous religions by foregrounding relationality and an approach to ethnography articulated through the practice of "guesthood" (Harvey, 2003). She concludes with a series of methodological provocations for how researchers might use guesthood, reciprocity and the nurturing of relationships with other-than-human persons to decolonise our perspective.

A number of theoretical, methodological and ethical demands jostle for space across the chapters. Emergent in the ethnographic encounter, they constitute small but vital steps to a pluriverse of interactions with humans and non-humans. We would like to take this opportunity to thank all the authors for their commitment to this book. We would also like to take this opportunity to thank Graham for his humour and his gentle guidance. We hope that he enjoys these essays that we hope reflect the diversity of his theoretical, methodological and political projects and engagements.

References

Dreyfus, H.L. and Rabinow, P. 1983. *Michel Foucault: Beyond Structuralism and Hermeneutics*, 2nd edn. Chicago, IL: University of Chicago Press.

Forster, E.M. 1910. *Howard's End*. London: Edward Arnold.

Harvey, G. 2017a. "Tylor, 'fetishes' and the matter of animism", in Tremlett, P., Sutherland, L. and Harvey, G. (eds), *Edward Tylor, Religion and Culture*. London: Bloomsbury. pp. 29–46.

Harvey, G. 2017b. "Performing indigeneity and performing guesthood", in Hartney, C. and Tower, D.J. (eds), *Religious Categories and the Construction of the Indigenous*. Leiden: E.J. Brill. pp. 74–91.

Harvey, G. 2013. *Food, Sex and Strangers: Understanding Religion as Everyday Life*. Hoboken, NJ: Taylor and Francis.

Harvey, G. 2010. "Animism rather than shamanism: New approaches to what shamans do (for other animists)", in Schmidt, B. and Huskinson, L. (eds), *Spirit Possession and Trance: New Interdisciplinary Perspectives*. London: Continuum. pp. 14–34.

Harvey, G. 2005. *Animism: Respecting the Living World*. London: Hurst; New York: Columbia University Press; Adelaide: Wakefield Press.

Harvey, G. 2003. "Guesthood as ethical decolonising research method", *Numen* 50(2): 125–146.

Harvey, G. 1996. *The True Israel: Uses of the Names Jew, Hebrew and Israel in Ancient Jewish and Early Christian Literature*. Leiden: Brill.

Latour, B. 2013. *An Inquiry into Modes of Existence: An Anthropology of the Moderns*. Trans. Porter, C. Cambridge, MA: Harvard University Press.

Latour, B. 1996. "On interobjectivity", *Mind, Culture, and Activity* 3(4): 228–245.

Latour, B. 1993. *We Have Never Been Modern*, trans. C. Porter. Cambridge, MA: Harvard University Press.

Latour, B. 1990. "The Force and the Reason of Experiment", in Le Grand, H.H. (ed.), *Experimental Inquiries: Historical, Philosophical and Social Studies of Experimentation in Science*. Dordrecht: Kluwer, pp. 44–80.

Conrad, S. 2016. *What Is Global History?* Princeton, NJ: Princeton University Press.

Schmidt, B.E. and Huskinson, L. (eds) 2010. *Spirit Possession and Trance: New Interdisciplinary Perspectives* (Continuum Advances in Religious Studies series). London: Continuum.

Smith, L.T. 1999. *Decolonizing Methodologies: Research and Indigenous Peoples*. Dunedin: University of Otago Press.

Tremlett, P.-F., Sutherland, L.T. and Harvey, G. (eds), 2017. *Edward Burnett Tylor, Religion and Culture*. London: Bloomsbury.

Tylor, E.B. 1913 [1871]. *Primitive Culture*. London: John Murray.

Indicative Bibliography

Books

Harvey, G. 2017. *Animism: Respecting the Living World*. Second, revised UK edn. London: Hurst.
Harvey, G. 2013. *Food, Sex and Strangers: Understanding Religion as Everyday Life*. Hoboken, NJ: Taylor and Francis.
Harvey, G. (ed.) 2013. *The Handbook of Contemporary Animism*. New York: Routledge.
Harvey, G. 2005. *Animism: Respecting the Living World*. London: Hurst.; New York: Columbia University Press; Adelaide: Wakefield Press.
Harvey, G. (ed.) 2003. *Shamanism: A Reader*. London: Routledge.
Harvey, G. (ed.) 2002. *Readings in Indigenous Religions*. London: Continuum.
Harvey, G. (ed.) 2000. *Indigenous Religions: A Companion*. London and New York: Cassell.
Harvey, G. 1997. *Listening People, Speaking Earth: Contemporary Paganism*. London: Hurst & Co.
Harvey, G. 1996. *The True Israel: Uses of the Names Jew, Hebrew and Israel in Ancient Jewish and Early Christian Literature*. Leiden: Brill.
Harvey, G. and Astor-Aguilera, M. (eds) 2018. *Rethinking Relations and Animism: Personhood and Materiality*. New York: Routledge.
Harvey G. and Ralls MacLeod, K. (eds) 2001. *Indigenous Religious Musics*. Aldershot: Ashgate.
Harvey, G. and Thompson, C. (eds) 2005. *Indigenous Diasporas and Dislocations*. Aldershot: Ashgate.
Harvey, G. and Wallis, R. 2006. *Historical Dictionary of Shamanism*. Lanham, MA: Rowman & Littlefield. Paperback edition (2010) entitled *The A to Z of Shamanism*. Second, revised edition (2016).
Harvey, G. and Whitehead, A. (eds) 2019. *Indigenous Religions: Critical Concepts in Religious Studies*. Four volumes (350pp each): *Vol 1: Place, Language, and Community; Vol 2: Cosmology: World-making and Environmentalism; Vol 3: Spirits, Possession and Witchery; Vol 4: Animism, Totemism and Fetishism*. New York: Routledge.

Chapters

Harvey, G. 2023. "Indigenous Religions", in George Chryssides and Amy Whitehead (eds), *Contested Categories in the Study of Religions*. London: Bloomsbury. pp. 57–62.
Harvey, G. 2022. "What makes a religion an 'Indigenous religion'?", "Why study Indigenous religious traditions?" and "What is animism?", in Bassett, M. and Avalos, N. (eds), *Indigenous Religious Traditions in Five Minutes*. Sheffield: Equinox. pp. 6–8; 37–39, 104–106.
Harvey, G. 2020. "Introduction: Indigenizing in European religious movements" and "Bear Feasts in a land without (wild) bears: Experiments in creating animist rituals", in Harvey, G. (ed.), *Indigenizing in European Religious Movements*. Sheffield: Equinox. pp. 1–11; 31–49.

Harvey, G. 2018. "Adjusted Styles of Communication (ASCs) in the Post-Cartesian World", in Harvey, G. and Astor-Aguilera, M. (eds), *Rethinking Personhood: Animism and Materiality*. New York: Routledge. pp. 35–52.
Harvey, G. 2017. "Tylor, 'fetishes' and the matter of animism", in Tremlett, P., Sutherland, L. and Harvey, G. (eds), *Edward Tylor, Religion and Culture*. London: Bloomsbury. pp. 29–46.
Harvey, G. 2017. "Paganism and animism", in Grim, J., Tucker, M.E. and Jenkins, W. (eds), *Routledge Handbook of Religion and Ecology*. New York: Routledge. pp. 209–217.
Harvey, G. 2017. "Performing indigeneity and performing guesthood", in Hartney, C. and Tower, D.J. (eds), *Religious Categories and the Construction of the Indigenous*. Leiden: E.J. Brill. pp. 74–91.
Harvey, G. 2016. "Art works: A relational rather than representational understanding of art and buildings", in Hutchings, T. and McKenzie, J. (eds), *Materiality and the Study of Religion: The Stuff of the Sacred*. London: Routledge. pp. 103–118.
Harvey, G. 2013. "Animist realism in indigenous novels and other literature", in Harvey, G. (ed.), *Handbook of Contemporary Animism*. Durham: Acumen. pp. 454–467.
Harvey, G. 2013. "Why study indigenous religions?", in Cox, J. and Adogame, A. (eds), *Critical Reflections on Indigenous Religions*. Aldershot: Ashgate. pp. 19–28.
Harvey, G. 2012. "Indigenous spiritualities", in Cobb, M., Rumbold, B. and Puchalski, C. (eds), *Spirituality in Healthcare*. Oxford: OUP. pp. 49–54.
Harvey, G. 2010. "Animism rather than shamanism: New approaches to what shamans do (for other animists)", in Schmidt, B. and Huskinson, L. (eds), *Spirit Possession and Trance: New Interdisciplinary Perspectives*. London: Continuum. pp. 14–34.
Harvey, G. 2005. "Guests and hosts: transforming academic paradigms in conversation with Māori diaspora communities", *Proceedings of the Indigenous Knowledges Conference – Reconciling Academic Priorities with Indigenous Realities*. Auckland: Ngā Pae o te Māramatanga. pp. 17–22.
Harvey, G. 2005. "Performing identity and entertaining guests: Māori diaspora in London", in Harvey, G. and Thompson, C. (eds), *Indigenous Diasporas and Dislocation*. Aldershot: Ashgate. pp. 121–134.
Harvey, G. and Whitehead, A. 2018. "Introduction: Critical concepts in studying Indigenous Religions", in Harvey, G. and Whitehead, A. (eds), *Indigenous Religions: Critical Concepts in Religious Studies*.

Journal Articles

Harvey, G. 2022. "Afterword: what staffs and paths do – a new animist contribution to studying pilgrimage", *Religion, State & Society* 50(2): 199–207.
Harvey, G. 2022. "Belonging to (not 'in') land as performed at Indigenous cultural events", *Material Religion: The Journal of Objects, Art and Belief* 18(1): 16–31.
Harvey, G. 2021. "Animist contributions to rethinking wellbeing and healing", *Curare* 42(3–4): 27–34.

Harvey, G. 2019. "Animism and ecology: participating in the world community", *The Ecological Citizen* 5: 79–84. www.ecologicalcitizen.net/article.php?t=animism-ecology-participating-world-community.

Harvey, G. 2019. "Indigenizing by the assembling actors of Riddu Riđđu's ritual/spectacle", *Journal of Ritual Studies* 33(1): 27–37.

Harvey, G. 2018. "If not all stones are alive…: Radical relationality in animism studies", *Journal for the Study of Religion, Nature and Culture* 11(4): 481–497.

Harvey, G. 2016. "Indigenising in a globalised world: the re-seeding of belonging to lands", *Worldviews: Global Religions, Culture, and Ecology* 20 (Special Issue, "The Spatial Turn"): 300–310.

Harvey, G. 2012. "An animist manifesto", *PAN: Philosophy Activism Nature* 9: 2–4. https://bridges.monash.edu/articles/journal_contribution/An_animist_manifesto/4308479 (first published in 2005 in *Strange Attractor* 2: 124–131).

Harvey, G. 2003. "Guesthood as ethical decolonising research method", *Numen* 50(2): 125–146.

Other Notable Publications

2021 *Contemporary Religion in Historical Perspective* (departmental blog): "Totem Latamat has retired" www.open.ac.uk/blogs/religious-studies/?p=1330.

2021 OpenLearn COP26 Hub blog: "Indigenous ceremonies and climate change" www.open.edu/openlearn/nature-environment/creative-climate/indigenous-ceremonies-and-climate-change.

2021 *Contemporary Religion in Historical Perspective* (departmental blog): "Returning to Earth: Climate Change, COP26 and Indigenous Voices" www.open.ac.uk/blogs/religious-studies/?p=1282.

2021 *Contemporary Religion in Historical Perspective* (departmental blog): "Indigenous festivals and the re-making of the +world" www.open.ac.uk/blogs/religious-studies/?p=1242.

2020 *Contemporary Religion in Historical Perspective* (departmental blog): "Africa at the forefront of global scholarship" www.open.ac.uk/blogs/religious-studies/?p=1132.

2018 *Extraordinary Rituals* (The Open University/BBC). Academic advisor/contributor. https://connect.open.ac.uk/history-and-the-arts/extraordinary-rituals.

2017 *Contemporary Religion in Historical Perspective* (departmental blog): "Pocahontas and colonialism" www.open.ac.uk/blogs/religious-studies/?p=387.

2015 *Indigenous in London*. Academic advisor/contributor. www.youtube.com/watch?v=4gBNgXHRAQc.

About the Authors

Paul-François Tremlett is a Senior Lecturer in Religious Studies at the Open University. His research interests include classical and contemporary anthropological and sociological theories of religion and the broad constitution of religion as a site of study in societies experiencing rapid social change. He is currently co-leading two research projects exploring religion and literacy. He is the author of *Religion and Marxism: An Introduction* (2023) and *Towards a New Theory of Religion and Social Change: Sovereignties and Disruptions* (Bloomsbury 2020). He co-edits the Bloomsbury Series "Religion, Space and Place".

David G. Robertson is Senior Lecturer in Religious Studies at the Open University. His work focuses on the social dynamics of knowledge in religions, conspiracy theories and beyond. He is the author of *UFOs, the New Age and Conspiracy Theories* (2016), *Gnosticism and the History of Religions* (2021) and *Religion and Conspiracy Theories: An Introduction* (2024), and co-editor of *After World Religions* (2016) and the *Handbook of Conspiracy Theories and Contemporary Religion* (Brill, 2018). He co-founded the Religious Studies Project podcast and is currently co-editor of *Implicit Religion: Journal of the Critical Study of Religion*. Twitter: @d_g_robertson.

2 In Search of Ceremony: Dialogues with Indigeneity and Graham Harvey at the ORIGINS Festival

Michael Walling

> The act of Performance and the act of Ritual
> meet at the level of the higher self,
> the next dimension closest to this human world
> where spiritual beings dwell.
>
> <div align="right">Floyd P. Favel (Cree) <i>Red People, Red Magic</i>
(in Archibald-Barber, Irwin and Day 2019 p. 208)</div>

> We call upon…Indigenous and non-Indigenous artists to undertake collaborative projects and produce works that contribute to the reconciliation process.
> (Call to Action 83 of the Truth and Reconciliation Commission of Canada[1])

Ceremonies of Welcome

It is May 5th 2009, and I'm in The Scoop outdoor auditorium by the Thames, next to London's City Hall for the Opening Ceremony of the first ORIGINS Festival of First Nations. Beside me is the actor Pete Postlethwaite, who takes a great interest in Indigenous issues,[2] and has agreed to stand as an "Elder of British theatre". On the other side of Pete is someone I've never met before, who has been invited to speak at this event by Rosanna Raymond (aka Sistar Spacific), an Indigenous artist of Samoan heritage and the curator of this ceremony. This man's long grey hair and beard, his boar-tusk necklace and tartan trews, leave me in no doubt that he is the person Rosanna has referred to as "Graham the Druid". It's only some time later that I discover he is also Professor of Religious Studies at the Open University.

---

1 https://www2.gov.bc.ca/assets/gov/british-columbians-our-governments/indigenous-people/aboriginal-peoples-documents/calls_to_action_english2.pdf (accessed 27 February 2023).
2 See, for example, https://insidestory.org.au/petes-legacy/ (accessed 25 February 2023).

Rosanna's structure for the Opening Ceremony follows the format of the pōwhiri: a traditional Māori ritualised welcome, involving whaikōrero (formal speeches), waiata (songs) and kai (food). We are able to offer this version of a pōwhiri because of the presence of Ngāti Rānana: the London Māori Club who have practised the Indigenous cultural traditions of Aotearoa/New Zealand since 1958.[3] In the 2009 Festival, there is a significant Māori contingent among the visiting artists, as Taki Rua[4] will be performing *Strange Resting Places* at Soho Theatre. The actor Maaka Pohatu (Ngāti Tāmanuhiri) takes up the challenge laid down by Ngāti Rānana's warrior, and the process of mutual recognition can begin, with a series of speeches from each side, offering or acknowledging welcome, and – crucially – explaining why.

On the host's side, the speeches are given by the Chair of Ngāti Rānana, Pete as our Elder, myself and Graham Harvey. And that's when I first become aware of Graham's nuanced and reflexive approach to the dialogue with Indigeneity. In a fully Indigenous ceremony, Graham points out, a welcome would be offered on behalf of the ancestors. That would seem deeply inappropriate in the context of ORIGINS, where we are welcoming Native Americans, Aboriginal Australians, Inuit and Māori to the very city that once sent out expeditions to invade and colonise their lands, and which continues to draw its wealth from those lands' resources. "I cannot welcome you in the name of my ancestors," says Graham.

And that, of course, goes to the heart of the matter.

Since that first Ceremony of Welcome in 2009, Border Crossings has presented the ORIGINS Festival every two years (with the exception of the Covid period, which led to a different kind of Festival that I will discuss below). The Opening has tended to follow a similar pattern to that established by Rosanna in 2009, with variations according to the nature of that year's programme and the artists present. Ngāti Rānana has often been involved, as has the GAFA Arts Collective[5] – a London-based group of Samoan artists, led by Sani Muliaumaseali'i, with whose help we have offered another Welcoming Ceremony rooted in Indigenous practices. This is the 'ava ceremony, during which honoured guests are called by name to receive a drink made from the roots of the 'ava plant (*Piper methysticum*). Within these Indigenous structures, there is considerable flexibility and openness to other traditions. In 2019, for example, our guests included two Chiefs of the Powhatan, visiting from the land now usually called Virginia, and their mode of response to the 'ava welcome was informed by their own cultural protocols. Their speeches were followed by a round dance, to the drum of Canadian artist Moe Clark

---

3   www.ngatiranana.co.uk/ (accessed 25 February 2023).
4   www.takirua.co.nz (accessed 25 February 2023).
5   www.gafa-arts-collective.com/ (accessed 25 February 2023).

Figure 2.1 The Opening 'Ava Ceremony at the 2019 ORIGINS Festival. Photo: John Cobb.

(Métis),[6] in which the entire assembled group, including Embassy officials and British academics, was expected to participate. It was gloriously inclusive and highly celebratory as inhibitions dropped away and the body took over from the brain. As the round dance ended, Sani and his team performed the final ritual within the 'ava ceremony structure, and we were then able to eat and drink together, sealing the act of welcome by offering to share food with our guests. After long journeys, people are hungry and thirsty: Indigenous tradition, which includes significant doses of practicality in its various spiritual systems, acknowledges this with the shared meal that concludes a ceremonial welcome (Figure 2.1).

In ceremony, something happens. Something changes. This is the quality that separates it from ritual. There's a ritual in the way we start our days – choosing clothes, drinking tea, checking the email – but the whole point of this sort of ritual is its sameness, the security of daily repetition. Ceremony, while it may be ritualised, is made distinct by its facilitating a transition. People might go into a ceremony as single, and emerge from it married. They might begin a ceremony as a child and emerge as an adult. In the case of a Welcoming Ceremony, the journey is slightly different according to whether you experience it as host or guest, but in each case it moves

---

6   http://moeclark.ca/ (accessed 25 February 2023).

from suspicion to trust, from distance to proximity, from separation to conviviality. In this sense, the Welcome Ceremony reconciles host and guest in their common etymological root. Ghos-ti, meaning someone with whom you share reciprocal duties of hospitality, is the Indo-European word-root from which we derive both "host" and "guest", as well as "hospital", and even "hostility" (see Griffiths, 2022: 210). So, however warmly a welcome may be given or received, however profoundly shared the space may become as a result, language tells us that a degree of difference can and indeed should remain between the parties. As Christopher Logue puts it in his epic poem *War Music*: "The host requires the guest to make himself at home. The guest remembers he is not." (Logue, 2001: 94.)

At ORIGINS, however potent the Welcoming Ceremony may be, the distinction between the visiting Indigenous artists, activists and thinkers and the British hosts remains clear, and is indeed crucial to the generation of meaning through the festival experience. If the welcome were simply to wipe out difference, then there would be little point in doing it. Rather, our welcome might be conceived as a clearing of space that may be shared, an establishment of common ground – but common ground as an area of contention. Helen Gilbert writes that "The festival opens and closes with ceremonies (often led by London's sizeable diaspora of Māori and Pacific peoples) that anchor the event in time and place, paying due regard to the politics of its location in the erstwhile centre of British imperialism" (Gilbert, Pigram and Swain, 2021: 229); while Graham Harvey himself argues:

> Much of this could happen on Indigenous lands. That it happens in London makes it distinctive. Colonialism in its many forms and manifestations is not ignored. ORIGINS is not about decorating the dominant culture with spectacles of diversity, and appropriation is discouraged. In his opening speech, Michael Walling uses words like conversation, equity, justice, complexity and provocation. When he speaks of loss, he does not evoke an imaginary pre-contact purity and subsequent disappearance but addresses the diminishment of all lives and cultures under the continuing impact of colonisation. (Harvey, 2020a: 69–85)

This takes us back to Graham's speech at the first ORIGINS opening, and his crucial point that we could not offer a welcome in the name of our European ancestors precisely because of the ongoing and unresolved tensions between colonising and colonised peoples. In the years since 2009, these tensions have not diminished but increased, partly because of the continuing state-supported incursions into Indigenous territories of international corporations intent on mining or logging; and partly because of the increased confidence and articulacy of the global Indigenous movement, buoyed up by historical developments like Standing Rock and #BlackLivesMatter. We have become increasingly conscious of ORIGINS having a political role as a space for negotiation, for having a conversation that society is not having, for embracing difficulty and rejecting simplification. It is a space in which we force ourselves to reckon with our differences. It is to this reckoning that we bid people welcome.

This is why I find myself uneasy with the concept of "indigenisation", which seems to come perilously close to cultural appropriation, a colonisation of culture that adds spiritual insult to the genocidal injury of empire. Graham's edited collection *Indigenizing Movements in Europe* (2020b) examines a range of minority religious or spiritual movements that aim to "reconnect" with a perceived (and romantic) notion of authentic connection to land. Both his introduction and Bjørn Ola Tajford's concluding remarks are rightly sceptical of such movements' claims to be "indigenising". At the same time, it seems important to recognise that there is a process of appropriate learning from Indigenous cultures, which is distinct from cultural appropriation, and which is indeed essential to processes of post-colonial healing and ecological revitalisation. In this sense, I would be more than happy to align the ceremonial (and hence spiritual) elements of ORIGINS with contemporary paganism and other practices seeking to establish genuine relationships between human and other-than-human communities. The Potawatomi botanist Robin Wall Kimmerer grapples instructively with these issues in *Braiding Sweetgrass* (2013), when she argues within two pages both that "By honouring the knowledge of the land, and caring for its keepers, we start to become indigenous to place" (2013: 210) and that "an invitation to settler society to become indigenous to place feels like a free ticket to a housebreaking party" (2013: 211). She settles for a notion of becoming "naturalised to place", which only serves to underscore the nature of the Indigenous as an historical and political identity that is (at least currently) exclusive. Exclusivity has caused all sorts of problems, including for Indigenous people themselves, for example the absurd disputes over blood quantum that results from colonial law. However, in the current historical moment it is strategically necessary and of great use both to Indigenous people and their allies in settler communities or former imperial centres who seek post-colonial justice together with its economic and environmental corollaries. At this moment in history, difference is the point. We cannot welcome Indigenous people in the name of our ancestors.

For some time, I have also been wondering whether it is really appropriate to offer that welcome within the structure of Indigenous ceremony either. If we are offering Indigenous travellers the kind of welcome to our city that acknowledges the levels of respect and decorum they would themselves show to honoured travellers arriving on their lands, then surely we need to find our own cultural form within which we can express such sentiment? Isn't asking our Māori and Pacific friends to plug the spiritual gap in our culture on some level just another instance of "indigenisation", another appropriation of Indigenous ceremony for our own ends? After the 2017 Festival where she presented her powerful video installation *The Lost World*, the Tasmanian artist Julie Gough (Trawlwoolway, Scottish and Irish) told me that she felt the Opening Ceremony should not be Indigenous, but rather of the land on which it happened. Her thoughts were all the more compelling, given her installation's preoccupation with the slow violence of ongoing colonial processes, whether through mapping, naming or repurposing of land and lives. Ceremony is itself an interaction with land and place, and a mark of custodianship over the space in which it happens. Isn't good hosting therefore about finding a form which does that for yourself, rather than resorting to the existing forms of others?

The problem, of course, is that contemporary Britain has no communally agreed and appropriate cultural framework within which to offer welcome. The colonial process did violence to our own spiritual lives, as well as those of the colonised. Because the capitalist-colonial structure generated national mythologies to underpin violent conquest and sustained brutality, the postcolonial era has left us divorced from ceremony. Julie Gough throws down the same challenge that Graham Harvey hinted at when he said we could not welcome our guests in the name of our ancestors: what is an appropriate and meaningful ceremonial form for the current moment?

In 2022, Border Crossings had the opportunity to explore this dilemma in the context of the Birmingham 22 Festival that accompanied the Commonwealth Games. We worked closely with Avatâra Ayuso, a Spanish choreographer living in England, who had already worked with ORIGINS in her 2019 production *No Woman's Land*, a collaboration with Inuk Elder Naulaq LeDrew. Responding to the deeply problematic structure of the Commonwealth – a post-colonial hangover if ever there was one – and the glib ceremonial forms used for the Games' opening and closing events, we elected to develop a structure which was clearly of the moment, at once welcoming Indigenous visitors and acknowledging the tensions inherent in that action. This also necessitated a genuinely dialogic process, in which the Indigenous people being welcomed would also have a voice. We spoke to the First Nations contemporary dance artist b.solomon//ELECTRIC MOOSE (Anishinaabe), who was keen to respond to the welcome with his own dance piece. With a certain irony, the structure began to head towards that of the pōwhiri. We would begin with Avatâra's dancers, themselves representing a cross-section of multicultural Britain, and their initial call would be answered by

Figure 2.2 *Remembrances*. Birmingham, 2022. Photo: Avatâra Ayuso.

the First Nations artists (Figure 2.2). And then we would try to find a way to come together.[7]

As well as dance, this piece, called *Remembrances*, involved texts. The Dënësųłiné & Métis poet Matthew James Weigel wrote a new piece, and I contributed a further text which was heard near the start of the performance, as the dancers began to perform a process of self-discovery, both personal and cultural, in front of their Indigenous guests. The challenge of welcoming First Nations artists had become even more acute and immediate with the

---

7 The process of collaboration, and the politics behind it, are discussed in Smyth et al. (2022: 42–47). See also www.birminghamworld.uk/whats-on/birmingham-commonwealth-games-british-empire-3794548 (accessed 28 February 2023).

discovery of the mass graves across Canada, and so this working towards a Ceremony of Welcome became very specific to the historical moment.

> Who are we now to welcome you?
> After the desecration of the sacred places
> After the unearthing of the children's bodies
> After the cynical breakage of the binding treaties
> Who are we now to welcome you?
>
> After the genocide against the buffalo
> After the coming of the measles and the smallpox
> After the systematic reduction of reservation land
> After the demonising of spirituality, culture and language
> After the banning of institutional generosity
> Who are we now to welcome you?
>
> After the forced removal of children
> After the trauma of abuse
> After the disappearances of so many women
> After the rape of the land
> After the suppression of hunting and fishing
> Who are we now to welcome you?
>
> After the imposition of alien governance
> After the wrangling over blood quantum and status
> After the unfettered arrogance of missionaries and teachers
> After the propagation of a multicultural myth
> After the tacit acceptance of sexual abuse
> Who are we now to welcome you?

Ceremony, Light and Shadows

It's July 12th 2013, and I'm sitting on the ground in a yurt, next to Graham Harvey. We are at the Riddu Riđđu Festival[8] on Sámi land in Kåfjord, Norway. Graham and I have not arranged to meet here, but neither of us feel surprised to bump into the other. Riddu Riđđu is, after all, the Indigenous Festival within easiest reach of Britain: we both have good reason to be here.

I'm not at all sure what time of day it is. Here in the Arctic, at the height of summer, it never gets dark. The sun is constantly overhead, even though it's far from hot. The yurt provides a welcome space of rest and warmth, where a group of Festival-goers, mainly Indigenous people from around the Arctic

---

8   https://riddu.no/en (accessed 27 March 2023).

Circle, gather around a wood fire. The darkness of this interior space is enlivened by the flames, and suddenly my body remembers that it is night.

Everyone is looking at the fire. After a long time, a young man's voice says "Somebody should tell a story." There's a short pause, and then an Inuk woman from Greenland replies "I'll do it." And she tells us a tale of Sedna, Mother of the Sea.

The story told by the fireside is at the origin of both theatre and ceremony. In *Ireland's Master Storyteller* the great *seanchaí* Éamon Kelly recalls communities gathering to hear stories: "Many of the kitchen floors in the old days were made of mud but there was always a large stone flag in front of the fire... I call this form of entertainment 'theatre of the hearthstone' – a diversion having its seed in the time when our forefathers sat at the mouth of a cave and listened to the happenings of a day's hunting" (Kelly, 1998: 8–9). Another Irishman, Seamus Heaney, saw the removal of fire from the living space as symptomatic of "the desacralisation of space... something my generation experienced in all kinds of ways... grates being removed from living rooms, hearths blocked up, central heating installed, with the consequent loss of focus." (O'Driscoll and Heaney, 2008: 309). This sacredness of fire is common to many spiritual traditions. There is the miraculous fire that runs every Easter Saturday through the streets of Jerusalem, the Zoroastrian Atar, the Vedic Agni that focuses many Hindu rituals, the perpetual flames in the Roman temple of Vesta and the more recent tombs of Unknown Warriors. Indigenous practice in particular lays great stress on the spiritual importance of fire: North American smudging and Australian smoking ceremonies are just two examples. The sacred flame, focusing the eyes of congregations and audiences, is also present in the superficially more secular ritual of theatre, where practitioners like myself develop our own forms of ceremony. It is present in the lit stage that contrasts with the darkened auditorium, in the shining silver screen of the cinema, and even in the new domestic hearth of the ubiquitous television.

What was especially potent in the experience of storytelling as ceremony that Graham and I encountered at Riddu Riđđu was that it took place in a specific and unusual space of shadow, surrounded by the perpetual sunlight that illuminated the rest of the festival for its entire duration. It was in the darkened space, focused on the fire, that people felt the need for story, theatre, ceremony – for the sacred.

In Plato's famous Allegory of the Cave, human "prisoners" experience the world through the shadows that a fire casts on the cave walls. It is only when one of them escapes the cave, emerging into the sunlight, that "reality" becomes clear. It is, of course, an allegory for Plato's ideas about educating and civilising processes, leading people out of dark ignorance and into the light of scientific understanding. Plato's is a foundational myth of Western thinking, which became particularly important during the period of "The Enlightenment" and Empire. As Edward Said pointed out: "Every empire… tells itself and the world that it is unlike all other empires, that its mission is not to plunder and control but to educate and liberate."[9] Plato's prisoners do not simply walk out of the cave: they have to be "dragged out of there by force" and "forced to look at the light itself". There is a violence to the Enlightenment, a violence made manifest in the genocidal and enslaving nature of the imperial project.

By contrast, Indigenous knowledge, spirituality and ceremony operate more profoundly and poetically within the shadowy space of the cave itself. This culturally distinct way of seeing, artistically constructed by conscious interplay with the light source, has become the site of what we might term a sacred resistance in the aftermath of colonisation. History casts long shadows, and the current moment is emphatically in their shade. If we simply place colonial histories with their attendant atrocities in the stark objective sunlight of academic discourse, then we will look at them as spectators, objectively and impassively. We will see the object, but not our own relation to it. However, if we dare to undertake a self-critical and self-reflexive creative interaction with the shadows of the past, then we can perhaps begin to engage self-consciously in a meaningful relationship with a history in which we recognise our own implication. Because it is about light and shade, this kind of creative interface does not offer simple solutions, whether to condemn or to absolve, but it does recognise the processes of exchange in which we have to participate in order to respond with any kind of moral depth and ethical receptivity.

What I am discussing here is, I suppose, the need to embrace the different ways of knowing that operate within Indigenous cultures, and to engage with these on their own terms. This can be deeply challenging for scholars operating within the ever more scientifically based research parameters of the Western academy. The combined forces of Enlightenment and Entitlement hold little sway in Indigenous knowledge-systems. Here, not all knowledge is open or available: much is secret or privileged, confined to initiates, offered only when the suppliant is ready to receive it. It is good for Western researchers to learn humility in this way; although it may not help their academic careers.

---

9   www.latimes.com/archives/la-xpm-2003-jul-20-oe-said20-story.html (accessed 27 March 2023).

During ORIGINS 2017, we brought together three Native American women who were living in Britain to create a ceremony in memory of Pocahontas (or, more correctly, Matoaka), the young Powhatan woman who had come as an ambassador to London four hundred years before. Graham Harvey made this ceremony the focus of one in a series of short films created for the Open University around ceremonial actions within the festival.[10] What made this film a particular challenge for him as a researcher was that the ceremony itself was felt to be too sacred to be videoed, or even explicitly described. As a result, the film talks around the ceremony, but does not directly address its content or what may have happened or changed as a result. The secret, sacred nature of the knowledge contained in ceremony is respected, and the beginnings of an intercultural dialogue can perhaps be perceived in consequence.

The very first work I did with Indigenous people was a play called *Bullie's House* by the Australian writer (and sometime seminarian) Thomas Keneally, which I directed for Border Crossings in 2004. The play is based on a monograph by the anthropologist Ronald Berndt (1962), describing events that had occurred the Elcho Island mission station, in Australia's Northern Territory, in 1958. A group of Indigenous people decided to build a monument that displayed the most secret and sacred totems of their tribe, known as the *ranga*. Following Indigenous protocols, the people with whom these secrets were shared (in this case, the "white" world of missionaries, anthropologists and civil servants), would be obliged to share their own secrets in return. As Bullie, the instigator, explains in the play:

> One thing they got, they got a house of books, bigger than anything on the pictures, bigger than Cape Grant. The British Museum, they call it. We need, Jimmie, we need a kind of British Museum. But I know they keep the patterns from us. The patterns of marrying. The patterns of the machines. The patterns for keeping your house up. You know why? *(Pause)* Because we keep the ranga from them. (Keneally, 2004: 25)

In our production, Bullie made this case to his friends at night, in the shadows, with the *ranga* present but concealed, wrapped in sacking (Figure 2.3). After the interval, the stage was ablaze with bright Australian daylight, and the *ranga* were on open display, set in cement (Figure 2.4). The contrast was startling and horribly telling. Bullie's attempted rapprochement with the colonial power would not lead to a reciprocal sharing of secret knowledge. Indeed, there is no such knowledge at the heart of Western civilisation. The

---

10   www.youtube.com/watch?v=7pq4dkKtyMY (accessed 27 March 2023).

Figure 2.3 *Bullie's House*. The argument in the shadows. Photo: Dave Ennis.

exposure of the *ranga* leads inexorably to tragedy, as Bullie is murdered, and to spiritual catastrophe, as the ceremonial beings at the heart of the culture lose the power derived from their very invisibility.

Ceremony, Politics and Passing

It's November 20th 2021, and I'm in the extensive grounds of the Crichton in Dumfries, southern Scotland. I'm pulling a rope, and beside me, pulling another rope, is Graham Harvey. The ropes are attached to a 4.5 metre high Totem, carved in Mexico by Totonac artist Jun Tiburcio, and brought to Britain by ship. Over the last couple of months, it has slowly made its way across the country, standing in a series of culturally and spiritually significant spaces, drawing links between Indigenous and local experiences. *Totem Latamat*, as

Figure 2.4 *Bullie's House*. The *ranga* by daylight. Photo: Dave Ennis.

it is known, finally arrived in Glasgow for the 2021 United Nations Climate Change Conference (COP-26), where it stood in the Indigenous camp at the Hidden Gardens.

After COP-26, we brought the Totem here to Dumfries, which will be its final resting place. This morning we have welcomed it to the Crichton, and thanked it for what it has done. And now is the time for it to rest, to return to the Earth, to be regenerated through the natural process of decay.

We pull the ropes, and *Totem Latamat* falls to the ground. It will remain there until it is no more.[11] (Figure 2.5).

---

11 The totem's journey, including this ceremony, is documented in our film: *Totem Latamat: Carving a Message for Climate*. www.youtube.com/watch?v=gebkkrKQy0I.

Figure 2.5 Graham Harvey and Michael Walling at the Return to Earth Ceremony for *Totem Latamat*. Photo: Mike Bolam.

The 2021–22 ORIGINS Festival was very different from previous editions. It took shape during the Covid-19 pandemic, which meant that we couldn't gather in theatres and we couldn't bring Indigenous artists from overseas. At the same time, it served to highlight the environmental agenda of ORIGINS: the virus had transferred to humans from other animals as a result of the destruction of natural habitats, and it had spread rapidly across the world because of the extreme mobility inherent in the globalised capitalist system. This made it more than a specific crisis in itself: it also served as a warning of the much greater catastrophe to come, in the form of climate change. The coincidence of the pandemic with COP-26 happening in the UK made our need for a presence there particularly urgent. *Totem Latamat* was a response to the need we felt to bring Indigenous voices into Glasgow's global conversation.[12]

---

12 The environmental meaning of *Totem Latamat* is discussed in the film, and by Anna Perdibon in the ORIGINS 2021–22 online programme: https://issuu.com/border_crossings/docs/origins_21-22_-_programme, pp. 16–17.

In doing this, the totem project also contributed to our evolving approach to ceremony as it relates to Indigenous cultures in dialogue with the West, and the possibilities of renewal that this dialogue contains. Part 1 of this chapter has looked at ceremonies of welcome for Indigenous visitors as complex spaces of negotiation, while Part 2 has emphasised the importance of Indigenous ceremony not being made overly public. The implication of this could be to reinforce divisions and undermine efforts at reconciliation, never mind ecological or spiritual renewal; but the experience of *Totem Latamat*, and particularly the Return to Earth Ceremony, suggested the potential for different relationships and dialogues between Indigenous cultures and the former imperial centre. Precisely because it emerged from Totonac lands as a fully-formed artefact, travelling alone (albeit with some awareness of culturally specific meanings and of spiritual and ecological contexts), *Latamat* became a site of negotiation, creativity and ceremonial focus for communities that are usually deprived of these things. There had been a Totonac ceremony when the tree was felled, thanking it for giving its life, but the responsibility of care for the totem and its Indigenous message passed entirely to us, the British, once it had arrived on our lands. This in itself represents a deeply Indigenous understanding of welcome, hosting and duty. The totem's journey impelled the series of communities through which it passed into a relationship that was reciprocal and dialogic: and again, that at the heart of Indigenous ideas is the role of ecology and of the human. Far from being excluded from ceremony, people felt impelled to make their own. The groups who sang to *Latamat* in Chiswick, Enfield, Milton Keynes and by the Rollright Stones were acknowledging the holiness inherent in its form, at the same time as investing something of themselves in its message. Wherever it went, we would find little offerings left on its base, or tucked into its carving: an apple, a nut, a flower, a ribbon, a note or a prayer. When the totem spoke to people, they were impelled to speak back to it. And this was at once a spiritual and a political action.

There is something about ceremony that places it in direct opposition to the capitalist, materialist, colonial worldview. Because ceremony brings humans into an active, engaged, reciprocal relationship with the other-than-human, including the numinous and the cosmic, it refutes the reduction of the world (including humans themselves) to a set of material objects to be bought and sold at profit. It is deeply telling that the ceremony most distrusted by colonial forces in North America was the potlatch of the Pacific North-West, which was completely banned for more than 60 years.[13] Why?

---

13 See https://umistapotlatch.ca/potlatch_interdire-potlatch_ban-eng.php (accessed 29 March 2023).

Because at a potlatch, people who have accumulated wealth give it all away. This action of redistribution underlines our equality as a spiritual aspiration, which is of course rooted in mortality.

Capitalism, by way of contrast, is a denial of mortality. By making the world into a space of competition through acquisition and exploitation, it propounds the lie that some people will somehow "win" in life, denying the absolute equality inherent in the certainty of death. While I was writing this essay, the 92-year old press baron Rupert Murdoch announced his engagement to Ann Lesley Smith, who is a mere 66, commenting (apparently without irony) that "We're both looking forward to spending the second half of our lives together."[14] The underlying assumption that extreme wealth overcomes death is truly extraordinary, but Murdoch's preposterous pronouncement betrays just how deeply the myth of the immortal capitalist has managed to embed itself in Western consciousness. As the Korean philosopher Byung-Chul Han argues:

> The society of production is dominated by the fear of death. Capital acts like a guarantee against death. It is imagined to be accumulated time because money allows you to have others work for you, that is, to buy time. Infinite capital creates the illusion of an infinite time. Capital works against death as absolute loss. It is meant to suspend the temporal limits of a life. (Han, 2020: 50)

Because it is a denial of death, capitalism is also a denial of life, since life is defined by death. In reducing the world to the mere material, the currently dominant global culture sets itself in direct opposition to the ceremonial and the performed. Because performance is temporal and finite, operating through the living body, it exists only in the moment of its happening, and therefore resists commodification. There are, of course, theatre tickets sold in "the experience economy", but the reality is that culture is not a place of profit and requires a different form of public investment if it is to fulfil its essential social role. What theatre, performance and ceremony truly represent is a space to commune with the dead. For most of history, in most cultures, theatre hasn't even been intended for a living audience so much as a dead one. As Border Crossings' Patron Peter Sellars explains:

> In Korea, in Africa, in aboriginal Australia, you danced for the spirits of the dead. To let them know you're still thinking of them, you still care about them, you still cherish them. And if they died in pain, if they died in unhappiness, if they died with something incomplete, or in the midst of injustice, you spend

---

14 https://nypost.com/2023/03/20/rupert-murdoch-engaged-to-ann-lesley-smith/ (accessed 29 March 2023).

those years making it up to them. And letting them know that your life won't be in balance either, until it's made up for them.[15]

The Return to Earth Ceremony which animist celebrant Gordon McLellan created for *Totem Latamat* in Dumfries was a performance about mortality in this sense, placing something that had once been literally alive as a tree, and had become symbolically alive as an active subject in art and ceremony, as the central figure in a meditation on passing out of the world. Or maybe that's the wrong phrasing: maybe what *Latamat* actually did was to pass back into the world. By allowing the wood to decay and so enrich the soil beneath it, by allowing wasps to make their home in its crown and worms to feed on its trunk, *Latamat* encapsulates the Indigenous idea of death as part of the ongoing processes of regeneration and decay; of being in constant relationship to the world, animated in whatever form you may currently occupy. This is not only an Indigenous worldview: it is also a scientific truth.

When I started to talk about the Return to Earth Ceremony, a lot of people were very surprised. We had, after all, spent a lot of Arts Council money on commissioning this piece. Would it not be better if it were preserved in a museum or art gallery as a precious object? If we had done that, we would have turned *Latamat* into another object, another acquisition, another denial of death, and that would totally have undermined its ecological and ceremonial meaning. *Latamat* means "life" in the Totonac language. Like anything that lives, it owes it to the Earth to perish.

References

Archibald-Baker, J., Irwin, K. and Day, M.J. (eds) 2019. *Performing Turtle Island: Indigenous Theatre on the World Stage*. Regina: University of Regina Press.
Berndt, R.M. 1962. *An Adjustment Movement in Arnhem Land*. La Haye: Mouton.
Gilbert, H., Pigram, D. and Swain, R. 2021. *Marrugeku – Telling that Story*. Aberystwyth: Performance Research Books.
Griffiths, J. 2022. *Nemesis My Friend – Journeys Through the Turning Times*. Beaminster: Little Taller Books.
Han, B.-C. 2020. *The Disappearance of Rituals*. London: Polity.
Harvey, G. 2020a. "Indigenous rituals re-make the larger than human community", in Harvey, G., Pike, S., Houseman, M. and Salomonsen, J. (eds), *Reassembling Democracy: Ritual and Cultural Resource*. London: Bloomsbury, pp. 69–85.
Harvey, G. (ed.) 2020b. *Indigenizing Movements in Europe*. Sheffield: Equinox.

---

15 www.pbs.org/wgbh/questionofgod/voices/sellars.html (accessed 29 March 2023).

Kelly, É. 1998. *Ireland's Master Storyteller – The Collected Stories of Éamon Kelly*. Dublin: Marino.
Keneally, T. 2004. *Bullie's House*. London: Border Crossings.
Kimmerer, R.W. 2013. *Braiding Sweetgrass – Indigenous Wisdom, Scientific Knowledge and the Teachings of Plants*. Minneapolis, MN: Milkweed.
Logue, C. 2001. *War Music: An Account of Books 1–4 and 16–19 of Homer's Iliad*. London: Faber & Faber.
O'Driscoll, D. and Heaney, S. 2008. *Stepping Stones: Interviews with Seamus Heaney*. London: Faber.
Smyth, L., Goodacre, J. and Elsayed, S. 2022. *International Collaborations: Evaluation of Birmingham 2022*. London: The Audience Agency. Available at: https://indd.adobe.com/embed/90992cff-078c-4a46-bb20-b925c4bae86a?startpage=1&allowFullscreen=true.
Walling, M. (ed.) *ORIGINS Festival of First Nations 2009 – Programme*.

About the Author

Michael Walling is Artistic Director of Border Crossings and Visiting Professor of Intercultural and Multicultural Performance at Rose Bruford College in Sidcup, Kent. He directs the ORIGINS Festival, which generates exchanges between Indigenous people and UK audiences. www.bordercrossings.org.uk, www.originsfestival.com

3 Indigenous Tourism: A Perfect Site for "Guesthood" Research?

Helen Jennings

Introduction

I first encountered Graham Harvey's theory of "Guesthood" when working on my PhD on articulations of indigeneity and spirituality in Indigenous Tourism in British Columbia, Canada.[1] The idea came as a welcome breath of fresh air to me, having heard enough academics bragging of having gained special access into private and personal spaces of the people they were researching. As Māori scholar Linda Tuhiwai Smith notes, this objectification of those being researched turns them into "donors" and epitomises a colonial approach to research long campaigned against by Indigenous scholars and activists.[2] Graham Harvey's notion of "guesthood" is an important response to this problem. His idea challenges researchers to avoid abusing their positions of power, entering spaces through force or deceit, or conducting research "on" or even against Indigenous people. Such problematic practices have been prominent for too long, have promoted narratives of "otherness" and produced work with little or no benefit to the people being researched. In attempts to overcome these issues, Harvey notes how academics have debated terms such as "insiders", "outsiders" or "participant observers", each striving to be more reflective about researcher roles. "Guesthood" offers a new approach premised on a different relationship that goes beyond "us" and "them" binaries and moves towards a more reciprocal relationship of hosts and guests – a different type of "social contract" that can be beneficial to all participants (Harvey, 2003: 141).

Harvey's concept of "guesthood" was inspired by the Māori people's *marae* protocols, whereby strangers, through a series of steps, are turned into either

---

1 This article is based on material from my PhD dissertation (Jennings, 2023) and from Graham Harvey's article on Guesthood (2003).
2 Smith (1999). For scholars writing about Indigenous peoples and academic research in a Canadian context see: Kovach (2009), Cruikshank (1998, 2005), McCall (2012), Niezen (2004, 2008, 2009).

Figure 3.1 Andy Everson giving his tour of the totem poles at The Royal BC Museum for the annual "Indigenous Cultural Festival" hosted by ITBC. Helen Jennings, June 2018.

guests or enemies (Harvey: 140). This process may look very different to each person or community one is hoping to become a guest in, but what is important is that the researcher recognises the hosts' right to accept or reject their requests. Researchers must recognise "the powerful priority, sovereignty and intellectual property rights of hosts" (Harvey, 2003: 140). This requires the researcher to acknowledge their own positions of power, and recognise that they come with ideas, perspectives and languages that affect the research. The process of becoming a guest is a less threatening start to a relationship than presenting as a scholar coming from a privileged position with an agenda packed with loaded questions. "Guesthood" acknowledges "power" on all sides and of different kinds. Knowledge – rather than being "out there", ready to be discovered – is gained in the relationship. This approach has numerous implications: it highlights the need to be reflective about the process of commencing research, negotiating a relationship and establishing a route forward. It also increases awareness of contexts to research, as for example in my work, Indigenous Tourism was flourishing in British Columbia aided by the political context of a process of Truth and Reconciliation.[3]

The history of Canada as a settler colonial state is important because since the 1800s state-sanctioned policies have controlled who does and does not count as Indigenous, contributed to a dramatic decline in the number of fluent Indigenous language speakers, restricted Indigenous peoples to reserves, imposed colonial governance on those areas and prohibited traditional land-use practices.[4] Moves towards reconciliation stemmed partly from a government report published in 2008 as part of the "Indian Schools Settlement Agreement", which officially launched the Truth and Reconciliation Commission (TRC). One purpose of the TRC was to document the history and impact of residential schools, institutions run by the state and the church for much of the twentieth century, designed to separate Indigenous children from their families, languages, and practices, and assimilate them into new Canadian ways of being.[5] The TRC report included "94 calls to action" to the government regarding reconciliation. The development of Indigenous Tourism in British Columbia relates to many of these calls to action for a space to learn and engage with different Indigenous languages and cultures, as well as the ability to partake effectively in the economy.

As proclaimed on *The Indigenous Tourism Association* website, "Indigenous Tourism has the power to change perspectives, preserve culture, language and community and provide our relatives with a platform to be the leading voice in reclaiming our space in history – both ancient and modern."[6] Indigenous Tourism in British Columbia, where the hosts own, control and manage these spaces, can serve as an invitation to tourists to learn more, do more and potentially become guests. The individuals and companies engaged in Indigenous Tourism that I witnessed had established boundaries, planned topics of conversation and different explicit protocols for showing respect. This growing provincial industry is regulated and marketed by an umbrella organisation called *Indigenous Tourism British Columbia (ITBC)*.[7]

---

3   The Truth and Reconciliation Commission report http://trc.ca (accessed January 2024).
4   Settler colonialism is a particular form of colonialism that describes the process by which settlers came, stayed, and formed new governmental structures (Aikau and Gonzalez, 2019: 4).
5   The first residential school opened in 1827; the last one closed in 1997.
6   www.indigenoustourismconference.com/2018 (accessed January 2024).
7   ITBC www.indigenousbc.com/ (accessed January 2024)

Unlike many other areas of research, tourism is not a private sphere, where people are forced to be hosts and translators to people whom they have not invited. Tourism is public and performative and an arena I have found to be a comfortable entry point for research.

Past research on indigeneity in Canada has been largely preoccupied with histories of encounters between Indigenous people and Europeans.[8] Much of this work has adopted the viewpoint of the settlers, often placing Indigenous people as passive victims; the work has focused not on what Indigenous people were doing at the time of the encounters, but what they had done, made or thought before the arrival of the Europeans. My research aims to contribute to the growing body of work that demonstrates how Indigenous people have always been "active assertive contributors to the unfolding of Canadian history" (Miller, 2018: x). It works towards a shift in focus to writing instead about how, for example, Canadian national histories have mapped on to Indigenous histories.[9] Indigenous Tourism in British Columbia is testimony to the active participation of Indigenous people in Canadian politics, the economy and history making. It also works to challenge notions of indigeneity as fixed in the past and lacking a future, a discourse that pervades both scholarly and public literature.

For my PhD research, I saw myself as a tourist-researcher, noting the similarities between the two roles, particularly in the way they both create value from their curated encounters, be that with people, places, stories, art or objects.[10] I started the process as a tourist, there to learn and enjoy myself like everyone else who had signed up and paid for the experience, event or workshop. Some tourist experiences I visited several times, others due to their more remote locations, high cost or frequency of events, I only visited once. During this time as a tourist, I learned a lot about the places, histories and current politics of a place, largely through the tours and the carefully considered performances and stories told to us by the guides, but also through the books I read and general conversations. It was during this early stage of setting up my research that I was learning how to prepare to be a guest. It is perhaps worth noting that I was a guest in more senses than one, as I had been fortunate to be given a fellowship at the University of Victoria (UVic) where I could learn from their approaches and ideas towards research with Indigenous peoples.

---

8   For research on settler histories see: Nichols (2013), Davis (2010), Davis et al. (2017), Regan (2010), Wolfe (1999, 2006), Lutz (2007), Miller (2009, 2018).
9   E.g. Nick Estes (2019).
10 My use of tourist-researcher was inspired by Peter Phipps' chapter in the book *Touring Pacific Cultures* (2016: 246).

I acknowledge that I was not entering this work as an average tourist, curious to learn about a particular place, its people, and interested in gaining different experiences. I arrived with background knowledge gained through a particular education in England, Finland and Norway studying Anthropology, Indigenous and Religious Studies. I had thus gained a particular training in research and was perhaps more aware than the average tourist of certain political contexts that framed work on Indigenous Tourism in British Columbia. Whilst I had done a certain amount of fieldwork in my studies, much of what I had learned had come through books. For this project fieldwork was vital.

The Transition from Tourist to a Guest-Researcher

My way of changing from being a tourist to someone hoping to do research entailed revelations and requests. On some occasions, at the end of a tour, I would reintroduce myself to the guide, explain my research interests and ask if I could email with more information. It was important to me that I was not putting anyone on the spot by requesting that they agree to be interviewed there and then. By requesting their email, I could send more information, which gave them a chance to consider my request more fully and reply or not. In this initial email correspondence, I would describe my interests and obligations, indicate how I would like to proceed with my research, and make it clear that I would keep them informed throughout. I gave everyone the option to read what I eventually wrote, and have the right to check, amend and approve my account of our encounters. Each one of the seven participants took me up on this offer. They would also have the right to leave the project at any time. This way the decision to play host to me in this new capacity as a researcher remained an active one, and this relationship influenced the course of my research, gave me freedom to change and adapt, and held me to the promises I made upon becoming a guest.

I conducted interviews with seven people: some lasted several hours, a few of them I had met several times prior to an interview, others just once or twice in person. The seven people were: Andy Everson an artist and chief and member of K'omoks First Nation; Tana Thomas a cultural guide and member of the Ahousaht First Nation; Roy Henry Vickers, an artist, author and Chief; Tsimka Martin, educator, musician and entrepreneur and member of the Tla-o-qui-aht First Nation; K'odi Nelson, a cultural guide/teacher, Business Director and member of the Kwakwaka'wakw First Nation; Alix Goetzinger, cultural guide and member of the Haida Nation; and Linda Calla co-ordinator for Indigenous Tourism British Columbia. Most interviews began with a meal, drink or walk so that we could reacquaint ourselves, build trust and get comfortable.

The process of writing my dissertation took many turns as I debated on the best ways of structuring the work. I wanted to ensure that whilst my voice was clear throughout, so too were the voices of the guides. I opted for extensive use of quotations, something I feel is lacking in many academic accounts of fieldwork. This process involved careful listening to my interviews, allowing for the "messiness" and contradictions that come with conversations; it also reinforced the differences between my perspective and that of the guides. The process helped with transparency and avoided some of the traps of speaking over those researchers are trying to hear.

One complaint about past colonial research might be that it has failed to take full account of ethical considerations. Whose code of ethics are prioritised, and how are they regulated? As part of the requirements of being a Visiting Fellow at UVic, I was asked to write an ethics contract to be signed by all parties in the research. This made me aware of tensions between forms completed for university purposes and agreements reached between researcher and host. For example, an important dimension of Harvey's notion of "guesthood" is that in acknowledging a transition from visitor to guest, control of ethical matters is shared rather than imposed. Whilst university ethical procedures have no doubt improved over the last few decades – and are clearly well intended – there is a danger that they become bureaucratic forms as opposed to mutually useful, shared agreements. In actual use, the university form needed some explanation to avoid people feeling that they were signing away their rights and interests and simply complying with a process designed to protect the University. Each time I introduced the form, I felt it was met with suspicion and ambivalence, and it came as an awkward disruption to the trust and relationship we were in the process of building. Transparency from start to finish helped to gain agreement to use names in my eventual thesis and further articles; this gave me a greater sense of responsibility about what I wrote – and how I wrote it – than any ethics form I was required to complete.

Another problem with these ethical agreements is that they do not allow for how the research process unfolds and changes as does the relationship of those involved. Following Harvey's process of becoming a guest-researcher, sound ethical procedures should attempt to embody that process. The reception these forms received served as a reminder to me that first and foremost, my ethical considerations needed to come from – and be led by – the people who were generously giving me their time and care. Many specific and local ethical protocols of showing respect were explained during the tourism experience and some were given to me personally. Tsimka Martin told me about a "prayer of intent" that she often invokes: "acknowledge where you stand, state that you come with good intentions, and that you will do your best". I thought of this often throughout the whole research process. Tsimka and Tana Thomas told me about a Nuu-chah-nulth philosophy of *Heshookish tsawalk* which they translated to mean "all is one"; this reminded me to appreciate the dynamics and interactions present in any encounters and be aware and consider any contribution and outcome.

Roy Henry Vickers shared with me three lessons that he had learned from his mother. (1) You have not because you asked not. (2) To whom much is given, much is required. (3) You are responsible for the knowledge you carry. Reflecting on these three lessons, I agree that researchers should not be afraid to ask, but they also have to be willing to accept set boundaries they may face. The second point fits many aspects of Indigenous methodologies, for as Linda Tuhiwai Smith (1999) requests, scholars should reflect on the design, framing and dissemination of their work and always question who is benefitting, bearing in mind sharing is the responsibility of research. The third lesson is a reminder to be active, to speak up, use your voice and reflect on the privilege of your position.

An important lesson I received from Tsimka – something in which I think Graham Harvey leads by example – is to write in a way that everyone can understand, to not tell stories just for fellow academics. James Cox (1998 in Harvey, 2003) notes that researchers have powerful ancestors from whom we have inherited a language which requires constant translation. Part of the process of recognising the "priority, sovereignty and rights" of hosts is to acknowledge these translations, to try not to take categories for granted and be open to complexities and contradictions. Another advantage of thinking about "guesthood" lies in the need constantly to reflect on the language used in interactions, to listen carefully to the words used by hosts, the concepts they employ and what they avoid. This also entails refusal to attempt to engage too quickly in acts of translation. An early realisation for me was to not limit my inquiries to experiences marketed in explicitly spiritual ways, such as ceremonies, but rather to attend all and any Indigenous Tourism events, and listen to if, how, when and in what ways spirituality might be invoked.

In shifting from a tourist to a guest-researcher, my hope was to learn more about the complexities of roles, including how, why and what the hosts choose to speak about with tourists. As a tourist I appreciated that I was getting a carefully curated performance. Whilst this could also apply to my developing role as a guest-researcher, I wanted to learn more about how and why those performances came about. Our conversations still took place within boundaries, but now we reflected on the messages the hosts hoped to put across to academics as well as tourists.

Boundaries

The issue of boundaries is important, even when the notion of "guesthood" suggests that they might be changed by giving greater power to hosts. Boundaries were clearly established in tourist events and remained in my conversations; what I perhaps learned was more about why those boundaries were placed where they were. In tourist activities boundaries were laid out clearly as guides spoke about certain things not being made available, and signs pointed to protected areas, only accessible to members of the community. I regularly saw signs placed in graveyards and memorial sights stating that these areas were for the community only and requesting tourists not to take photographs. Some people spoke about how there are stories or songs connected to a place or totem pole or history, but that they personally did not have the right to share them, as they did not belong to them, or they were for a different nation to tell, sing, etc. I read this as a direct message to the public, and specifically academics.

Ceremonies like the *potlatch* were largely unavailable for tourists to attend but the topic regularly came up on tours and was referenced in museums and cultural centres: we were informed about the historic potlatch ban, the many uses the potlatch had and still holds for communities. The potlatch was considered a threat to the Christian Canadian state and was legally banned between 1885 and 1951 (Noakes, 2023). All six guides described the potlatch as a multifaceted ceremony, as – in Andy's words – a place where "we do our legal business", "an essential part of our society", "a way to symbolise wealth", "a way of passing down knowledge", "a ceremony that combines elements of culture, traditions, legalities and spiritualities" (Jennings, 2023: 40). Tsimka stated that the "the potlatch is a really important societal ceremony for us, it encompasses our governance, our spirituality, feasting and economy" (Jennings, 2023: 110). It was through the potlatch ceremony that Alix received her Haida name, SGaana Gaahlandaay meaning "spirit of the killer whale", which she described as a "rite of passage", as "recognition of her work, and dedication to learning about her history and culture" (Jennings, 2023: 156). She explained that when you receive a name through a ceremony, you have to speak it publicly three times and then dance your name as a new person. Then you hug a line of Matriarchs and Chiefs to cement it and show that this is part of your new identity, and that is how it went with her naming ceremony.

The potlatch ban is highlighted as one of the most damaging parts of colonial legislation. Even dances associated with the potlatch, such as the Tamanawas, were prohibited and seen as evidence of devil worship (e.g. Bracken, 1997). An "illegal" potlatch was held in Kwakwaka'wakw territory in 1922. Much of the sacred regalia used in that potlatch was confiscated, with many items ending up in museums around the world (Cole and Chaikin, 1990). The Kwakwaka'wakw have fought for the return of that regalia and much of it is now housed, partly in the U'mista Centre, and partly in the Nuyumbalees Cultural Centre on Quadra Island.[11] Andy and K'odi argued that one reason for banning the potlatch was the sharing of wealth, which contrasted with Victorian values of accumulating wealth. The ban failed, Andy added, and, if anything, the potlatch became bigger in response. K'odi said they once again celebrate important events with the potlatch and are in the process of relearning many old dances. He explained that a potlatch can also help you to grieve, say an official goodbye and be an occasion to burn things that the departed will need on their journey, like food and clothes.

During the tours I attended I would often hear people talk about or demonstrate laws and protocols, for example, around songs and totem poles, either by explaining why they could not speak about something as it was not theirs to share, or by explaining the origins or person or nation a story or song belonged to. Tana shared a song on her tour and later in an interview explained:

> There is a lot of protocol around songs, and it is part of our law. Songs can only ever be gifted and you must share the origins and meanings of songs, it's very bad if you don't, I think many people are scared that they will get it wrong. I have my song now and I have been singing it on whatever platform I have (Jennings, 2023: 62).

This was my first introduction to the laws and protocols around songs, something that I later heard and saw a lot during my time on Vancouver Island. I think the term "law" is used to signal, maintain and reinforce its importance as a practice. Tana described how she enjoyed singing in tourist settings as it was free from the rules and hierarchies around singing that exist in her community. I was told men typically sing and women dance. K'odi, however, was resolute that he would not share any songs or dances in tourist settings or any "sacred stuff"; he explained that he has so much to share that they don't need to share everything, and some stuff they can keep for the community (Jennings, 2023: 142). He described tourism as "dancing with the devil" and needing to be careful with it (Jennings, 2023: 144).

Similar practices were performed regarding totem poles – which are something of a tourist symbol of indigeneity on the Northwest coast. On his

---

11 The Umista Centre: https://www.umista.ca/ (accessed January 2024); The Nuyumbalees Cultural Centre: https://www.museumatcapemudge.com/ (accessed January 2024).

tour of totem poles, Andy pointed out that some of the "mythological" and historical stories about the poles could not be shared by him, as, for example, he is "not Haida and can therefore not tell Haida stories" (Jennings, 2023: 179). Much like the potlatch, instead of being invited to witness the ceremonies, protocols and special meanings that the poles invoke, tourists got to learn about their various purposes, their important historical and colonial significance, and particular figures relating to different nations. Showing diversity of the poles and connected peoples and practices is important, as historically the varying styles of these structures have been collapsed and homogenised. Totem poles, for example, were given special significance when erected by a chief, when used for personal connections with the creator, and they can be used as teaching tools to communicate specific stories with tourists, and to mark boundaries by indicating spiritual significance of the poles that will not be shared.

Andy Everson spoke with me of the boundaries he puts in place for his own work as an artist, navigating between his commercial work and that which he does for his communities. Andy is most famous for his iconic Star Wars prints. He explained that he mostly does two-dimensional art and sometimes traditional work which he reserves for communities and ceremonies. He noted that he likes to make things that people want to hang on their walls. Partly for that reason he does not do a lot of carving, as "in our culture and our teachings, we don't hang carved art like masks on our walls" (Jennings, 2023: 43). These he said are carefully stored away ready to be used in ceremonies. Carving is for traditional use; flat designs are for sale, which is how he mediates between two worlds. Andy explained that he was uncomfortable with the colonial notions of some tourists who buy masks to display on their walls like trophies and that for him, making and selling limited edition prints "feels a more honest encounter" (Jennings, 2023: 43).

Everyone I interviewed spoke about the importance of navigating these boundaries for themselves and their communities. They all described having specific messages they wanted to get across, much of which was based on their historic and ongoing colonial treatment as well as the creativity, resilience and hopes they share for the future. Each person described their own personal motivations for why they were engaged in tourism and what they hoped their involvement would do/bring for themselves and others, how they decided what to share or not with tourists. All of them described having specific messages and topics they wanted to discuss, many of which were common to all, and all spoke about making personal, familial or community-based decisions about what feels right to share with tourists. Whilst asserting and holding to their own boundaries with their work in tourism, they all described a need to share in tourism, with and for each other, and for tourists.

Navigating Tourist Imaginaries and Expectations

Another common theme that emerged from the interviews was how the guides navigate tourist expectations and imaginaries. "Tourist imaginaries" refers to widespread notions about a particular destination, spread through various media and likely to be known by visitors prior to their visit. Imaginaries connected to Indigenous peoples comprise a range of ideas, "from the most banal stereotypes to deep respect and knowledge of historical and cultural transformations and often located in the past in ways which complicate the efforts of Indigenous peoples to be heard in contemporary struggles" (Mathisen, 2004: 4). Indigenous Tourism can offer a space where imaginaries are pulled upon for different purposes, such as selling or enhancing a product, and to challenge, expose, teach, reformulate and reject them.

The guides have chosen to be hosts to tourists who have chosen to sign up and pay for the experience. But tourists can come loaded with ideas and expectations that the hosts might not meet. Tourists are not yet guests. Alix described how most tourists who travel as far as the Haida Gwaii do so ready to learn; they might ask some ignorant questions, but remain open and willing to learn, while others are there to pass judgement and cause offence. Such people, she described, become known island-wide very fast and are swiftly turned into "enemies".

One "tourist imaginary" that the women I interviewed all spoke about was the expectation of not being, looking or sounding Indigenous enough. This idea fits colonial narratives of who can claim indigeneity and on what grounds, and this has affected women in particular. Indigeneity has long been heavily regulated on cultural, religious, biological or legal grounds, or some combination of these. After confederation in 1867, Canada erected mechanisms to legislate "Indian" identity. For example, the original Indian Act of 1867, which has gone through many iterations, imposed a definition of "Indianness" that distinguished between "status" and "non-status Indians", and notably on grounds of gender. Between 1867 and 1951, women and their children who were "status Indians" lost their status if they married a man who did not have "status"; this policy did not apply to men. The designation of "status" had real political implications as it determined who had access to treaty rights and services. In the early twentieth century, anthropologists made evaluations of "Indianness" based on biological features.[12] Debates around authenticity are still prevalent today and remain rooted in colonial assumptions of purity and stasis. This has contributed to benchmarks being drawn and fractures emerging about and between people who identify with

---

12   E.g. Raibmon (2004, 2006, 2008), Lawrence (2003, 2004, 2011), Garroutte (2003).

some form of indigeneity. Colonial constructions of "Indianness" closely contributed to the dispossession of Indigenous lands as the government sought to restrict the number of those who could claim access and rights. Although these ideas and policies have been criticised and dismissed, their effects still linger.[13]

Tana expressed her concerns about how she had not grown up on Nuu-chah-nulth territory and that her main connection to her culture growing up was "tribal journeys" – annual canoe gatherings that take place up and down the Northwest coast. Tsimka commented on her mixed lineage, with her father being Tla-o-qui-aht and her mother being a non-Indigenous Catholic woman from Quebec. She said owing to this she has dealt with discrimination from both her community and from tourists. She also acknowledged certain privileges she feels because of it, for instance that "even in my appearances, people don't know what I am when they look at me, and there's so much racism so it's a different take when people meet me" (Jennings, 2023: 114). She described being very "mindful and sensitive" about this (Jennings, 2023: 114). Likewise, Alix spoke about how strange it can be when speaking about your own identity with tourists:

> They'll say something like "oh are you Haida?" and I'm there, as a Haida guide, on the boat wearing my Haida crew hat, and it's a Haida owned and operated company. I've had that question so much it becomes exhausting! People question saying, "you don't look like you're native", or "oh do they allow non-native people to work here?" Faced with such questions she would think to herself, "if they knew me, knew my identity, they would understand how hurtful that accusation really is" (Jennings, 2023: 159).

She recalled a recent visit of a large tour group to the Centre, when one visitor – everyone on the island now knows who that person is – became angry and vocal because he thought his tour had been given by white people. Alix said:

> The four female guides were Haida, who had worked hard to learn their lineage, introduce themselves in Haida, learned to dance in traditional ceremonies, but just because of the shade of their skin, because they don't look like "Pocahontas-style native", these people make accusations and then leave. That's the hard part about tourism, being stereotyped. It's a really weird thing to deal with. You want to reply, like what's your heritage, you don't look ⅛ Italian or whatever. Geographically, anthropologically we are all different, with different skin colours, different hair. It has nothing to do with who we are or how much

---

13 Lawrence (2003, 2004, 2011), Harris (2004).

we are native. It's a real jaw dropper. You don't know how to fill that space. They want their version of authenticity (Jennings, 2023: 160).

This had become so common that Alix worked on a stock response about how everyone looks and sounds different, warning people not to judge. Expanding on the topic of judgement and stereotypes, Alix brought up her age and gender, saying she had started doing tours at 18, and is now 22.

> I am young, Indigenous and a woman and these three things kind of work against me. Not to stereotype old white men in return, but it's often them that judge, that want to "mansplain", get on their high horse and interrupt you whenever you are speaking (Jennings, 2023: 160).

People would often mistake her for a dockhand and when she introduces herself as the guide, "people click and are surprised, but then they realise I know my shit" (Jennings, 2023: 160). Alix thinks these issues will always be there but is hopeful they will improve with time.

These tourist expectations go beyond what people are supposed to look and sound like, and include what they do and how they do it, like being engaged in tourism, selling knowledge, skills, etc. Both Andy and Roy spoke about their fears of being accepted as contemporary artists and moving away from the traditional iconography more widely associated with their specific Indigenous nations. However, both described becoming more popular and successful as artists as a result.

One tourist imaginary that was highlighted and challenged through my tourism experiences and interviews was the notion of a wilderness. Iconic images of supposedly vast and untouched nature have been and still are used to sell and market Canada. British Columbia was once marketed as untamed and its resources unexploited. Nature plays a huge role in the Canadian narrative and has helped forge an "imagined community"; ideas of wilderness are highly valued in the national rhetoric. On their tours of Meares Island, Tsimka and Tana told the tourists that where we are is not a wilderness, which she said is a word often used to describe islands like this. "Wilderness" implies that it is untouched by people; instead they informed tourists that this is an "ancestral garden" and that this land looks like this and is flourishing because it has been, and continues to be, cared for. Tsimka explained that you can see the selective harvests and places that have been gardened and that whilst some areas don't see as many humans as others, you can always see the stewardship if you know how to look for it.

The idea of a "wilderness" served colonial governments when claiming ownership of land. It is fundamentally a colonial vision and is central to

Figure 3.2 Sign on Meares Island, welcoming guests to Tla-o-qui-aht tribal parks with a canoe and sea serpent engraved. Helen Jennings 2018.

settler colonialism's notions of *terra nullius* and the Frontier. Geographer Bruce Braun (2002) argues that the notion of wilderness suggests that nature lies outside of history, and by so doing denies other histories, specifically those of Indigenous peoples. Through representations of the wild frontier "the Indigenous worldview, the land and the people have been radically transformed in the spatial image of the west" (Smith, 1991: 51). In other words, "Indigenous space has been colonised. Indigenous peoples are either collapsed into the notion of wilderness, namely, made part of nature, or have somehow disappeared to later re-enter the scene as protectors and guardians of that so-called wilderness" (Smith, 1991: 51). Challenging notions of wilderness opens questions about how to conceptualise a place and its histories, corrects perceptions and teaches guests new ways of thinking. Rejecting the term in favour of words that are seen to better illustrate the ongoing relationship to the land is, as Tana said, serving current Indigenous land right claims. The tours, as well as the Boardwalk and welcome sign written in Nuu-chah-nulth, which have been erected on Meares Island work as a physical claim to sovereignty. In this way, Tana and Tsimka respond to an established discourse about indigeneity and reject it for a term that better speaks to the Nuu-chah-nulth speaking peoples. This discussion of "wilderness" versus "garden" illustrates the importance of Graham Harvey's advice for scholars to be alert to the complexities of language in use in any encounter, be mindful of preconceptions, and open to new interpretations and translations. People choose and employ words to do particular work.

Motivations

Tsimka said that one of her main motives for working in tourism was her ability to train guides, not just with the hard skills needed to be a guide, but with the time and care it gave them to learn about their own pasts, to speak with relatives and learn the stories of their families. Tana, a guide who had been trained by Tsimka, said that she had been "thinking a lot about healing" for:

> There is so much work to do in our communities. To start with we need to know about what our parents went through. They need to heal, and we need to understand. We need to understand where all the hurt and pain comes from (Jennings, 2023: 69).

Tana valued tourism as a good start to this work as it "engages the community in our culture and in our surroundings and for it to be multidisciplinary, so everyone can find their space within it… I think tourism can provide that opportunity for the new generation" (Jennings, 2023: 69).

Reinforcing the importance of and need for healing, Tana noted that "We cannot thrive if we are not healthy people" (Jennings, 2023: 69). Responding to the pain and loss brought on by colonial policies and with hope for the future she remarked:

> We need to be learning from our elders and teaching our youth. We, my generation, need to be good mentors and role models so then we can share our culture in tourism. We need a culture that we know well and that we are proud to share, communities have been so displaced. Not all families were able to hold on to so many teachings so those that can, now need to search for them (Jennings, 2023: 69).

She explained that:

> The older generations went through the residential school system. They learnt not to talk about their ceremonies. They were taught to be ashamed, and some people do not realize that they are passing that sense of shame on by keeping

it all so hidden. We need to change, I think we need to share, we need to stop keeping things secret (Jennings, 2023: 69).

Tana described how the spaces tourism provides can serve as an opportunity to do some of this important healing, not just for herself and her communities, but for everyone involved. "Being a tour guide gives you the time to do that cultural work, to dig into the past and dig up those teachings and to share them; I think tourism is a great platform for that and one that everyone can benefit from" (Jennings, 2023: 72).

Tana commented that working in tourism could, however, be problematic:

I have seen some communities get lost in tourism, they have too many tourists and just start to entertain with their culture and that's when it becomes inauthentic. There's a fine balance, it can be repetitive and strange, sharing your story, time and again and you can get bored of yourself, so if one day you are tired and bored of a particular job, you have the space to do something else...tourists can sometimes dehumanize their guides. They can think of them just as entertainers and lose sight of the fact that they have a story. it's not just someone on stage. I think the space needs to be safe and reciprocal. If it's too one sided, it can be draining for both the guide and the tourist. Tourism should be about an exchange and connection and then it's all worth it (Jennings, 2023: 73).

Tana's point here really cuts through a lot of academic arguments about tourism which often focus on commodification and consumption and uphold rigid binaries concerning the roles played by guides and tourists.

Tsimka's business is one of only a few in the area that are Indigenous-owned and operated. She explained that one of the obstacles stopping Indigenous peoples from entering the market is a lack of money and inheritance. Tsimka added that the Tla-o-qui-aht people have a rich history of hosting people which she felt gave them an advantage for working in tourism. She saw tourism as a way of making money and was proud of how she was training the guides through which she and they gain time to learn and talk about histories and families and what they think is appropriate to share with tourists. She stressed how important it is for the guides to decide for themselves what they feel is appropriate to share and in that seek appropriate permissions. She added:

I think we have a great opportunity with tourism, to get around in a different way, and set up something more positive. I hope that as our community sets up more tourism it does so in a way that is more grounded in our values (Jennings, 2023: 121).

Tsimka is currently working on a project with "Tourism Tofino" about a "value initiative" for tourists visiting Tofino. She explained:

> The first part is for a brochure to be distributed around Tofino about Tla-o-qui-aht values, to give a welcome from our people. At the moment people can come here and not even know what Nation lives here or what area they are in. So I think it's important to offer some understanding and core principles (Jennings, 2023: 113).

Andy described how he hoped his artwork served as a kind of "gateway drug", that people would be drawn into the recognisable images, like the Star Wars storm trooper, and through that become more interested in Indigenous art forms and explore the work of other Indigenous artists. He said that some traditional art pieces and stories can be hard to understand and because of that tourists can feel intimidated, but with pop culture iconography Andy asserted that the viewer is already halfway there. Andy hoped that his images help to bridge the gap for people approaching his art and:

> It also gives me space to talk about colonisation, treaties, my concerns, negotiations, settlements and the current relationship between Indigenous peoples and the colonial government. So, it is loaded with so many different things, not only does it draw people in visually, but it also enables me to hack it with more meaning than I could if I just drew a thunderbird for example (Jennings, 2023: 45).

Andy spoke about the responsibilities he feels to his grandmothers, his ancestors, and his community, and that with that responsibility he enjoys showing that his people are still here, and his culture is still relevant. For several of the guides, tourism gave them an opportunity to be stewards of their lands once more, or as Kodi expressed it, he was able to be the "eyes and ears on the land" to watch over the work of developers, loggers and others.

Conclusions

Indigenous Tourism offers a perfect site for – and illustration of the value of – Graham Harvey's theory and method of "guesthood". It affords the researcher clear entry points for learning local protocols and provides a pathway from the position of tourist to that of guest-researcher. Initiating and negotiating the starting point of any research project can be a minefield for academics; adopting the role of guest, and all that comes with that, emphasises the need for respect, consideration and acceptance of boundaries. The role of guest automatically implies greater humility than that which has been revealed in the work of many scholars in the past. The role of guest sets up more scope for constructive interaction and transparency. Tourists, like researchers, seek new knowledge, knowledge that their hosts have and are free to give, or not, on their territory. As Alix said jokingly, guests are perhaps especially respectful on tours to remote sacred sites as "we are their only ride home." Indigenous tourist guides – at least the ones I spoke with – are always acting as discriminating hosts, treating each tourist on their merits, making decisions on what to share.

Yet, as Graham Harvey warns, researchers should not assume that becoming a guest is as easy as turning up and asking for a dialogue. It is an evolving process which helps to bring about deeper and more respectful understandings of topics of research and is well worth the extra effort involved. When it works well it can enhance understanding for all concerned. I hope my research has been useful to the people I spoke with. Guided by Tsimka, my thesis was written in an accessible way, relatively free from academic jargon. I think Harvey's methodology helps to keep researchers attuned to this goal.

The concepts of "Learn, Teach, Heal," which I used in my thesis, grew directly from my discussions with the guides about their work. This involved their personal development, that of their communities – both near and far – and also tourists and the wider project of reconciliation and decolonisation. I did not commence my project with these ideas in mind and would not have derived them without the full involvement of the guides; their participation in my research was essential. Thanks to my role as a guest-researcher, the guides discussed aspects of their work – such as their intentions and values – that I could not have gained in other ways. The guides were very open that they were in a process of learning much of what they wanted to share in tourism, be that about their cultural practices and traditions and/or their colonial pasts and presents. This process of reclaiming and re-narrating was expressed as one of healing.

My encounters with the guides resembled and differed from that of other tourists. Among the methodological lessons – foregrounded by all the guides and directed explicitly for my research – was to be careful about stereotypes, to provide space for complexity, particularities and to respect boundaries. They each made it clear to me that they did not speak with one voice and that they related to their indigeneity in different ways. Indigenous Tourism is not something that is happening to them, and their role in this industry does not make them, or the practices they choose to share, inauthentic. Instead, they are looking to learn and teach other guides and tourists, and in that process heal.

My role as a guest-researcher has helped me to appreciate just how research is negotiated through encounters. "Learn, Teach, Heal" emphasises agency, process and change; it challenges notions of indigeneity as fixed in the past and lacking a future. Learning signals change and development. Teaching denotes knowledge, rather than merely entertainment, something often associated with tourism, and a relationship between teacher and pupil, rather than spectacle only. Teaching implies learning for all parties involved. For the younger guides, tourism also offers a space in which to deepen their knowledge of the land and associated traditions and can offer a practice ground free from rules and hierarchies that might exist in their communities and from expectations held by the public. The upholding of "pure" traditions has long been seen by both scholars and tourists as a mark of authentic indigeneity; yet tourism is being used by many guides to disturb the constraints of tradition for both themselves, and for tourists. Their very engagement in tourism challenges notions of authenticity which exclude them from participating in the economy.[14] For older guides, tourism offers a way to share their knowledge, "play" with traditions and develop gateways; channels through which tourists may be invited in, learn more and join them in their causes. To teach signals control in these contexts over what to share, with whom and in what circumstances; it signals competence, authority and responsibility.

Without the transfer to becoming a guest-researcher, the research described above would not have come about; it all depended upon building a relationship based on trust and respect. Without this, my appreciation of what is going on in Indigenous Tourism in British Columbia would have been more superficial and my engagement with the hosts less transformative. Graham Harvey's concept has been invaluable and opened avenues for further development in research methodology, particularly in the field of research ethics. It has also proved to be an effective method of conducting research in a decolonising context. Tourism has for too long been dismissed as shallow entertainment, a product of colonial capitalism, an arena in which the hosts are expected to meet the demands of their visitors to their own detriment. The concept of "guesthood" changes that dynamic completely; it forces the researcher to listen to hosts and take what they say and do seriously. And this may have the added benefit of challenging assumptions all round.

---

14 E.g. The Truth and Reconciliation Commission report http://trc.ca (accessed January 2024). Alexis Bunten (2010) addresses this issue and writes about what she calls "Indigenous Capitalism".

References

Aikau, H.K. and Gonzalez, V.V. 2019. *Detours: a Decolonial Guide to Hawai'i*. Durham, NC and London: Duke University Press.
Bracken, C. 1997. *The Potlatch Papers: A Colonial Case History*. Chicago, IL: University of Chicago Press.
Braun, B. 2002. *The Intemperate Rainforest: Nature, Culture, and Power on Canada's West Coast*. Minneapolis, MN: University of Minnesota Press.
Bunten, A, 2010. "More like ourselves: Indigenous capitalism through tourism", *The American Indian Quarterly* 34(3): 285–311.
Cole, D. and Chaikin, I. 1990. *An Iron Hand Upon the People: The Law Against the Potlatch on the Northwest Coast*. Vancouver: Douglas and McIntyre.
Cruikshank, J. 1998. *The Social Life of Stories: Narrative and Knowledge in the Yukon*. Vancouver: University of British Columbia Press.
Cruikshank, J. 2005. *Do Glaciers Listen? Local Knowledge, Colonial Encounters, and Social Imagination*. Vancouver: University of British Columbia Press.
Davis, L. 2010. *Alliances: Re/envisioning Indigenous-Non-Indigenous Relationships*. Toronto: Toronto University Press.
Davis, L. et al. 2017. "Complicated pathways: Settler Canadians learning to re/frame themselves and their relationships with Indigenous peoples", *Settler Colonial Studies* 7(4): 398–414.
Estes, N. 2019. *Our History is the Future: Standing Rock Versus the Dakota Access Pipeline, and the Long Tradition of Indigenous Resistance*. London: Verso Books.
Garroutte, E, M. 2003. *Real Indians: Identity and the Survival of Native America*. Berkeley: University of California Press.
Harris, C. 2004. "How did colonialism dispossess? Comments from an edge of an empire", *Annals of the Association of the American Geographers*. 94 (1).
Harvey, G. 2003. "Guesthood as ethical decolonising research method", *Numen* 50(2): 125–146.
Jennings, H. 2023 "Learn, Teach, Heal: Articulations of indigeneity and spirituality in British Columbia, Canada", https://hdl.handle.net/10037/27718.
Kovach, M. 2009. *Indigenous Methodologies: Characteristics, conversations and contexts*. University of Toronto Press.
Lawrence, B. 2003. "Gender, race, and the regulation of Native identity in Canada and the United States: An overview", *Hypatia* 18(2): 3–31.
Lawrence, B. 2004. *"Real" Indians and Others: Mixed-Blood Urban Native Peoples and Indigenous Nationhood*. Lincoln: University of Nebraska Press.
Lawrence, B. 2011. "Legislating Identity: Colonialism, land and indigenous legacies", in Wetherell, M. and Mohanty, C.T. (eds), *The Sage Handbook of Identities*, 508–529. Thousand Oaks, CA: Sage.
Lutz, J. 2008. *Makúk: A New History of Aboriginal White Relations*. Vancouver: University British Columbia Press.
McCall, S. 2012. *First Person Plural; Aboriginal Storytelling and the Ethics of Authorship*. Vancouver, B.C.: University of British Columbia Press.
Miller, J, R. 2009. *Compact,Contract,Covenant:AboriginalTreaty-Making in Canada*.Toronto, ON: University of Toronto Press.

Miller, J, R. 2018. *Skyscrapers Hide the Heavens: A History of Indian-White Relations in Canada*. Toronto, ON: University of Toronto Press.

Mathisen, S.R. 2004. "Hegemonic representations of Sami culture from narratives of noble savages to discourses on ecological Sami", in Siikala, A.L. Klien, B. and Mathisen, S.R. *Creating Diversities: Folklore, Religion and the Politics of Heritage*. Helsinki: Finnish Literature Society.

Nichols, R. 2013. "Indigeneity and the settler contract today", *Sage Publications* 39(2): 165–186.

Niezen, R. 2004. *The Origins of Indigenism: Human Rights and the Politics of Identity*. Berkeley: University of California Press.

Niezen, R. 2008. "The Global Indigenous movement", in *Handbook of North American Indians* (Vol. 2), G. A Bailey (ed.), 438–445. Washington: Smithsonian Institution.

Niezen, R. 2009. *The Rediscovered Self: Indigenous Identity and Cultural Justice*. Montreal and Kingston: McGill–Queen's University Press.

Noakes, T.C. 2023. "Potlatch ban", in *The Canadian Encyclopedia*. Available at: www.thecanadianencyclopedia.ca/en/article/potlatch-ban (accessed February 2024)

Phipps. P. 2016. "Performing Indigenous sovereignties across the Pacific", in Alexeyeff, K. and Taylor, J. (eds), *Touring Pacific Cultures*. Acton, A.C.T.: Australian National University Press. pp. 245–267.

Raibmon, P. 2004. *Authentic Indians: Episodes of Encounter from the Late-Nineteenth-Century Northwest Coast*. Durham, NC and London: Duke University Press.

Raibmon, P. 2006. "The practice of everyday colonialism: Indigenous women at work in the hop fields and tourist industry of Puget Sound", *Labor: Studies in Working-Class History of the Americas* 3(3): 23–56.

Raibmon, P. 2008. "Unmaking native space: A genealogy of Indian policy, settler practice, and the microtechniques of dispossession", in Harmon, A. (ed.), *The Power of Promises: Rethinking Indian Treaties In the Pacific Northwest*. Seattle: Center for the Study of the Pacific Northwest in Association with University of Washington Press. pp. 56–85.

Regan, P. 2010. *Unsettling the Settler Within: Indian Residential Schools, Truth Telling, and Reconciliation in Canada*. Vancouver, B.C.: University of British Columbia Press.

Smith, L.T. 1999. *Decolonising Methodologies: Research and Indigenous Peoples*. London: Zed Books.

Wolfe, P. 1999. *Settler Colonialism and the Transformation of Anthropology: The Politics and Poetics of an Ethnographic Event*. London: Cassell.

Wolfe, P. 2006. "Settler colonialism and the elimination of the native", *Journal of Genocide Research* 8(4): 387–409.

About the Author

Dr Helen Jennings is currently an independent scholar; she completed her PhD in Religious Studies at UiT – The Arctic University of Norway.

The dissertation was about articulations of indigeneity and spirituality as presented in Indigenous Tourism and was based on fieldwork in British Columbia, Canada. Her current interests build on this work as she has publications forthcoming on: Indigenous Tourism as a site for reclaiming and becoming, religion making in a decolonial mode, and women and fieldwork. Helen wrote this paper on "guesthood" whilst benefiting from a "transitional scholarship", for which she thanks UiT.

4 "Guesthood" as a Scientific Method: Principles Supporting Relational Research

James L. Cox

Graham Harvey has contributed significantly throughout his academic career to the study of Indigenous Religions, particularly by reflecting on the relationship between research methods and colonisation. Following the lead of Linda Tuhawai Smith in her landmark book *Decolonizing Methodologies* (1999, 2022), Harvey contended that "researchers have appropriated from people whilst being party to their subjection to a culture that diminishes them" (2003: 127). As an alternative to traditional approaches to the study of Indigenous Religions, which tended to treat the people who comprise the subject matter of academic projects according to Western dualisms such as "objective" vs "subjective", "insider" vs "outsider" and "science" vs "superstition", in an important article published in 2003 in *Numen*, Harvey (2003: 125–46) proposed a new method he called "guesthood". In this chapter, I examine guesthood in Harvey's terms as an "an ethical decolonising research method", compare it with my own interpretation of "relational research" derived from phenomenological principles and suggest that taken together, guesthood and relationality, rather than violating the objective intentions of scientific investigations, following the conclusions of the internationally acclaimed physicist, Carlo Rovelli, actually conform closely to theories rooted in quantum mechanics.

Harvey's Use of "Guesthood"

Harvey attributes the notion "guesthood" to his study of Ngāti Porou, a traditional clan located on Aotearoa-New Zealand's east coast, and Ngāti Rānana, a diasporic Māori group living in and around London. Harvey is particularly concerned to explain protocols associated with the *marae*, which is an open space with an identifiable entry point, where traditional Māori ceremonial and social functions occur. Across the space is located a carved or decorated meeting house, often called a *whare nui*, or *whare tipuna* (ancestral house) (Harvey 2003: 133). Harvey's concern is to explore the significance of Māori protocols connected with the "opportunity for strangers to express one or other side of their potential to be enemies or guests" (Harvey 2003: 133). He describes how this relationship was expressed in his observations of a *marae* in the *whare* Hinemihi, located on the grounds of Clandon Park House, a National Trust property situated around 30 miles southwest of London in Surrey, near Guildford.[1] Since the 1990s, the *whare* Himemihi has been used as a meeting house of the Ngāti Rānana and other Māori communities around the UK. Harvey (2003: 134) explains that Māori and their guests are regularly welcomed to the *whare* Hinemihi, but only "a descendant of the particular ancestor is sufficiently intimate to have the right of entry with impunity". Guests are not descendants and thus have different relationships to the ancestors associated with the *whare*, even if they have lived for a prolonged time among the group. The protocols that are in place describing the relationships between members of the ancestral body and guests, Harvey (2003: 135) explains, are "intended to enable… intimacy to take place appropriately".

According to traditional convention, the protocols determine if the strangers who approach the *marae* are enemies or guests. Strangers must stop at the entrance to the *marae* and wait for the call of invitation that is issued by women. They then take a few steps into the open space and distinctions between members of the ancestral clan and those that are outside it are highlighted, such as "different ancestry, traditions, habits, 'normality', taken-for-granted everyday-ness, knowledge and prestige" (Harvey 2003: 135). In a series of stages, the proper relationships between the hosts and guests are clarified, which Harvey suggests "aim to highlight the prestige and precedence of locals" (2003: 135). The stages include a local warrior laying down a *taki*, a symbol of wielding weapons, frequently a small branch, which visitors pick up to show they come in peace. This is followed by the performance of

---

1   The National Trust website for Clandon Park House explains that Hinemihi was a woman of great authority who lived in Aotearoa/New Zealand in the mid-sixteenth century. Hinemihi is depicted on the building located in the grounds of Clandon Park House with intricate carvings of various parts of her body. Her head sits on the top of the house, her arms surround the veranda and her heart is represented in the central supporting column inside the house. In November 2019, nearly twenty years after Harvey conducted his research on the *whare* Hinemihi, an agreement was reached between the National Trust UK and Heritage New Zealand for the original carvings of Hinemihi to be returned to Aotearoa/New Zealand. As a substitute, a new meeting house is planned at Clandon Park which will feature carvings of Hinemihi created by expert Māori artists (www.nationaltrust.org.uk/visit/surrey/clandon-park/a-new-future-for-hinemihi, accessed 25 April 2023).

haka, warrior posture songs displaying the local group's pride, which is well known to those familiar with how Aotearoa-New Zealand players begin international rugby matches. Harvey explains: "The visitors are expected to pick up the *taki* and face the challenge of *haka* without reciprocating violence" (2003: 135). In this way, "locals and visitors initiate the process of accepting the roles and responsibilities of host- and guesthood" (Harvey 2003, 135).

Although Harvey goes into detail about how guests and hosts interact and solidify their respective roles in further interactive stages, I want to focus on what he calls "*marae* as method" (Harvey 2003: 137), through which he uses traditional Māori etiquette as a model for constructing a proper relationship between academic researchers and the communities they are investigating. The starting point is for researchers to "confront their potential hosts as possible guests and possible enemies" (Harvey 2003: 138). This is based on the acknowledgement that researchers as guests do not share a common ancestor with their hosts, which means that they cannot really "go native" nor can they simply assume that they understand what is "self-evident" to their hosts (Harvey 2003: 138). It is important to note, according to Harvey, that traditional "colonialist" methods based on Western dualisms have resulted in academic assumptions that researchers have the "right to observe and discover whatever they desire to know" (Harvey 2003: 138). The resulting emphasis on academic objectivity minimises the fact that those being studied are also observing the researchers.

Following Māori rules, researchers must actively seek the invitation of those they are researching, which means that "the priority of locals is fundamental… as is their prestige" (Harvey 2003: 138). Then Harvey makes an important point: the knowledge scholars seek to uncover, understand and interpret "is the property of their hosts" (Harvey 2003: 139). Researchers must recognise and accept that "guests are made by hosts" and not the other way around (Harvey 2003: 139). The academic as guest means that the hosts may decide, rather than being a guest, the researcher is actually an enemy. If this conclusion is reached, it is likely that members of the researched community will deliberately mislead the researcher or provide false or incomplete information. If the host accepts the researcher as a guest, however, research proper can begin. The hosts possess the knowledge and understanding that the researcher desires. The researcher in turn attempts to translate this for the academic community. Or it could be that neither the local community nor the academic investigator acting alone can achieve understanding of each other's aims. Although the process is dialogical, the host-guest relationship means that the researcher gives priority to the agency of those being studied and accepts that local knowledge belongs to local communities. Harvey

(2003: 142) concludes: "To become a guest-researcher is to bow to the power/prestige of hosts".

Guesthood as Phenomenology

I have written in numerous publications on the phenomenology of religion by relating it to key thinkers in religious studies and by outlining the method as a step-by-step process (Cox 2006, 2010, 2022a). From the 1930s until the 1970s, phenomenologists of religion played pivotal roles in departments for the study of the history of religion and thus helped shape the direction taken within the field of religious studies through a large part of the twentieth century. Key thinkers in the phenomenology of religion became household names among students of religion: W. Brede Kristensen, Gerardus van der Leeuw, C.J. Bleeker, Raffaele Pettazzoni, Mircea Eliade, Ugo Bianchi, Ninian Smart, Geo Widengren, to name just a few. In the sociology of religion, phenomenological principles were made prominent in the writings of Joachim Wach and Alfred Schutz, and in theology by Rudolf Otto, Karl Heim, Wilfred Cantwell Smith and John Hick. The list, of course, is far wider than those I have named, but they serve to demonstrate how influential the phenomenology of religion was through most of the twentieth century. Although in his article on guesthood Harvey does not draw direct parallels between his description of the relationship between hosts and guests and phenomenological methods, I believe a case can be made for depicting "guesthood" as an example of an extended type of phenomenology.

To demonstrate this point, I refer to a discussion of phenomenological approaches derived from a field not commonly associated with the humanities, business studies. In their comprehensive guide for students entitled *Business Research Methods*, British scholars Alan Bryman and Emma Bell include a section on "epistemological considerations", under which they list a method they call "interpretivism". They define "interpretive research" as "involving a dialogical process between theory and empirical phenomenon", which requires the researcher to produce "reflexive narratives" rather than "explanatory models or theoretical propositions" (Bryman and Bell, 2015: 26). Of particular interest to Bryman and Bell (2015: 31) are what they call "the hermeneutic-phenomenological tradition and the *Verstehen* approach".

For Bryman and Bell, the hermeneutic-phenomenological method requires the researcher to adopt a position in relation to those who comprise the subjects of research based on the conviction that "social reality has a meaning for human beings and therefore human action is meaningful" (Bryman and Bell, 2015: 30). Then, in a key phrase, they write, "it is the job of the social scientist to gain access to people's 'common-sense thinking' and hence to interpret their actions and their social world from their point of view" (Bryman and Bell, 2015: 30). The contribution of phenomenology to the social sciences, according to Bryman and Bell, results from the application of phenomenological methods to social action, which broadens traditional academic interpretations beyond abstract ideas by relating them to the pragmatic concerns of the researched communities. This approach makes it possible to forge not only interpretative links with those being studied but involves both researcher and the researched in practical planning for social action that reflects fundamental local concerns.

In previous writings, I have argued that one of the primary aims of the phenomenological method in the study of religious communities is to foster understanding of them among a broad range of audiences who otherwise might misrepresent them, suppress their goals or even oppress them because of widespread biased interpretations of their cultural values. I have suggested that the stage in the phenomenological method I have called "empathetic interpolation" is intended to limit the tendency of scholars to impose their own pre-judgements on their research subjects by cultivating a feeling for the practices and beliefs that initially to them may appear strange, inexplicable or culturally offensive. To interpolate means to insert what is apprehended from another religion or culture into one's own experience by translating seemingly alien behaviours into terms outsiders can understand (Cox, 2010: 49–70). Understanding in this sense is related to the German word *Verstehen*, which extends the English meaning to stress "understanding in depth".

In my book *Restoring the Chain of Memory* (2018), I illustrate how the linguist and anthropologist T.G.H. Strehlow used empathetic interpolation to foster understanding of the songs, stories and ceremonies he observed and recorded during the 1930s among Arrernte-speaking groups in Central Australia. In his book *Songs of Central Australia*, Strehlow (1971: xvi) defined one of the principal aims of his research among the Arrernte as drawing "attention to the mental attitudes, common human emotions, uninhibited subconscious drives which seem to find a safe and convenient outlet for their expression through the medium of these songs". Communicating to outsiders a sense of what it is to think like an Arrernte person required Strehlow to interpolate symbols and meanings gained from studying the Indigenous cultural context in terms familiar to a European audience. Strehlow applied this method repeatedly throughout *Songs of Central Australia* by drawing parallels between Arrernte beliefs and practices, which to the Western reader appeared bizarre or even offensive, and themes commonly found in European, and particularly Old Norse, literature and poetry. He summarised his reason for doing this in the Introduction to his book:

The European parallels are designed to achieve a more sympathetic attitude in the mind of the white reader towards aboriginal verse and towards the aboriginal world of ideas. For once it can be shown that some of these apparently crude, cruel, strange, or disgusting ideas were once found also in ancient pagan Europe, then more thoughtful readers may hesitate to reject them as utterly valueless (Strehlow, 1971: xl).

To resolve the problem created by potential conflicts between academic and community interests in research projects, phenomenologists of religion have maintained widely that scholarly interpretations which offend the religious communities being studied are illegitimate because they distort the data on which the interpretations are based. In my view, phenomenologists of religion correctly asserted that religious adherents, who cannot recognise themselves in the scholarly explanations offered, are not being described or interpreted accurately nor are scientific principles being observed. This is because phenomenologists have insisted that the validity of explanations must be judged on criteria that include believing communities themselves, without which there would be no data on which to build academic theories and without which genuine understanding (*Verstehen*) cannot be achieved. This conviction lay behind W. Brede Kristensen's famous declaration that "the believers were completely right" (Kristensen, 1960: 14), a position expanded by Wilfred Cantwell Smith's "verificationist principle" of humane knowledge, which Smith argued requires agreement of a scholar's interpretations by believing and academic communities alike (Smith, 1981: 97).

Although this conventional phenomenological approach has contributed much to fostering empathetic interpretations of religious and cultural practices, it does not redress the power imbalance between the academic who describes, interprets and compares religious beliefs and practices among a diverse range of groups. Later stages in the phenomenological method, as I have outlined it, call for the creation of religious typologies derived from comparative studies, which lead in turn to broad and generalised interpretations of religion in general, the phenomenological "eidetic intuition" or "eidetic vision" (Cox, 2010: 63–68). On this model, academic researchers remain almost totally responsible for any broad interpretations concerning the communities they have studied. The scholar Gavin Flood refers to this as granting epistemic privilege to the phenomenologist which unduly limits "the range of methodological possibilities within the study of religions" (1999: 93). He argues that this is because, in its philosophical roots, phenomenology is wed to the idea it derived from the German philosophical phenomenologist Edmund Husserl that "assumes the universality of the rational subject...who can, through objectification, have access to truth external to any particular cultural standpoint" (Flood, 1999: 108).

This problem can be overcome by directly connecting the role of the researcher to the immediate concerns of the communities under study. Following Bryman and Bell, research conducted in dialogue with local communities will inevitably result in action plans worked out jointly by the researcher and those being researched. This is where hermeneutical phenomenology that promotes understanding (*Verstehen*) and action research coincide. If dialogue is taken seriously and the priority of the host is acknowledged, when seen in the light of empathetic interpolation, the phenomenological aim of promoting tolerance and good relations between local communities and wider audiences bears clear practical consequences, including influencing policy decisions by governmental, religious, educational and other agents that affect the local community's wellbeing.

In this sense, Graham Harvey's contribution to the discussion, by identifying the research method he calls guesthood, goes further than developing interpretations that reflect fairly the point of view of the groups under study, because ultimately such interpretations are dictated by academic researchers themselves. Guesthood acknowledges the legitimate ownership of knowledge by local communities and it reverses conventional power relationships by affirming that local communities possess agency and therefore have the right to welcome or reject the researcher as a guest. Through a process of carefully constructed dialogue, the interests of hosts and guests are communicated and points of commonality identified. The interpretations of the communities being investigated are jointly owned and accepted before the research findings are disseminated. This approach is fully consistent with phenomenological aims, but extends the conventional phenomenological emphasis on the researcher reflecting believers' perspectives to one that insists that all interpretations are jointly owned, having been made possible only by the invitation of those being studied and ratified through dialogue and consensus.

Guesthood, Academic Freedom and Relational Research

If communities that are the subjects of academic research must be involved at every stage of a research project, including endorsing academic interpretations based on informed scholarly analysis, the issue of the freedom of the academic to offer critical reflections on the beliefs, attitudes, practices and behaviours of religious groups would appear to be restricted severely. One of the commonly accepted lynchpins of scholarly analysis depends on the academic having the freedom to describe and interpret religious communities in terms the communities themselves may not endorse. Otherwise, it would appear that the role of the researcher is limited to nonanalytical summaries of what adherents believe and non-critical reports as to how members of local groups themselves interpret the meanings of their ceremonial practices. The distinctive roles of the academic and religious communities would appear blurred on this model, with the scholar seemingly not only describing what believers say and do, but in fact endorsing their faith positions. Two advocates of separating or at least clearly delineating the legitimate places of the researcher and the researched are the late Robert Segal, formerly Professor of Religious Studies at the University of Aberdeen in Scotland, and Laurie Patton, Professor of Religion at Middlebury College in the USA.

In a critique of Wilfred Cantwell Smith's dialogical interpretation of the relationship between academics and religious adherents, Segal (2017: 174) objects that all dialogical approaches to the study of religions make the error of granting adherents the right to "hold veto power over any outsider's proffered interpretation". He adds: "If adherents can decide which interpretations are wrong, then they can decide which ones are right" (Segal, 2017: 174). In place of a dialogical approach to the study of religion, which Harvey's method "guesthood" certainly fits, Segal argues that the best term to describe the association between a researcher and a religious person is "diagnosis", following the analogy of a doctor–patient relationship. Segal contends that "there is nothing reciprocal in the relationship of adherent to scholar". Rather, "just as the patient has the disease but is not thereby the authority on it, so the adherent has the religion but is not thereby the expert on it" (Segal, 2017: 174). He admits that both scholars and doctors require subjects to perform their functions, but they rely on their subjects solely for information. The scholar has studied a community's religion in detail according to scientific protocols, which makes the roles of the researcher and the adherent fundamentally different. Even if the believer is able to convey a large amount of information to a scholar, just like a doctor, the researcher is the expert on the religion being studied.

In support of likening the relationship of the scholar and the subjects of research to that of a doctor and patient, and in sharp contrast to traditional phenomenological aim of achieving *Verstehen* in the study of religious communities, Segal (2017: 177) counters that "the goal of medicine is not 'understanding' but explanation". A doctor's job is to classify "the patient's symptoms", determine "the origin of the illness" and predict "the course of the illness" (Segal, 2017: 177). Medicine does not seek to understand "what it feels like to a patient to have cancer" but to try to figure out how it can be treated (Segal, 2017: 177). Segal concludes that religion should be studied in the same way because "like disease, religion has a cause, and the social sciences strive to find out what it is" (Segal, 2017: 178).

Another position relevant to Harvey's concept "guesthood" has been developed by the American scholar of religion, Laurie L. Patton, in her book *Who Owns Religion?* (2019). Although Patton considers religion a conceptual category, she primarily focuses on the conflicts created by interpretations of specific religious communities proposed by academics that are rejected or criticised by the members of the communities themselves. Through a series of case studies highlighting controversies, or what she calls "scandals", occurring during the late 1980s and through the 1990s, Patton considers the problem for scholarly interpretations of religion created by giving priority to hosts, as explained by Harvey, which seems to privilege the interpretative right of adherents over the analytical perspectives of scholars.

Patton (2019: 41) highlights conditions that create conflict between what she calls "the scholar's right to interpret" and the "agency" of religious groups. She insists that "the understanding of the university's ability and obligation to represent a religious tradition is at harsh odds with the community's understanding" (Patton, 2019: 35). The "trigger" for a conflict in representation, she argues, usually results from the publication of a scholarly work, which when it reaches a wider, public audience may have negative impacts on the communities being described (Patton, 2019: 36). The justification for promoting academic conclusions that may offend religious groups, she says in an argument similar to that developed by Segal, "derives from the discourse of objectivity" (Patton, 2019: 41). Then, in sharp contrast to Harvey's theory of "guesthood", Patton contends that "religious communities have no agency in endowing scholars with the right to interpret" (Patton, 2019: 41). She admits that religious groups are free to pass judgement on the interpretations developed by academics about them, but she maintains that "there is no social contract between religious communities and university communities" because there are "no commonly understood norms, no agreed-upon standard as to who has the 'right' to interpret" (Patton, 2019: 41). The relationship between religious studies departments and religious communities, according to Patton, is "tension-filled" due to the inherent conflict over "*the rivalry to represent*" (2019: 43, emphasis in original). She admits that frequently academics in a phenomenological tradition adopt a sympathetic attitude towards the communities they are studying, but she insists that "such bonhomie cannot obscure the fundamentally irreconcilable views about the right to interpret the same religious texts and artifacts" (Patton, 2019: 43).

Segal and Patton, by constructing strict boundaries between the roles of academics and adherents, pose a question that is relevant to Harvey's position: "What qualifies as genuinely scientific research?" For Segal, the answer is clear-cut. Just like a doctor, who is the expert on illness, the academic possesses the training, knowledge and skills to explain religious phenomena objectively and submits any analyses proffered to empirical testing. The believing communities, by the very nature of their commitment to confessional truths, cannot adopt an objective position and hence cannot provide empirically testable interpretations of their beliefs and practices. Examples of empirically testable interpretations of religious behaviour include analysing the social and economic conditions in which a religious community functions, classifying the psychological predispositions of individuals who claim to have experienced spiritual agents or tracing the historical antecedents on which groups of believers have developed their traditions. If we follow Segal, the scholarly researcher possesses the knowledge derived, just like a doctor, from specialised fields of study in order to describe, classify, interpret and explain the data of religion. The scholar's descriptions, interpretations and analyses are developed according to clearly identified methods, procedures and theories which are subject to critical analysis and, as such, can be verified, modified or falsified. Religious beliefs and experiences are not subject to similar scrutiny and, what is most important, cannot be falsified. For religious adherents, if such interpretations are used to explain (or explain away) their belief in the reality of spirits or supernatural beings by reference to empirically testable social, psychological or historical factors, these cannot be accepted because believers possess a prior confessional commitment to the real existence of invisible spiritual agents.

Patton's position largely supports Segal's analogy, but she is more hesitant to refer to the explanations developed by believers as "non-scientific". Rather, she concludes that how communities are represented defines the fundamental conflict between the academic and those being researched. The academic is committed to representing believers according to guidelines requiring empirical verification or at least logical justification, whereas believers, as "insiders", are dedicated to representing their faiths in ways that support arguments for their worth and validity. By contrast, in agreement with Harvey, in my most recent publications, I have argued that a way to overcome the barrier between academic and adherent roles advocated by Segal and Patton can be found through a method I have called "relational research", which although consistent with both phenomenological methods and Harvey's explanation of "guesthood", takes both a step further by exploding the myth of objectivity while at the same time remaining fully scientific.

Relational Research, Academic Freedom and Trust

Relational research, of course, is not a new or novel idea, but its application within the study of religions has been limited largely to phenomenologists and liberal theologians. In my book *Rational Ancestors* (1998), I hinted that relationality occupies a central place in the study of African religions. In that book, I discussed a method called "diatopical hermeneutics", which I derived from the Spanish Roman Catholic priest and scholar of comparative religions, Raimundo Panikkar (Cox, 1998: 91–97). I explained that for Panikkar, diatopical hermeneutics requires the one seeking to understand a person of another faith to move into a space between religious confessions. Panikkar (1979: 9–10) put it this way: "Diatopical hermeneutics stands for the thematic consideration of understanding the other without assuming that the other has the same basic self-understanding and understanding as I have". This suggests, as I stated, "it is in a place between confessions that genuine dialogue leading to understanding can occur" (Cox, 1998: 91). Although this may sound a bit tame, Panikkar made this much more radical by insisting that understanding requires conviction, or as one of Panikkar's interpreters, the theologian David Krieger argued, genuine understanding requires conversion. In support of this conclusion, Krieger endorsed Panikkar's contention that "to understand something as false is a contradiction in itself" (Krieger, 1991: 51). Krieger expanded this point by proposing a distinction between confessional and methodological conversion. A confessional conversion, according to Krieger (1991: 53), is characterised by "a model of *rejection and acceptance*", a rejection of one's old convictions and an acceptance of the new faith (emphasis in original). This, he suggests, is the way conversion is usually understood. Diatopical hermeneutics, however, is better described as a "methodological conversion", which is rooted in the assumption that the other with whom a dialogue takes place, in Krieger's words, "is not just an other (*alius*), and much less an object of my knowledge (*aliud*), but another self (*alter*) who is a source of self-understanding, and also of understanding, not necessarily reducible to my own" (Krieger, 1991: 213–14).

By using the term "relational research", I am following a similar theme to that I explored in my discussion of Panikkar and Krieger, but in a more deliberate way by focusing not only on understanding and interpretation of the other, but by providing the principles on which academic research proceeds. Relational research requires that all parties in a research programme, including those who constitute the subjects of the researcher's interests, become involved actively in the planning, descriptions, interpretations and explanations of a community's beliefs, practices and alleged experiences. If they accept this premise, academics will voluntarily impose a limitation on their research design by involving the subjects of research not only in the descriptions of their traditional practices, but also in the content and scope of the interpretations and explanations achieved. Research on this model is relational and intersubjective.

In an article appearing in *The New Centennial Review*, I describe relational research in the context of the work of a group of researchers who participated in a study funded by the Social Science Medicine Africa Network (Soma-net) which aimed at restoring ecologically damaged land in Kenya (Cox, 2022b: 68; Ahlberg et al., 2016: 258). After encountering numerous problems caused by a multifaceted set of cultural and gender issues, the researchers adopted a method, which they acknowledge was derived from the German philosopher Jürgen Habermas (1987), called "communicative action", an approach, they explain, that "allows participants to consciously and deliberately reach intersubjective agreement as the basis for mutual understanding about what to do in their particular practical situation" (Ahlberg et al., 2016: 259). The beginning point for implementing "communicative action", as interpreted by Soma-net researchers, is to acknowledge that what traditionally scholars have regarded as the objects of their research actually play an active part in how they are investigated, and consequently have a right to participate in what is said about them, to engage with researchers on how information is obtained from them, and to be consulted on how the findings of a research project are disseminated, including the practical recommendations resulting from the project.

The Soma-net project represents an example of action research, sometimes called "collaborative action research" (Reason, 1999) or "participatory research" (Park, 1999). Peter Reason, Emeritus Professor in the Centre for Action Research in Professional Practice at the University of Bath, describes this type of research as

> an inquiry strategy in which all those involved in the research endeavour are both co-researchers, whose thinking and decision-making contributes to generating ideas, designing and managing the project, and drawing conclusions from the experience; and *also* co-subjects, participating in the activity which is being researched (Reason, 1999: 207, emphasis in original).

Reason argues that in conventional terms, research "is usually thought of as something done by people in universities" and the researcher as someone "who has all the ideas, and who studies other people by observing them, asking them questions, or by designing experiments" (1999: 207). In this traditional approach, Reason explains, "there is often very little connection between the researchers' thinking and the concerns and experiences of the people who are actually involved". This results in treating those being studied as "passive subjects rather than active agents" (Reason, 1999: 207).

Reason counters this problem by employing a co-operative research strategy that combines four types of knowledge: experiential, presentational, propositional and practical. Experiential knowledge requires empathy and is obtained through "direct face-to face-encounter with a person, place or thing" (Reason, 1999: 211). Presentational knowing is related to experiential knowledge but is expressed oftentimes symbolically through "story, drawing, sculpture, movement, dance and so on" (Reason, 1999: 211). Propositional knowing, as the word suggests, reflects knowing "through ideas and theories" and practical knowledge emphasises the "how to" aspect of knowing as embodied "in a skill, knack or competence" (Reason, 1999: 211). Reason concludes:

> In co-operative inquiry we say that knowing will be more valid – richer, deeper, more true to life and more useful – if these four ways of knowing are congruent with each other; if our knowing is grounded in experience, expressed through our stories and images, understood through ideas which make sense to us, and expressed in worthwhile action in our lives (Reason, 1999: 211).

Further distinctions between types of knowledge have been developed by Peter Park, Emeritus Professor at the Fielding Graduate University in Boulder, Colorado, in a way that pushes relational research beyond Reason's emphasis on the researcher and researched as "co-researchers" and "co-subjects". Park uses the term "relational knowledge", which he likens to knowing someone intimately like a mother, a close friend or a lover. This kind of knowledge involves "one of acquaintance and sharing that resides in the thick of the relationship itself, not one of depicting or portraying that person as an object of scrutiny" (Park, 1999: 147). This, of course, is not the only type of knowledge. One can "know" another representationally, as Patton has explained, with the resulting interpretations depending on the perspective of the one who constructs the representations. Relational knowledge, however, is "distinctive": "Where representational knowledge separates the knower and the known, acting merely as a window that allows one to get a glimpse of the other, the relational unites the two in a union" (Park, 1999: 147). Park concludes that "relational knowledge, experienced in various degrees, is the foundation of community life", which when implemented through participatory research, augments "that knowledge deliberately" (Park, 1999: 147).

We now reach the critical point in my discussion of guesthood, phenomenological empathy, relational research and various terms for action research. Park observes that by acknowledging and empowering local agency through relational knowledge, the actual research results are influenced and potentially altered. This is because relational knowledge forms the basis for the generation of interpretive knowledge. Park (1999: 148) explains: "Much of the information about what goes on in the community is generated by methods involving some form of human interaction, including dialogue, which requires that people open and speak frankly and authentically." The most important element in relational research methods, according to Park, is "trust". He concludes: "Where there is no trust emanating from relational knowledge, the picture of the community situation that people gain from their investigation is a mere shadow of the reality" (Park, 1999: 148).

The interaction between the host and the guest, as described by Harvey, can be interpreted as building trust between the two parties. What appears as hostility initially by the host, the performance of a war dance, and the offer of friendship on the part of the guest is resolved in acceptance of the guest by the host because the host trusts the intentions of the guest. If applied to the model of relational research, this means that the community being researched, as the host, has the power to accept or reject the researcher as guest. If the researcher is offered guesthood, a level of trust is immediately extended based on the assurance that both parties will live by the conditions of the invitation. The ensuing research results, including the empirical findings, will be determined by the relations that have been endorsed and adhered to both by the local community and academic researchers. This process has the potential of advancing knowledge by producing new and even unexpected outcomes.

Relational Research as a Scientific Method

Although relational research has a close affinity with action research, it does not end exclusively with the academic researchers and researched communities agreeing on practical solutions to problems affecting individuals and groups in the local regions being investigated. In a firm rejection of Robert Segal's objectivist definition of the role of the social scientist in interpreting religious communities, relational research can be demonstrated to affect the actual data from which theoretical results are obtained and therefore potentially alters matters of empirical fact. This position has been endorsed by leading scientists in theoretical physics, particularly Carlo Rovelli, who is Director of the Quantum Gravity Research Group of the Centre of Theoretical Physics in Marseille, France. In an article published in the *Journal of the British Association for the Study of Religions* (*JBASR*) (Cox, 2022c), I provide a detailed account of an experiment Rovelli described in his book

Helgoland (Rovelli, 2021: 44–48) in which he demonstrated that by simply observing what would appear to be an objective study of the reaction of photons, the actual direction of the photons altered (Cox, 2022a: 16–17). For Rovelli, this illustrates in practice a radical discovery, which he traces historically to the development of the uncertainty principle central to quantum mechanics as posited by the young German physicist Werner Heisenberg in his retreat to the North Sea island of Helgoland in 1925 (Rovelli, 2021: 9–20), that the primary factors in studying the physical world are observation and relationality. I will summarise briefly what I wrote for the *JBASR* before referring to another book in which Rovelli makes his case even stronger for relational knowledge.

The experiment described by Rovelli illustrated the principle of "quantum superposition", which he defined as occurring "when two contradictory properties are, in a certain sense, present together" (Rovelli, 2021: 44). He explained that this means that "an object could be here but at the same time elsewhere" (Rovelli, 2021: 44). A superposition, however, can never be observed: we can only see the consequences of it through "quantum interference" (Rovelli, 2021: 44). Rovelli witnessed quantum interference in the laboratory of the Austrian experimental physicist, Anton Zeilinger, who set up an experiment using optical instruments. These included a small laser, lenses, prism mirrors, which separate the laser beam and reintegrate it, and photon detectors. Rovelli describes that during the experiment photons were split into two parts by the prism, one following a left path and the other the right path, before reuniting and dividing again, eventually one set going up and the other going down. When Rovelli blocked either one of the two paths with his hand, half ended in the up position and half in the down position, If he did not block the path, all the photons went into the down detector; none travelled upwards. Rovelli (2021: 46) explains that "the disappearance of the photons from the upper detector when *both* paths are open is an example of *quantum interference*" (emphasis in original). This is demonstrated by the fact that "each photon behaves as if it passed through both trajectories, … but if we look to see where the photon is, we always see it on just one path". Rovelli (2021: 47) adds that "it seems that you need only to *observe* for what is happening to change!" (emphasis in original) He concludes:

> The very act of measuring which path the photon takes causes the interference to disappear! If we measure where they pass, half of the photons go upward again….This is quantum superposition: the photon is, so to say, 'on two paths'. But if you search for it, it is only on one path (Rovelli, 2021: 47–48).

In his discussion of the history of the development of theories about quantum mechanics in his book, *Reality is Not What It Seems*, Rovelli suggests that "the hardest key" in understanding quantum mechanics is "the *relational* aspect of things" (Rovelli, 2017: 100, emphasis in original). He asserts, for example, "electrons don't always exist. They exist when they interact" (Rovelli, 2017: 100). He explains:

> [Electrons] materialize in a place when they collide with something else. The quantum leaps from one orbit to another constitute their way of being real; an electron is a combination of leaps from one interaction to another. When nothing disturbs it, an electron does not exist in any place (Rovelli, 2017: 100–101).

In a later chapter, Rovelli contends that "we must not confuse what we know about a system with the absolute state of the same system. What we know is something concerning the relation between the system and ourselves" (Rovelli, 2017: 223). This leads to the conclusion, which as we have seen echoes the position of action-researcher Peter Park, in Rovelli's words: "Knowledge is intrinsically relational; it depends as much on its object as upon its subject" (Rovelli, 2017: 223). To speak of the "state" of a system immediately implies a relation to another system. Rovelli says that classical mechanics misled us by suggesting that humans could construct a theory of reality "entirely independent of the observer" (Rovelli, 2017: 223). The development of quantum physics, however, shows that this is impossible because it confirms that reality is a "network of relations, of reciprocal information, which weaves the world" (Rovelli, 2017: 224).

If we apply Rovelli's vision of reality based on his conviction that "properties exist only in relation to something else" to principles guiding research among living communities, we see how insightful Graham Harvey's analysis of "guesthood" as a research method was when he introduced it in 2003. Guesthood fundamentally embodies relationality; it is founded on relationships of trust between hosts and guests, between local communities and those who want to conduct research among them. As we have seen, notions of cooperative inquiry and participatory research were already being discussed and modified in the late twentieth century within numerous disciplines related to organisational management, business studies and some of the social sciences, but the main challenges to conventional research methods in religious studies, so aptly articulated by Robert Segal and Laurie Patton, tended to be phrased in dialectical terms such as insider versus outsider, emic versus etic, subjective versus objective, theology versus the academic study of religion. Although these debates are important and necessary, they suffer from perpetuating the opposition between science as objective truth and living faiths of religious communities as subjective and confessional. Harvey's "guesthood", as I have likened it in this chapter to "relational research" seen as the next step in the phenomenology of religion, discloses a new interpretative method that overcomes dichotomous thinking by recognising the significance of Carlo Rossi's claim that the "hardest key" in understanding how the world works is to acknowledge, act on and implement the "relational aspect of things".

References

Ahlberg, B.M, Maina, F., Kubai, A., Khamasi, W., Ekman, M. and Lundqvist-Persson, C. 2016. "'A child, a tree': Challenges in building a community research project in a Kenyan context", *Action Research* 14(3): 257–275.
Bryman, A. and Bell, E. 2015. *Business Research Methods*, 4th edn. Oxford and New York: Oxford University Press.
Cox, J.L. 1998. *Rational Ancestors: Scientific Rationality and African Indigenous Religions*. Cardiff: Cardiff Academic Press.
Cox, J.L. 2006. *A Guide to the Phenomenology of Religion: Key Figures, Formative Influences and Subsequent Debates*. London and New York: Continuum, T & T Clark.
Cox, J.L. 2010. *An Introduction to the Phenomenology of Religion*. London and New York: Continuum.
Cox, J.L. 2018. *Restoring the Chain of Memory: T.G.H. Strehlow and the Repatriation of Australian Indigenous Knowledge*. Sheffield: Equinox.
Cox, J.L. 2022a. *A Phenomenology of Indigenous Religions: Theory and Practice*. London and New York: Bloomsbury Academic.
Cox, J.L. 2022b. "Delimiting religion: From religious experience to relational research", *CR: The New Centennial Review* 22(2): 41–77.
Cox, J.L. 2022c. "The collective ownership of knowledge: Implications for the study of religion/s in local contexts", *Journal of the British Association for the Study of Religions* 26: 1–22.
Flood, G. 1999. *Beyond Phenomenology: Rethinking the Study of Religion*. London and New York: Cassell.
Habermas, J. 1987. *Theory of Communicative Action, Vol 2: A Critique of Functionalist Reason*. Cambridge: Polity Press.
Harvey, G. 2003. "Guesthood as ethical decolonising research method", *Numen* 50(2): 125–146.
Krieger, D. 1991. *The New Universalism: Foundations for a Global Theology*. Maryknoll, NY: Orbis Books.
Kristensen, W.B. 1960. *The Meaning of Religion*, trans. Carman, J. The Hague: Martinus Nijhoff.
National Trust. "A New Future for Hinemihi", www.nationaltrust.org.uk/visit/surrey/clandon-park/a-new-future-for-hinemihi (accessed 25 April 2023).
Panikkar, R. 1979. *Myth, Faith and Hermeneutics*. New York: Paulist Press.

Park, P. 1999. "People, knowledge, and change in participatory research", *Management Learning* 30(2): 141–157.
Patton, Laurie L. 2019. *Who Owns Religion? Scholars and their Publics in the Late Twentieth Century*. Chicago, IL and London: University of Chicago Press.
Reason, P. 1999. "Integrating action and reflection through co-operative inquiry", *Management Learning* 30(2): 207–226.
Rovelli, C. 2017. *Reality Is Not What It Seems: The Journey to Quantum Gravity*, trans. Carnell, S. and Segre, E. London: Allen Lane.
Rovelli, C. 2021. *Helgoland,* trans. Carnell, S. and Segre, E. London: Allen Lane.
Segal, R.A. 2017. "Diagnosis rather than dialogue as the best way to study religion", in Aitken, E.B. and Sharma, A. (eds), *The Legacy of Wilfred Cantwell Smith*. Albany, NY: State University of New York Press. pp. 173–182.
Smith, L.T. 2022. *Decolonizing Methodologies: Research and Indigenous Peoples*, 3rd edn. London and New York: Bloomsbury Academic.
Smith, W.C. 1981. *Towards a World Theology: Faith and the Comparative History of Religion*. Philadelphia, PA: Westminster Press.
Strehlow, T.G.H. 1971. *Songs of Central Australia*. Sydney: Angus and Robertson.

About the Author

James L. Cox is Emeritus Professor of Religious Studies in the University of Edinburgh and Adjunct Professor in the School of Social Sciences, Western Sydney University. He has written widely on the phenomenology of religion and theories of Indigenous Religions, most recently *The Invention of God in Indigenous Societies* (2014), *Restoring the Chain of Memory: TGH Strehlow and the Repatriation of Australian Indigenous Knowledge* (2018) and *A Phenomenology of Indigenous Religions: Theory and Practice* (2022).

5   Harebrained?

Michael Houseman

A 3-year-old boy was examining his testicles while taking a bath.
  "Mama", he asked, "are these my brains?"
  "Not yet", she replied.

Introduction

I am forever grateful to Graham for having encouraged me to spend a week of the summer of 2014 at Druid Camp near Gloucester.[1] He knew that I had recently become interested in Contemporary Pagan ceremonial, but that I had little day-to-day experience with Pagan practitioners. My low-flying jet-set Californian upbringing, as well as a mixed bag of subsequent religious experiments, had made me more amenable to New Age sensibilities than to those of Contemporary Paganism. According to Graham, Druid Camp would be an ideal introduction to a Pagan world: the people who ran it were an easy-going, undogmatic bunch, he assured me, and the camp itself boasted good food, efficient drop toilets and, in a corner of the open field in which participants pitched their tents, working showers and a sauna. So, I went. Although I am an (Africanist) anthropologist by trade, I did not undertake fieldwork at Druid Camp, but applied myself to doing what Graham says he does as a religious studies scholar when visiting foreign lands: I hung out. Although a druidic fellow traveller at best, I returned to Camp five years running, and have only fond memories of the invigorating, interstitial times spent in the company of those quirky, generous folk.

In 2017, Graham, who was scheduled to give a talk at Druid Camp, came to stay for a few days, and we got the chance to hang out together. I remember that we were both quite taken with a woman who was herself very much taken with hares. F.B. had a tattoo of golden hares running up her right arm, and would rise well before dawn to get a glimpse of these commanding creatures in the surrounding fields.

---

1   I am indebted to Marika Moisseeff for her helpful comments on a previous draft.

Now, I can understand being enchanted by hares. I spent many years enthralled by rabbits. What began as a study of the widespread, North-Atlantic prohibition on transporting this animal or even saying its name aboard a boat (Houseman, 1990), turned into a bit of an obsession, sustained by friends' seemingly endless gifts of rabbit-related mementos. However, I was less inspired by time spent in the company of actual rabbits than by the remarkable features of *oryctolagus cuniculus* and the figurative qualities associated with them. Specifically, as nineteenth-century European folklorists, but also other, earlier and later sources show, a number of rabbits' attributes prompt them to be perceived as prolifically fertile creatures in whom sexuality and reproduction are inseparable. This, I argued, was the key to their prohibition. In a nutshell, I suggested that the conditions under which unisexual male productive activities like deep-sea fishing (or underground mining) are pursued are analogous to those of human reproduction, especially with respect to the potentially hazardous, two-fold position women occupy relative to men as both sexual protagonist and maternal environment. To avoid the calamitous repercussions of incest, it is important that the virtually agonistic relations a man enjoys with a female sexual partner remain distinct from those he entertains with she in whose womb he was once contained. Correspondingly, in order to steer clear of shipwreck and drowning (cave-ins and suffocation for miners), it is imperative that the inevitably combative relations sailors (miners) pursue with their partner the ocean (the earth) not be conflated with those they maintain with the unstable aquatic (subterranean) environment that encompasses them, for a physical environment that becomes a protagonist cannot but be disastrously overwhelming. Symbolically, the need to keep these two relational registers apart translates as a necessary dissociation of sex and reproduction while at sea (in or around the mine), in the context of which, rabbits, because they incarnate an unrestrained, inherently procreative sexuality, are to be avoided at all cost.

Regardless of how convincing this argument may be, one might think that in this day and age of ontological, animal and bodily turns, this type of symbolic interpretation is a decidedly outdated way of taking what are surely our most familiar other-than-human beings into consideration. I would maintain, however, that such speculative storytelling contributes just as much to a non-anthropocentric appreciation of animals, as does, for example, understandings born of personal encounters with the creatures in question. Attributing characteristic properties and dispositions to animal species lifts them out of generic otherness by providing them not so much with individual personhood than with distinctive personalities as representatives of peculiar kinds of being humans have to deal with. Indeed, an important aspect of animal symbolism consists in acknowledging that while humans and animals often intervene physically in each other's lives – through hunting or damaging crops for example – animals can also affect humans in other ways, such as by portending or bringing about fortune or misfortune. A black cat, for example, can betoken bad luck or be a witch in disguise. Animals have this power because, in a given cultural context, certain of their intrinsic qualities are associated with particular ideas, values or bodily traits that humans find both meaningful and emotionally stirring. As virtually all folklore traditions attest, these associations are often made explicit in language and in the form of memorable stories. This emblematic recognition of animals, by affording them with conceptual and affective contours, hollows and ridges that humans can come to grips with, encourages something akin to what Graham has called an "etiquette of interspecies relationality" (Harvey, 2013: 215) in which appreciations of alterity and likeness go hand in hand. In other words, it discourages taking avowedly self-motivated non-human creatures for granted as entities reducible to their sheer materiality.[2] In doing so, it admits "an underlying level on which humans and non-human animals share the *same* existential status as living beings or persons" in the world (Ingold, 1994: xxiv, italics in the original). It is in this spirit that I propose to consider briefly certain cultural representations of the hare.

My somewhat meandering demonstration regarding maritime prohibitions drew on documentary and ethnographic material dealing mainly with rabbits, but also in a subsidiary manner with hares, for not only are these species closely related, but some of their shared traits have received similar interpretations. However, focusing on hares as I intend to do here brings out important differences between the two. In many ways, the rabbit seems like a less mature, more gregarious, domesticated version of the hare. Rabbits were introduced into northern Europe fairly recently (thirteenth century). Born helpless, hairless and blind, they dwell in collective burrows underground, and are for the most part either raised by humans or constrained by them to dedicated places such as warrens or islands. Hares, on the other hand, who are native to continental Europe and well established in Britain by the late Iron Age (Lauritsen et al., 2018: 290), are larger and faster and with longer

---

2   While accompanying my wife to Australia where she was undertaking anthropological fieldwork in an Australian Aboriginal community, I was disappointed to discover that my beloved rabbits, presumably due to their plague-like proliferation ("the grey invasion"), were seemingly reduced to their material parts (meat, fur, etc.) and bereft of any symbolic dimension whatsoever. I found that for Settler populations, rabbits were a commercial resource to be exploited, but mostly vermin to be exterminated by an impressive variety of means: trapping, poisoning, warren ripping, fumigation, releasing viruses, and so on. For Aboriginal communities, they were welcome but unexciting "easy tucker", readily available in the nearby sandhills-cum-larder.

ears. Lacking family life, hunted as wild game, they are more solitary animals that nest above ground, and are born fully-furred with their eyes open (Flux and Angermann, 1990). In short, rabbits are cosmopolitan, eminently sociable yet kept creatures, whereas hares are more like lone, free-ranging locals.

Taking into account other, more expressive qualities associated with rabbits and hares further enriches the distinction between them. Insofar as reproduction is concerned, the rabbit, who has no oestrous cycle, is notorious for its potentially alarming fecundity, as the disparaging expression "breed like rabbits" as well as any number of popular images suggest (Marcia Scrivan's multiplying bunny slipper cartoons come to mind, Figure 5.1). In contrast to this, the hare, who is much less prolific in spite of its capacity for superfetation (conception by an already pregnant female), is better known for the frenzied, mad-as-a-March-hare boxing and chasing behaviour that takes place both among males and by females toward males during the breeding season. On a related, more explicitly symbolic, cosmological plane, rabbits, with their month-long gestation period, are easily associated with lunar phases that are themselves linked with both tidal patterns and menstrual cycles, whereas hares tend to be connected to yearly, solar periodicities, often evoking sacrificial death and rebirth, as in Frazer's account of cutting or killing the "hare" (the last sheaf of corn) in Autumn (1922: 452–453).[3] As previously mentioned, the nominal or actual presence of rabbits are thought to bring about disastrous perturbations at sea or in the subterranean depths of mines, whereas, as we will see, hares portend storms or impending fire. I am tempted to suggest that rabbits are above all creatures of water and earth (in simplified Contemporary Pagan terms, they pertain to the realms of feeling and body), hares, creatures of air and fire (inspiration and action). Be that as it may, both rabbits and hares are associated with fertile, unchecked sexuality. However, in the case of the rabbit, a more confined, dependent and collectively oriented entity, this association is modulated in a gestation-related, female direction, whereas the hare, a wilder, more self-reliant, individual being, is readily appreciated as incarnating a male, eruptive potency. It is this virile aspect of hare symbolism that I wish to explore briefly here.

---

3 Note that hares are mythologically associated with the moon in Asia and Native America. However, I have purposely limited myself here to the cultural region of Europe and to the United Kingdom in particular.

Figure 5.1 Multiplying rabbit slippers.

Hares and "the Life in the Head"

Let's begin with what is perhaps not the most significant of the hare's manly qualities, but which has the advantage of bringing Graham to mind: hares are very hairy, to the point, observes Aristotle, of having hair growing inside their mouth (in fact these are jugal glands [Angermann, 1972: 383]). Now, for Aristotle, that DWEM's DWEM, this excessive pilosity is indicative of an abundance of semen, and more generally, of a particular kind of generative force residing principally in bone marrow and the brain (*Generation of Animals* IV.5.774b). This is part of a larger complex of ideas, documented for Greek and Roman Antiquity by Onians in his compendium *The Origins of European Thought* (2000 [1951]; see also La Barre, 1984 for a wider cross-cultural account), that sees cerebro-spinal fluid as the seat of the "life-principle" (*psyche*, ψυχή), of which sperm is the prime procreative vector. In this view, the head has little to do with ordinary consciousness; it is above all a generative organ, the creative faculty associated with it – the *genius* – being specifically linked to the propagation of new life. According to Aristotelian thought, highly influential in Western representations of procreation until

Figure 5.2 Giant jackalope at Wall Drug in South Dakota (USA). (cc) Mbailey.

the seventeenth century, the apparent thickness of seminal fluid is a temporary consequence of its stay in the warm environment of the male body. Once transferred through coitus to a woman's colder body, it dissolves and evaporates, drying up the blood contained in the womb, which is then no longer evacuated in the form of menstruation. Like fig juice that turns milk, the desiccating vitality born by this male spiritual seed is held to endow female matter, blood, with form, movement and soul (for a synthetic account, see for example Sissa, 1989).

This generative potential identified with cerebro-spinal fluid and the head manifests itself in two ways, both of which are markedly present in hares. One is a prominence given to marrow, cartilage and bone, evinced not only by an abundance of hair and ever-growing teeth, but also by remarkably large ears that are often either likened to horns (Evans and Thomson, 1972: 209–10) or, as in the case of the chimerical jackalope (Figure 5.2), supplemented by a set of impressive antlers. Hares' close connexion with such capital extrusions as well as with osseus substances generally is further attested by traditional pharmacopoeia in which either the brains of a hare, or a tooth, a leg or other bone of this animal constitute certain remedies against rheumatism, lumbago and cramp in the lower limbs (sciatica); alternatively, these same things guard against toothache and/or encourage the growth of teeth in children and calm the agitations that accompany it.[4] Finally, Onians (1951: 174–182) provides

---

4   British references include Thiselton-Dyer (1978: 164), Layard (1944: 188), Glyde (1973 [1872]: 38), Burne (1883: 193-4), Porter (1969: 88) and Udal (1922: 235). In a recent article, Ashley (2001: 4) points out that "In 117 AD, the physician Soranus of

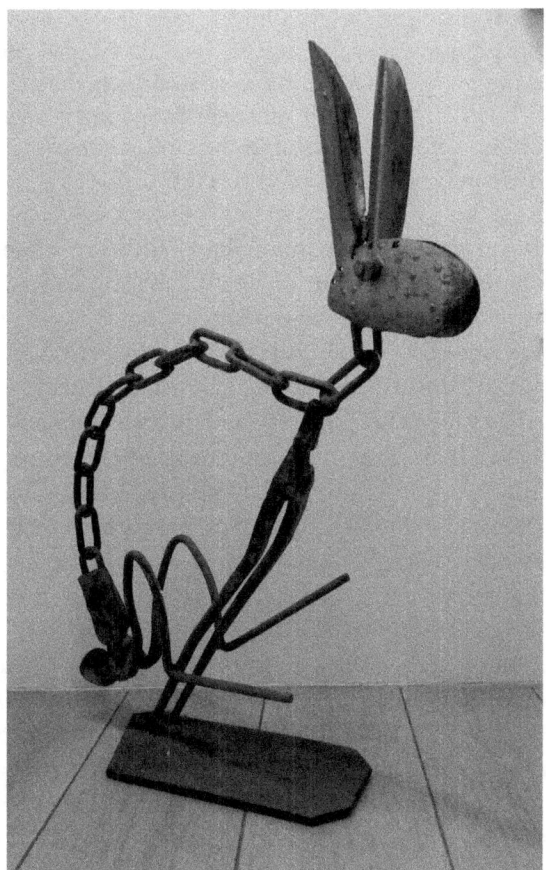

Figure 5.3 Golden headed iron hare. Author's collection.

extensive evidence that the knee joint's synovial fluid was also thought to be a source of germinal power. In this light, it is significant that the hare, a decidedly skeletal depiction of which is shown in Figure 5.3, is endowed with particularly prominent knees.

The other way the male life-principle expresses itself is through involuntary, usually heated behaviour, often centred on the head: unintentional nodding, yawning, or sneezing are such "spontaneous expression[s] of the life in the head" (Onians, 1951: 104), as is when the head, brain or face "burns" with shame, rage, passion or madness:

Ephesus was the first to suggest using hare's brain to ease teething. This remained a favoured remedy until the seventeenth century."

> In madness and what seems to be a brief spasm of madness, violent rage [...], when the head was thus "on fire", the normal rational consciousness, whose seat is in the chest, is no longer in control [...]. The man appears to be "possessed", dominated by some other spirit, and might well seem to be dominated by that potent other spirit in the head, more particularly in the brain (*cerebrum*), the *genius* (Onians, 1951: 148).

The most glaring example of this among hares is their excitable and unpredictable – harebrained – behaviour during the mating season. However, the inherently hotheaded, inflammatory nature of hares is also suggested not only by what appear to be their singed (black-tipped) ears and their association with immanent storms (Evans and Thomson, 1972: 214; Porter, 1969: 67), but especially by the belief once common in the south of England and the southern Midlands, that a hare running through a village portends coming fire. While arguing that the Grant, a sparkling-eyed "demon" mentioned only by Gervase of Tilbury (c. 1150–1228), whose appearance racing through the streets forewarns of fire, was "something of an exaggerated hare", Pentangelo (2019) provides an overview of nineteenth- and twentieth-century sources attesting to this belief (see also Roud, 2006). For Evans and Thomson's informants, the linking of the hare with fire and burning (a "tradition in many parts of the world" (1972: 121)) is due to the fact that hares try to escape a fire by running through it 1972: 123–126), whereas Pentangelo, citing Sokos et al. (2016), suggests that because hare populations increase following scrub fires, "people have a better chance of spotting hare in burnt landscapes than unburnt ones for several years after a fire strikes" (2019: 6). Along similar lines, Layard (1988: 106), in connexion with what he sees as the hare's self-sacrificial character, mentions its "attribute well known to all farmers" of not running before the fire like a rabbit, but of clinging till the last moment to its fold before rushing out with fur blazing.

The hare's eruptive vigour is also responsible for the congenital division of its upper palette, the unexpected sight of which is said to cause a pregnant women's unborn child to acquire a harelip, an outcome than can be avoided if the expectant mother has the presence of mind to tear her own dress (see for example Burne, 1883: 212–213; Hazlitt, 1905: 305; Evans and Thomson 1972: 220–22). Indeed, the spontaneous manifestation of the life in the head that is explosive laughter is the cause of the hare's cleft palette in virtually all European folktale traditions. In the most widespread of these legends (ATU tale type 70, see Uther, 2004), the racket a hare makes when approaching a pond frightens the frogs around it, causing them to dive in; seeing this, the hare laughs so much he splits his lip. In another version, the frogs, worried about a coming storm, exhort the hare to return home before it rains; observing the frogs jumping into the pond so as not to get wet, he laughs until his lip splits.[5] The situation is somewhat similar in the folktale Straw, Ember, and Bean (ATU tale type 295 collected by the Grimm brothers [1884]) in which uncontrolled hilarity explains why beans, those concentrated embryonic organisms, have an obtrusive seam: one day, Bean, Ember and Straw try to cross a stream; Straw makes a bridge between the two banks, but Ember, while crossing, lights it on fire and both fall into the water; Bean laughs so hard he splits his back (a passing tailor sews him back together).

This exuberant welling up of form-engendering life-force that splits the hare's head (the bean's spine) can be likened to a purely virile procreative act that, in the absence of additional bodily matter that (according to Aristotelian thought) maternal blood is held to provide, is destined to remain incomplete. This comes close to Lévi-Strauss's (1978) interpretation of a Northwest Coast Amerindian myth in which the hare, hidden under a log that causes a young woman to fall, catches sight of her genitals and makes fun of them; furious, she hits him with a stick causing his muzzle to split. The hare's cleft palette, Lévi-Strauss argues, linking this story with other myths, can be seen as the beginning of a twinning process: "[the young woman] initiates a fission in the animal's body which, if completed, would split it and transform it into twins".[6] If the hare's cleft palate can be understood in this way as a relative excess of generative form, its symmetrical inverse, that is, an equally unfulfilled, purely uterine procreative act, is the amorphous, boneless "mola" described by

---

5   In the moralising rather than etiological fable credited to Aesop (138 Perry Index), hares, upon discovering that frogs are afraid of them, take comfort in the realisation that cowardice is a relative matter; although the hare's laughter and split lip are not mentioned, in Jean La Fontaine's literary variant (Book 2 fable 14), the hare is likened to a powerful warrior in a way that evokes lightning and a coming storm: "they take me for the very thunderbolt of war! ("Je suis donc un foudre de guerre?").

    In other, less widespread stories, the hare's lip-splitting laughter is caused by a fox (or a bear) being carried off by a supposedly dead horse whose tail the animal has been convinced to bite (ATU tale type 47A), by Frost's unsuccessfully attempt to freeze the hare (ATU 71), or by the sudden emergence of a cloud of insects from a sac that the hare, contrary to God's instructions, opens to peek into (ATU 2003).

6   A contemporary, science-fiction flavoured illustration of the connection between male generative power and eruptive head-splitting is provided by a scene close to the end of the Peter Medak's 1998 film *Species 2*, in which the face of a remarkably exoskeletal male alien, about to submit a female of his species to a fertilising (but fatal) oral rape, violently divides into two. Also note that in a number of facetious folktales such as "Lie. The Split Dog" (ATU tale type 1089L), as in the stories reported by Evans and Thomson (1972: 83, 229–230), the hare's tremendous speed and/or its ability to double back sharply on itself causes the hare itself or the dog chasing it to be sliced in half.

Hippocrates, Aristotle and Pliny the Elder, and later translated as "mooncalf". Beginning in Antiquity, throughout the Middle Ages and until the seventeenth century, such undifferentiated growths, now called "molar pregnancies", were held to be generated either from female seed exclusively, or from an excess of menstrual- and/or moon-derived moisture due to an insufficient degree of form-inducing desiccation that sperm was thought to provide.[7]

Hares and Witches

Other than calling attention to the hare's inherent propensity for both form-producing fecundity and the coming of heat and light, I am going to steer clear of the highly debated historical connections between hares, the Anglo-Saxon goddess Eostre/Ostara and the laying/bringing of eggs at Spring Equinox/Eastertime.[8] On the other hand, the hare's close association with a formative capacity residing in cerebro-spinal fluid, semen and marrow casts a revealing light on the well-documented belief that hares entertain a privileged relationship with witches, notably as milkhares who make off with the fatty milk of others' cows. As Kittredge explains in *Witchcraft in Old and New England* (1929: 166–179):

> A witch, as we all know, often takes the shape of a hare, and in this guise she may suck your cow dry and drink up the milk. [...] Hares may be employed as familiar spirits, and as such may steal milk for their mistress hags by sucking a neighbor's cows. For witches in hare-form we have the authority Giraldus Cambrensis [Gerald of Wales c. 1146–1223] and of modern folk-lore in profusion. If you wound a witch-hare, the witch herself suffers the injury, of course.[9]

---

7   For a history of the interpretations of molar pregnancies, see Foscati (2021); for "mooncalf" (not to be confused with the spindly, bulging-eyed beast of the Harry Potter universe [Rowling, 2001]), see for example folklorist Sarah Allison's "Lorialets and Mooncalves" (https://writinginmargins.weebly.com/home/lorialets-and-mooncalves, 21 December 2020, accessed 1 August 2023).
8   For those interested in venturing into this minefield of contemporary folklore scholarship, see for example Newall (1971: 323–326), Cusack (2007), Lauritsen et al. (2018), Murphy and Ameen (2020) and Sermon (2022).
9   Along similar lines: "The hare is the most common disguise of a witch in all the northern countries of Europe, and was well known in the Northern Counties of England" (Glyde 1973 [1872]: 56). For additional references, see for example Billson (1892: 455), who cites a number of nineteenth-century sources, as well as Dhuibhne (1993) for Ireland, and Nildin-Wall and Wall (1993) for Nordic traditions.

Evans and Thomson (1972: 156–161) provide a number of typical accounts, recorded between 1930 and 1970, in which a man discovers a hare sucking milk from one of his cows. He sics his dog on the hare and/or attempts to shoot the animal who escapes with only a minor wound; the hare, jumping through a window or a hole in the wall, seeks refuge in a neighbouring house in which the man finds an old woman with an identical injury.

As Dhuibhne (1993) has argued, these stories convoke a set of normative contrasts – male vs. female, young vs. old, wild vs. domestic, open landscape vs. house – that the witch challenges by venturing outside her home, illicitly procuring another's cow's milk and confronting a young man in an open field. Calling into question her female-connoted, subordinate, nurturing role (see also O'Connor, 2016 on Dhuibhne's play *Dún na mBan trí Thine*), she acts more like a man whose aptitude for autonomous agency, we may suppose, is closely linked to the male-connoted "life in the head". It is indeed significant that in these accounts the witch is presumed to be a postmenstrual hag, that is, someone who, from a procreative point of view, can be likened to a man but also to a hare who embodies the generative power men are held to possess. Unlike men, however, the witch does not have an innate, ever-replenished supply of this virile life principle. To gain access to it, she must amass a substance of a similar, albeit less accomplished nature: the cow's milk she steals, more precisely the fatty cream and butter it contains, replaces the semen she is incapable of producing herself. According to enduring Aristotelian notions of physiology (cf. Héritier-Augé, 1985), both semen and milk are "useful residues" of food, passing through the intermediate stage of blood. The former, however, because it is elaborated in a man's warmer body, is a purer concentrate; the blood of women, whose bodies are colder by nature, produces a residue that is insufficiently cooked, providing only the matter of the embryo, nourishment for the foetus during pregnancy, and milk after birth (Bonnard, 2013). In keeping with this logic, it is perhaps not too far-fetched to assume that the passage of the cow's milk through the hare's hot body – or the witch's own unprocreant body – causes it to coagulate still further, rendering the pilfered fluid even more comparable to the seminal life force the witch seeks to make her own. In short, the witch's hare, or the witch herself in the form of a hare, by absorbing and transforming cow's milk into a semblance of sperm, enables her to acquire the *genius* necessary to act independently in a man's world.

This close connexion between hares and witches raises the possibility that the productive life-force life in the head that hares are held to embody may, under certain conditions, be possessed and wielded by both men and women. More precisely, it implies that when procreation, specifically gestation, is disregarded, masculinity becomes one thing and virility – "manly strength and vigour of action or thought; energy or force of a virile character" (Oxford English Dictionary) – quite another. From this point of view, the hare can be seen as epitomising a gender model that contrasts sharply with that exemplified by the rabbit. Both creatures are associated with fertility and unbridled sexuality, but as indicated previously, not in the same way.

The rabbit, by virtue of its extreme prolificity, is taken to embody the exclusively uterine functions of gestation and childbirth. As such, it betokens an irreducible asymmetry between male and female. In this prevailing gender model, as Marika Moisseeff (1985, 2010) has argued, anatomical differences between the sexes, those that provide the grounds for sexual identity at birth, are deemed inseparable from men's and women's postpubescent reproductive roles. Because individuals of both sexes develop in and emerge from females, this frame of reference grants a clear preeminence to women. As previously suggested, it is this hierarchical encompassment of the masculine by the feminine, in which women are appreciated at once as men's sexual partners and as those from whose bodies they are born, that underlies superstitions regarding rabbits on boats (or in mines). However, Moisseeff goes on to point out, this scheme usually goes hand in hand with what amounts to its inversion on the level of the cultural representations that underlie men's and women's socially elaborated gender roles. Women's reproductive capacities are typically seen as being dependent upon men's spiritual competencies – often exercised in the course of rituals – such that women are assigned a subordinate position. The notion that has permeated Western thought from Antiquity onwards, namely that cerebro-spinal fluid and semen partake of the same form-producing, immaterial life-force capable of animating the embryonic matter that women supply is, for Françoise Héritier (1996), a quasi-universal instance of such an inversion. Because it implies a continuity between creative thinking and engendering seed, this appropriation of women's procreative powers, she maintains, provides the ideological grounds for men's domination over women.

The hare, known for its exuberant sexuality and combative courtship behaviour pursued by individuals of both sexes, is more readily associated with another, more symmetrical gender paradigm identified by Moisseeff. In this culturally more marginal model, which she associates with certain contemporary Western aspirations, male and female procreative functions are suspended or put aside, allowing sociocultural gender complementarities to be grounded in anatomical sexual disparities instead of reproductive ones. Within the framework of this scheme, gender identity is largely irrelevant to the stormy, productive life in the head that, freed as it were from procreative concerns, becomes potentially available to all. Men and women, acting together or apart, may bring this spiritual life-force into play in different

Figure 5.4 *Lady Hare Sitting* by Sophie Ryder at Yorkshire Sculpture Park.

ways. However, as in the case of jacks and jills (male and female hares) who regularly interact in the course of their largely solitary, event-filled lives, such divergencies are not expected to call their parity into question. This different-but-equal gender ideal is what the menopausal, milk-plundering hare-witch hungers for. It is also that proclaimed by Sophie Ryder's monumental sculptures of Lady Hare (Figure 5.4), an equally powerful female counterpart of the Ancient Greek minotaur whom she sees as "not threatening, but strong, loving and protective" (www.sophieryder.com). As an emblem of such a gender-independent understanding of virility, it is significant that hares are notoriously hermaphroditic. Innumerable sources, beginning in Antiquity, though the Middle Ages and up until the nineteenth century, bear witness to the belief that male hares are able to give birth or that hares regularly change sex (for references see Houseman, 1990). A particularly explicit example is provided by "the old laws of Wales, which set out the value of many animals, [...] giving different prices for males and females of various ages, [but] put

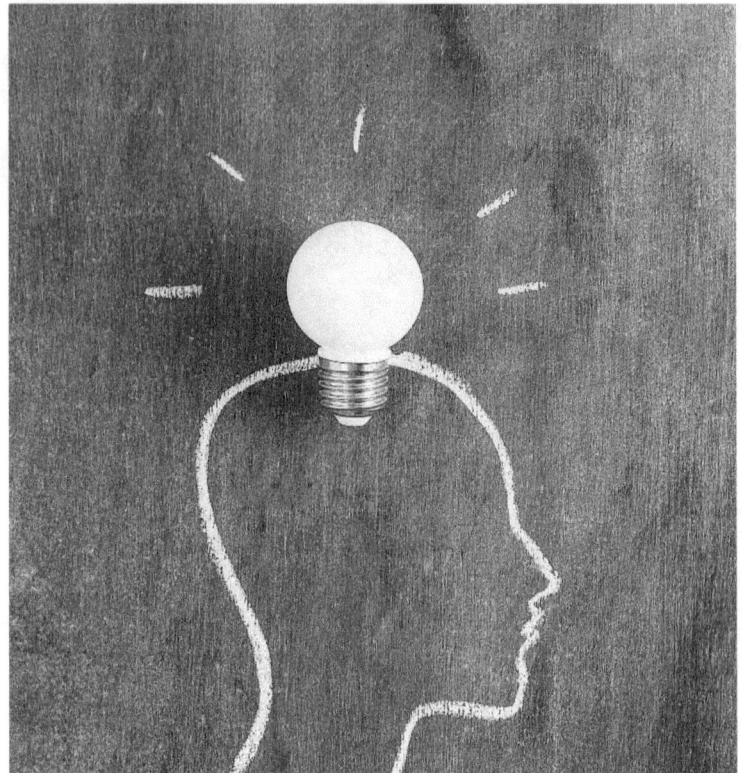

Figure 5.5 Image by Freepic.

no price on the hare because it was female one month and male the next" (Evans and Thomson 1972: 25).[10]

The hare, then, is reminding us that once procreative considerations are put to one side, something family-minded bucks and does (male and female rabbits) presumably find well-nigh impossible to do, the somewhat unruly, incandescent creativity in the head it so tellingly exemplifies is circumstantially rather than inherently masculine. There is indeed a fair bit of the spunky hare in us all, and we would do well to appreciate that fertile spark (Figure 5.5) for what it is: evidence that human and other-than-human

---

10 In preparing this text, I went back over the sources cited in my 1990 article in which the characteristic features of rabbits and hares are systematically conflated, and was surprised to discover not a single case attesting to the opinion that rabbits could change sex or that both male and female rabbits could give birth; in every instance, such beliefs concerned hares.

beings, like men and women, are not as hierarchically distant as we might imagine.

Conclusion

My intention in writing this tribute was not to construct air-tight interpretations out of hare-related scraps of British folklore. Nor was it to draw undue attention to Graham's hare-like ways (although, if the shoe fits…). My aim was to use these cultural snippets, and inspiration provided by Graham, to suggest how broadening one's focus from the strictly human to include other living creatures can bring about new self-understandings.

The druidic attitude Graham espouses, both privately and professionally, towards the world we live in consists mainly in acknowledging the personal dimensions of both human and other-than-human beings. Hence his overriding concern with the ongoing network of relationships they cannot but jointly take part of, and his insistence upon politeness as the exemplary ritualised posture with respect to humans and other-than-humans alike. As my country-bred wife keeps reminding me, taking into consideration the non-human entities that dwell in one's natural or supernatural environment is not that different from making do with one's human neighbours and acquaintances. It is less a matter of cultivating an all-embracing "connection" with the living world (cf. Houseman, 2023) than one of drawing and honouring boundaries with respect to particular others, of taking sides in concrete situations, of acknowledging limits of knowing, of recognising potential threats and possible affinities, and so forth. Being able to ascribe specific dispositions, points of view and intentional qualities to one's other-than-human familiars, on the basis of private conjectures but especially on the grounds of culturally sanctioned representations, is, I suggest, an essential aspect of this process. In this regard, animal symbolism can be a great gift. Like metaphor generally, it creates shared meanings that cut both ways: in prompting us to perceive ourselves in others, it inspires us to recognise others in ourselves.

References

Angermann, R. 1972. "Les Lagomorphes", in Grzimek, B. (ed.), *Le Monde Animal. Mammifères*. Zurich: Stauffacher.

Aristotle. 1942. *Generation of Animals* with an English translation by Peck, A.L. (Loeb Classical Library No. 366). London/Cambridge, MA: William Heinemann/Harvard University Press.

Ashley, M.P. 2001. "It's only teething… A report of the myths and modern approaches to teething", *British Dental Journal* 191(1): 4–8.

Billson, C.J. 1892. "The Easter Hare", *Folklore* 3(4): 441–466.

Bonnard, J.-B. 2013. "Male and female bodies according to Ancient Greek physicians", *Clio. Women, Gender, History* 37(1): 21–39.

Burne, C.S. 1883. *Shropshire Folklore*. London: Trübner & Co.

Cusack, C. 2007. "The Goddess Eostre: Bede's text and contemporary pagan tradition(s)", *The Pomegranate* 9(1): 22–40.

Dhuibhne, É. Ní. 1993. "'The old woman as hare': Structure and meaning in an Irish legend", *Folklore* 104(1/2): 77–85.

Evans G.E. and Thomson, D. 1972. *The Leaping Hare*. London: Faber & Faber.

Flux, J.E.C. and Angermann, R. 1990. "The hares and jackrabbits", in Chapman, J.A. and Flux, J.E.C. (eds), *Rabbits, Hares and Pikas: Status Survey and Conservation Action Plan*. Gland: International Union for Conservation of Nature and Natural Resources (IUCN). pp. 61–94.

Foscati, A. 2021. "'An mola sine viri congressu concipi possit?' The uterine mole in medical and philosophical texts between the Middle Ages and the Early Modern period", *Ágora. Estudos Clássicos em Debate* 23(1): 117–137.

Frazer, Sir J. 1922. *The Golden Bough. A Study in Magic and Religion*, abridged edn. New York: Macmillan.

Glyde, J. 1973. *Folklore and Customs of Norfolk*. London: E.P. Publishing [1872].

Harvey, G. 2013. *Food, Sex and Strangers: Understanding Religion as Everyday Life*. London/New York: Routledge.

Hazlitt, W.C. 1905. *Faiths and Folklore: A Dictionary of National Beliefs, Superstitions and Popular Customs*. London: Reeves & Turner.

Grimm, J. and Grimm, W. 1884. *Grimm's Household Tales*. Translated by Hunt, M. London: George Bell and Sons.

Héritier, F. 1996. *Masculin-Féminin I. La Pensée de la différence*. Paris: Odile Jacob.

Héritier-Augé, F. 1985. "Le sperme et le sang", *Nouvelle Revue de Psychanalyse* 32: 111–122.

Houseman, M. 1990. "Le tabou du lapin chez les marins: une spéculation structurale", *Ethnologie française* 20(2): 125–142.

Houseman, M. 2023. "Afterword: In among the more-than-humans", in Chamel, J. and Dansac, Y. (eds), *Relating with More-than-Humans: Interbeing Rituality in a Living World*. Cham: Palgrave Macmillan. pp. 237–245.

Ingold, T. 1994. "Preface to the Paperback Edition", in Ingold, T. (ed.) *What is an Animal?* London/New York: Routledge. pp. xviii–xxiv.

Kittredge, G.L. 1929. *Witchcraft in Old and New England*. New York: Russell & Russell.

La Barre, W. 1984. *Muelos. A Stone Age Superstition About Sexuality*. New York: Columbia University Press.

Lauritsen, M., Allen, R., Alves, J.M., Ameen, C., Fowler, T., Irving-Pease, E., Larson, G., Murphy L.J., Outram, A.K., Pilgrim, E., Shaw, P.A. and Sykes, N. 2018. "Celebrating Easter, Christmas and their associated alien fauna", *World Archaeology*, 50(2): 285–299.

Layard, J. 1988. *The Lady of the Hare. A Study in the Healing Power of Dreams*. Boston and Shaftesbury: Shabhala.
Lévi-Strauss, C. 1978. "Une prefiguration anatomique de la gémellité", in *Systèmes de signes. Textes réunis en homage à Germaine Dieterlen*. Paris: Hermann.
Moisseeff, M. 1985. "De la procréation à la sexualité: une approche anthropologique de la différence des sexes", *Cahiers de l'Institut Universitaire des Sciences Psychosociales et Neurobiologiques de l'U.F.R. de Médecine de Bobigny* 36: 14–31.
Moisseeff, M. 2010. "Alien ou l'horreur de la procreation dans la mythologie occidentale contemporaine", in Gouyon, P.-H. and Civard-Racinais, A. (eds), *Aux origines de la sexualité*. Paris: Fayard. pp. 446–465.
Murphy, L.J. and Ameen, C. 2020. "The shifting baselines of the British hare goddess", *Open Archaeology* 6(1): 214–235.
Newall, V. 1971. *An Egg at Easter: A Folklore Study*. London: Routledge & Kegan Paul.
Nildin-Wall, B. and Wall, J. 1993. "The witch as hare or the witch's hare: Popular legends and beliefs in Nordic tradition", *Folklore* 104(1/2): 67–76.
O'Connor, S. 2016. "Hares and hags: Becoming animal in Éilís Ní Dhuibhne's *Dún na mBan trí Thine*", in Kirkpatrick, K. and Faragó, B. (eds), *Animals in Irish Literature and Culture*. London: Palgrave Macmillan. pp. 92–104.
Onians, R.B. 1951. *The Origins of European Thought about the Body, the Mind, the Soul, the World, Time, and Fate*. Cambridge: Cambridge University Press.
Pentangelo, J. 2019. "The grant, the hare, and the survival of a medieval folk belief", *Folklore* 130(1): 48–59.
Porter, E. 1969. *Cambridgeshire Customs and Folklore*. London: Routlege & Kegan Paul.
Roud, S. 2006. *The Penguin Guide to the Superstitions of Britain and Ireland*. London: Penguin.
Rowling, J.K., credited as Newt Scamander. 2001. *Fantastic Beasts and Where to Find Them*. London: Bloomsbury.
Sermon, R. 2022. "Eostre and the *Matronae Austriahenae*", *Folklore* 133(2): 139–157.
Sissa, G. 1989. "Subtle bodies", in Feher, M., Naddaff, R. and Tazi, N. (eds), *Fragments for a History of the Human Body*. Part Three. New York: Zone. pp. 132–156.
Sokos, C., Birtsas, P., Papaspyropoulos, K.G., Rsachalidis, E., Giannakopoulos, E., Milis, C., Spyrou, V., Manolakou, K., Valiakos, G., Iakovakis, C., Athanasiou, L.V., Sfougaris, A. and Billinis, C. 2016. "Mammals and habitat disturbance: The case of brown hare and wildlife", *Current Zoology* 62(5): 421–430.
Thiselton-Dyer, T.F. 1878. *English Folk-Lore*. London: Hardwicke & Bogue.
Udal, J.S. 1922. *Dorsetshire Folklore*. Hertford: Stephen Austin & Sons.
Uther, H.-J. 2004. *The Types of International Folktales: A Classification and Bibliography Based on the System of Antti Aarne and Stith Thompson*. 3 vols. Folklore Fellows Communications 284, 285, and 286. Helsinki: Academia Scientarium Fennica.

About the Author

Michael Houseman, anthropologist, is Professor emeritus (chair of African religions) at the Ecole Pratique des Hautes Etudes, Université PSL (France).

He has undertaken research among the Beti of Southern Cameroon, in Benin, in French Guyana and in France. He has published extensively on kinship and social organisation, and on initiation and ritual performance. He is currently interested in emergent forms of ritual practice in contemporary Western societies. His publications include *Naven or the Other Self: A Relational Approach to Ritual Action* (1998, with Carlo Severi) and *Le rouge est le noir: Essais sur le rituel* (2012).

6 Spirit Possession and Trance as Humpty Dumpty Words: Reflection on Adjusted Styles of Communication

Bettina E. Schmidt

Introduction

Communication with other-than-human entities is at the heart of religious practices worldwide. For an anthropologist, however, it creates methodological problems. Even the terminology is problematic. For a long time scholars referred to them as spirits or gods, using therefore terms with a Christian connotation that – consciously or not – led to a hierarchical differentiation between these entities. Gods seemed more powerful than spirits, and a supreme creator god even more than deities. However, these hierarchical differentiations obscured the lived practice that is anchored on the relationship with these other-than-human entities.

Doing fieldwork in communities that communicate with other-than-human entities on a regular basis – the trademark of any anthropologist – usually leads to questions about the validity of the experience and consequently the reality of these entities. Anthropologists have been trained to avoid any probing questions about whether we believe in these spirits or gods, following Evans-Pritchard's advice not to comment on the reality from a Western perspective (1965: 17). But avoiding taking a stance in such an important issue just shows the methodological bias anthropology still struggles with, despite so many turns and new directions.

To be honest, this was also my own position. While I admired the performance of mediums channelling the messages from the spiritual world, I did not commit to say anything about the reality of them. For a while, the approach of performance studies was my way out of the debate. But when I began to focus on mediumship and so-called spirit possession I realised I could not avoid the confrontation with my own perception any longer. And here Graham Harvey helped me to find my way.

I met Graham in 2004, at the conference of the British Association for Study of Religions in Oxford where I joined the BASR. Our first conversations about common research interests took place at the following BASR conference in Bath. We soon realised our passion for not just vernacular religions but for our encounters with practitioners, i.e., "doing fieldwork". Graham made me feel welcome within the BASR and assured me that being an anthropologist did not affect my place among the British study of religions scholars. Coming from Germany, I was rather cautious about my shift from anthropology to the study of religions, as German scholars are rather defensive about their disciplines. However, Graham reassured me in words and actions that it does not matter; what joins us is our common interest in other religions and in things people do. Over the years, I worked with Graham in various positions and engaged with him in several debates. I organised a BASR conference when he was secretary. I became later secretary myself and persuaded him to take on the role of president. I managed to get him to speak at a conference about spirit possession I organised at Bangor, and he persuaded me to contribute to more books than I intended. He even invited me to submit a proposal for my translated book about my research about Caribbean religious communities in New York City, which became my first monograph published in English. When I was invited to contribute to this Festschrift, I did not hesitate, well, at least not long, as time is always an issue today for anyone working in a university! I owe Graham more than he probably knows.

When I considered what to write, I initially thought about his excellent article in *Numen* about Māori guesthood (Harvey, 2003), which I make all postgraduate students read, not just the ones doing fieldwork. It is now part of my Theory and Methodology in the Study of Religions course, and I enjoy my annual discussions with the students. However, I decided on a different topic, linked to our common research interest. As we all know, Graham is a wonderful storyteller and his presentations as BASR conferences and others quickly became the highlight for me. But what I remember most of these early meetings is his re-telling of a story from Irving Hallowell in which he coined the phrase "other-than-human-person". After I heard Graham mentioning it at a BASR conference, I suddenly recognised the importance of the phrase as a way out of the methodological conundrum. Graham elaborated and discussed it in numerous publications. But my starting point is his chapter in the book *Spirit Possession and Trance* (Schmidt and Huskinson, 2010) that came out of the conference I had organised around this topic so many years ago. In this chapter Graham presented "shaman", "spirit" and "possession" as Humpty Dumpty words, "words that are made to work hard, sometimes in eccentric ways, and sometimes 'paid extra' for their work" (Harvey, 2010:

32), referring to a conversation between Alice and Humpty Dumpty in Lewis Carroll's *Through the Looking Glass* (1872). "Spirit possession" became my Humpty Dumpty word, as I will show here. After I organised a conference around this term, I spent a sabbatical in Brazil speaking with people about their experience with it (Schmidt, 2016). However, due to the contested nature of the term, I used various other words to talk about it. While I am not such a gifted storyteller as Graham is, I include ethnographic *intermezzo* in this chapter that give insight into my fieldwork. In addition, I include excerpts from my conversations and interviews that show how people experiencing trance and possession talk about the practice. These *intermezzi* illustrate my engagement with a different ontology, as well as the Humpty Dumpty-ness of spirit possession.

Ethnographic *Intermezzo*

Shortly after I arrived in Brazil for research on spirit possession and trance, a colleague invited me to accompany a group of students to a Candomblé ceremony. Candomblé is one of the African-derived religions in Brazil, probably the best studied due to its popularity among anthropologists. One of the highlights are the encounters with the *orixás*, the African deities at the heart of the Candomblé pantheon. As I had just arrived in Brazil, I had not yet conducted any interviews about the practice, which would lead me much later to a new understanding of what went on. I attended the ceremony struggling with jetlag and getting increasingly tired throughout the evening, despite the engaging music, colourful costumes and inspiring dance. One of the photos I took at that evening is still my favourite despite (or perhaps because of) showing the dancer out of focus due to the movement – and the failing battery of my camera. The *terreiro* (compound of the religious community) where the ceremony took place was just outside São Paulo. When we arrived, the preparations were well in swing, people struggled finding space for their cars and members hurried inside to change into their ceremonial dresses. It was already quite busy, though it took some time until the start of the ceremony. For a while, my colleague showed us around the main ceremonial hall and indicated the name and role of some of the people around. At a later visit we were also shown the little museum which the community set up to teach visitors about their belief. After a while he stepped aside, and I began to immerse myself into the ceremony. I became rather overwhelmed by all of it, the music, the dance, the colourful and creatively decorated costumes. Suddenly I noticed a woman standing a little bit apart from the activities, nearly disappearing in the flower decoration at the edge of the room. Her costume and necklaces indicated her membership in the community, but she did not partake in any of the activities. Her eyes were shut, and she stood totally still, rather withdrawn from the rather hectic ongoings around her. What intrigued me was that she was constantly turning her hands, up and down, up and down, up and down. I kept looking back at her while trying to keep track of all the other activities. It was clear that she was in a deep trance and the hand movements were a form of communication. Later I learned more about it but at that moment her stillness kept me captivated. Reflecting on it much later, I realised that this moment opened the door for me to realise that "spirit possession" was an inadequate term and did not capture in even a slightest way the lived experience of what I observed. Together with the term "trance", another inadequate term so commonly used by academics, it is indeed a Humpty Dumpty word as Harvey had told me. While used in academic literature as well as referred to outside academia, people experiencing it reject the term, sometimes due to its biased connotation but also because of the inadequacy of it. However, according to Harvey, careful attention to its inadequacy allows us "insights into the richness of the human relationships, performances and experiences that it labels" (Harvey, 2010: 32). And here the "hard work" begins.

Irving Hallowell and Other-than-Human-Persons

Relations are at the core of Irving Hallowell's explanation of Ojibwe ontology. His contribution to the Paul Radin Festschrift, "Ojibwa ontology, behavior, and world view" (1960), is sometimes referred to as an early precursor of the ontological turn within anthropology, 50 years before its time. However, recent scholars tend to ignore his early contribution, even when they use the phrase "other-than-human", as Pauline Turner Strong notes (Strong, 2017, referring for instance to Eduardo Kohn, 2013). Decades before the ontological turn in anthropology Hallowell urged anthropologists to follow "observed practices" rather than formal linguistic analysis (Strong, 2017: 469). Using the term for "grandfather" as example, Hallowell explains that the Ojibwe apply the term not just to humans but also to other-than-human persons, and he argues that "the more deeply we penetrate the world view of the Ojibwa the more apparent it is that 'social relations' between human beings (anícinábek) and other-than-human 'persons' are of cardinal significance" (1960: 23). He illustrates the point in this much-cited anecdote: "Since stones are grammatically animate, I once asked an old man: Are *all* the stones we see about us here alive? He reflected a long while and then replied, 'No! But *some* are'" (1960: 24, original emphasis). As Harvey highlights, Hallowell's main point in this and other anecdotes is that stones and other inanimate objects are not attributed with living souls on their own, hence they "do not do things of their own volition" but when "they engage in relationships" (Harvey, 2010: 20). In Hallowell's words: "the Ojibwa are not animists in the sense that they dogmatically attribute living souls to inanimate objects such as stones. The hypothesis which suggests itself to me is that the allocation of stones to an animate grammatical category is part of a culturally constituted cognitive 'set'" (1960: 25). Hallowell's very nuanced differentiation between inanimate objects and animate persons is at the heart of not only the Ojibwe ontology but is the key to an understanding of religious concepts in other cultures. As Harvey summarises Hallowell, "Persons are known to be persons when they relate to other persons in particular ways" (2010: 20). Communication is one of these ways to engage in relationships, as well as gift-giving and movement. The conversation, however, is not always respectful and intimate but can also be hostile and aggressive as enmity is also a way to relate to each other. Consequently, "'person' is not a nominal category but a performance, and one that is both corporeal and corporate" (Harvey, 2010: 20). Crucial is to keep in mind that Hallowell does not define a person with humanlike characteristics but describes a person as a being that "communicate[s] intentionally and act[s] towards other relationally" (Harvey, 2010: 21). This point is important to repeat as for many, personhood is a uniquely human attribute (e.g., Klass, 2003). In order to point out this flaw in our thinking, Hallowell coined the phrase "human- and other-than-human persons", though the term "person" would capture this following Hallowell's definition of personhood. Hence, only because we seem to be preconditioned to apply the term "person" only to humans, Hallowell insisted on these clarifying adjectives as a reminder not to privilege humanity.

And it goes even further, as a person does not need to have a physical form such as a stone, tree or an animal, as often assumed when talking about animistic ontologies. Hallowell shows that conversations between persons take place across species boundaries, as this anecdote illustrates:

> An informant told me that many years before he was sitting in a tent one summer afternoon during a storm, together with an old man and his wife. There was one clap of thunder after another. Suddenly the old man turned to his wife and asked, "Did you hear what was said?" "No," she replied, "I didn't catch it" (1960: 34).

Reading this anecdote takes me immediately back to my own research area, as thunder is also a characteristic of one of the main *orixás*, and my PhD supervisor commented after my PhD viva that took place during a thunderstorm that Shango must have approved my defence full-heartedly. To be honest, I did not catch Shango's contribution, like the old couple in Hallowell's story, as I was too nervous and had my back to the window. But reading the anecdote, with which Hallowell illustrated that not all conversations are about us humans, reminded me of my own link to the god of thunder.

What these anecdotes also show is that "Hallowell is fundamentally concerned with phenomenological experience – 'the real experience of persons in a lifeworld' – not with constructing a theory of the real" (Strong, 2017: 471). Perhaps this is the reason why he is so often overlooked by anthropologists today. Even Tim Ingold, who praises Hallowell's article as one of the great classics in northern circumpolar ethnography (2000: 90), challenges Hallowell's lack of interest in the nature of reality. Instead his main concern is, as Ingold writes, "to understand the world view, not the fundamental nature of reality" (2000: 95). And Ingold is correct; Hallowell was not interested in a theory of reality but in the understanding of a different philosophy. With his anecdotes and reflections, Hallowell urged anthropologists, decades before it became popular, to consider our cultural subjectivity and abstain from projecting categorial abstraction derived from Western thought. We should adopt, he urged us, "a perspective which includes an analysis of the outlook of the people themselves as a complementary procedure" (1960: 21). This is the only way to gain an understanding of their world view and the way they conceive the nature of the world.

Ethnographic *Intermezzo*

Halfway through my research leave in São Paulo, I was invited to a Candomblé ceremony in a very small *terreiro* at the centre of São Paulo. It consisted of one house only, though it also housed various rooms for preparation (e.g., kitchen), consultation office, shrine, rooms where initiation took place, and more. I had visited the house before to interview the priest after having met him on several occasions. He then invited me to attend a small ceremony in honour of the *caboclo* White Feather (Pena Branca). Caboclos are more common within Umbanda, another African-derived religion in Brazil, which includes in addition to the African *orixás* also spirits associated for instance with the Amazon (*caboclos*) or other groups. While Candomblé communities had long incorporated these spirits in the pantheon, during a process of (re-)Africanising Candomblé they disbanded with these spirits and focus now on the veneration of *orixás* alone. However, there are still some exceptions like this community. When I saw the costume of Pena Branca and mentioned that so many others stepped away from *caboclos*, the priest explained that as a Brazilian he also needs to celebrate the Brazilian spirits, not just the African gods. Though he was very active in a Brazilian form of the Black Power movement and dressed proudly in colourful "African" clothes whenever he was asked to speak at public engagements, he was also proud of being Brazilian (see Schmidt, 2013).

I had invited a friend to accompany me to the ceremony. While we arrived at the time indicated to me, it was much too early Brazilian time. This allowed me to observe the final preparations and the arrival of other guests. Celebrations such as this one, for a particular spirit, are usually public occasions where members of the community invite friends, family and neighbours to join in. As time progressed, the crowd in the small hall where the celebration took place became nearly unbearable. The priest was thrilled to see so many and welcomed nearly everyone with a big hug and smile and passed joyfully through the crowd. After some singing and talking, Pena Branca arrived and took over the body of the priest. Members of the house helped him to another room where he was dressed in the costume of Pena Branca. When he reappeared, it was clear that Pena Branca had entered the room, not the priest. With some other people I also came forward to greet Pena Branca. However, I made a mistake in the way I greeted the caboclo and was told off by Pena Branca for not behaving in a respectful and accurate manner. After correcting my body posture, Pena Branca embraced me before moving on to the next guest. A short while later the celebration reached its peak.

While in other places I had attended first a ceremony and afterwards arranged to interview members to learn more about it, here it was different. I had met the priest several times, but mainly at public events, which then led to me gaining an interview with him. I was therefore already familiar with the priest at the start of the ceremony. However, it was my first encounter with Pena Branca and I learned it was not enough to know the priest, the human body; I had to establish also a connection with the *caboclo*. Pena Branca was a different person than the priest, though hosted for a while in the same physical body. I had to adjust my communication accordingly. It also indicated the inadequacy of the academic concept of spirit possession. The priest was not possessed by Pena Branca but Pena Branca used the priest's physical body to engage with the community.

Graham Harvey and Adjusted Styles of Communication

Harvey puts communication at the core of his approach to shamanism when he proposes re-using ASC to refer to Adjusted Styles of Communication, instead of Altered States of Consciousness (2010: 31). He explains that "shamans are persons (human or otherwise perhaps) who learn to communicate across species boundaries within a rich animate world full of persons who deserve respect but who might be eaten and might aggress, and who might control and be controlled" (2010: 31). The vagueness of the statement reflects his critique of the artificially construed boundaries between practices that he proposes to be types of communication between persons, human and otherwise. By challenging the widespread differentiation between animism and shamanism as well as between spirit possession and trance, Harvey puts forward a radical new approach to animism that rejects Western notions of well-defined categories. Instead, he highlights the lack of clear boundaries and insights into "the richness of human relationships, performances and experiences" that "arises from and affects the behaviour or both the shaman and the otherworld person" (2010: 32). While traditionally shamanism and spirit possession were seen as on the opposite ends of the spectrum with regard to control (e.g., Eliade, 1964), Harvey's new animism embraces different phenomena and even distinct ways of understanding. As he demonstrates so well in *The Handbook of Contemporary Animism* (2013), animism refers to "more than one thing or theory", it concerns "the nature of human-being and the nature of our world" (2013: 1). Further on he defines spirits – such a tricky term at the core of the traditional definition of animism as belief in spirits (Tylor, 1913) – as "a way in which some people try to convey an idea about their personal relationship with trees, animals, rivers or ancestors that others consider inanimate and inert" (2013: 4). Instead of limiting spirits to non-empirical realities as Tylor did, Harvey's all-embracing definition acknowledges the cultural context as well as diversity within. In this way, animism is just another word for tradition (Hogan, 2013), similar to ontology, just a new way to speak about culture (Strong, 2017: 468). However, Harvey's proposal of Adjusted Styles of Communication goes further. One could even see it as a new way to speak about any religious or spiritual tradition, avoiding hence any Western presumptions and labels. Let's apply it to mediumship (and my Humpty Dumpty word "spirit possession") to find out more.

Mediumship, Incorporation and Other Relations between Persons of Different Species

During my research in Brazil I struggled to find the correct terminology which had an impact on my conversations with people (Schmidt, 2022). While acknowledging the importance of academic categories (Johnson, 2011), I proposed seeing spirit possession as deictic term whose understanding depends on the cultural context (Schmidt, 2016). At the same time, I tried to avoid using this contested label in the ethnographic context and adapted various terms people used for their practice. Hence, while I kept the term in my academic writings, I stepped aside and followed the lived practice of my research partners. One of these rather successful terms is "mediumship", as it highlights the role of the human to facilitate the communication with the spiritual world. It is frequently used by Brazilian spiritists as well as members of some of the African-derived religions such as Umbanda, one of the most widespread African-derived religions in Brazil. However, it would be wrong to see the mediums just as means of communication, like "an immense metaphysical telephone" as Emilio Rodríquez Vázquez did (1994), because this viewpoint denies their agency (Schmidt, 2015). As a spiritist who vehemently rejected the term "spirit possession" once told me, spirits:

> cannot say "go and do this and do that". The most they can do is to direct a doctor to the proper diagnosis and help us [the mediums] to find the right words so that people feel obligated to take the medication, and empower them to modify, change, and improve their habits, and be happy (interview on 5 May 2010).

He referred to "free will" that would prevent a medium from being influenced by spirits, which is just a different term for agency. A similar point was made by another spiritist when I asked him about imperfect (i.e., bad) spirits. He asserted that a trained medium would be able to identify an approaching spirit based on the vibration and could take countermeasures. For him, mediumship does not offer an excuse for their actions:

> Mediumship does not leave everything up to the spirit, he [the medium] is not exempt from responsibility when he is unconscious. A medium would not be very honest, if he said, "Oh but I have nothing to do with it, I do not know what happens or how it happens." As in the case of a conscious medium, he knows absolutely for sure what happened (interview on 30 March 2010).

Mediums are therefore agents of their deeds and are not controlled by spirits, whether they are conscious, semi-conscious or unconscious. One of the teachers in a spiritist centre even insisted that mediums need to remain in control even when what they are saying is inspired by spirits. He suggested that:

> mediums need to know what they are doing, and that they can resist the spirits and say no if needed. Often the spirit has a load that is too heavy for us, and if we are not the masters of ourselves, and cannot say "No, not in that way, you have to keep quiet, have to remain conscious, you will remain calm, because

I do not accept you. You are not here to curse, nor to offend anyone, nor wish evil upon anyone." And we are aware of ourselves; we are directing this spirit in order to get a good resolution. Moreover, in order to improve, and become more trustworthy, we cannot let them do whatever they want to do. We have to have control and know what is going on (interview on 17 April 2010).

To sum up, while mediums can hear or see the spirits, or intuitively learn from them, their relationship with the spirit world is a style of communication, not more but also not less. To some degree, a similar problem around agency comes up when discussing the practice among Candomblé and other African-derived religious communities. While some prefer the term "incorporation" instead of "mediumship", they agree in their rejection of the term "spirit possession". However, even the term "incorporation" is seen as insufficient. While it acknowledges the agency of both human medium and divine entity, it is misleading as it seems to imply an encounter of two similar entities, one human and one divine. Yet, the *orixás* are perceived as forces of nature, much too powerful for a human being to be incorporated in a body. As a Candomblé priest explained, the energy of the *orixás* would destroy a human body during any attempt to incorporate into the body. While it is used, in conversations as well as in the literature, it comes therefore with a comment that incorporation does not mean actual incorporation of an *orixá* into a human body but more of a merger of two separate entities during the initiation ritual that creates, out of two separate and previously "unfinished" entities, one (see Schmidt, 2016 for more information).

Stepping aside for now from the difficult question of terminology, which illustrates the inadequacy of the term "spirit possession" despite its longevity in academic literature, I want to illustrate how the application of Harvey's ASC can improve our understanding of practice often categorised as spirit possession but also described as mediumship and incorporation (among others). I will reflect on two points here: on the practice as styles of communication and on the nature of the entities, hence the persons involved in the communication. As the discussion about the correct terminology above has shown, several of my interviewees stressed the free will of the mediums as well as the agency of the spirits. Yet, interestingly, several of the Candomblé priests I spoke with pointed towards divination as a form of communication with the *orixás* and not incorporation. By pushing for oracle reading as the main – sometimes only – way of communicating with the *orixás*, they remain in charge of the communication, as only priests are trained in reading oracles such as *buzios* or *ifa*. As an explanation, some of the priests mentioned that most Candomblé mediums do not speak during an episode of incorporation. Some even mentioned language as another problem. As the *orixás* are

African, they would be unable to speak Portuguese. However, communication does not need to be verbal. The *orixás* can convey messages by other means such as hand gestures, which I already mentioned above, in the first ethnographic *intermezzo*, but also other forms of body language. Whether dancing, walking or just standing, the *orixás* can express emotions such as contentment but also disappointment and anger, without saying a word. To some degree it is rather similar to the communication of the Thunder Birds in one of Hallowell's anecdotes mentioned above. While we can hear sounds, we usually don't understand what they are saying, even if it is directed towards humans. However, the conversation is not always with humans, which I noticed during the ceremonies I attended, too. Several times it seemed that the *orixás* were more interested in greeting each other and re-confirming the hierarchy among them. As I learned to notice, *orixás* regarded with a higher esteem are honoured by *orixás* at a lower level in a range of different ways, from a deep bow of the head to lying on the ground in front of them. This now links to the nature of the entities involved and their personhood. As already described above, across the traditions my interviewees stressed the agency of the entities, whether they were spirits of deceased humans, spirits of nature such as the *caboclos*, and the *orixás*, the African gods and goddesses. Each community has its own pantheon of spiritual entities, some more mixed than others. But a common theme in the conversations I had was the affirmation of their agency, i.e., the affirmation of their personhood though with a twist. In spiritism as well as in Umbanda, the African-derived Brazilian religion which is heavily influenced by spiritism, spirits are perceived as descended from humans, or, more precisely, the other way around, humans are perceived as embodying spirits for the duration of their lives on earth. After death the spirit becomes an entity without a physical form until reincarnated into another body or moving on to another world. Yet the nature of the *orixás* is perceived differently. In Umbanda some *orixás* are regarded as having lived on earth in a mythical time before having been transformed into a god or goddess. There are numerous myths about them, some of them rather like Ancient Greek and Roman stories. They present the source of specific *linhas* (lineages) that structured the spiritual world. In Candomblé, however, the *orixás* are perceived as surpassing individuality. Despite the myths which describe *orixás* with sometimes humanlike characteristics and behaviours, *orixás* are compared with forces of nature that surpass any physical entity. Nevertheless, they are still other-than-human persons.

To explain the nature of the *orixás* in Candomblé ontology, we have to look at the initiation ritual and the first encounter of the novices with their *orixás*. The Brazilian anthropologist Marcio Goodman explains that during the initiation ritual and the initial possession, two separate persons are created, a human and an individualised *orixá*. Goldman defines a person (and here he means a human person) as "multiple and layered, composed of agencies of natural and immaterial elements" which includes a main *orixá* and several secondary *orixás*, ancestral spirits and a soul (2007: 111). Humans are born imperfect, or as he writes "not ready-made" until the initial possession that makes the human self finally complete because it leaves an aspect of the *orixás* inside the human body. This element becomes part of the (human) self and constitutes a vital aspect of the individuality of this person.

Interestingly, the *orixás* are similarly transformed during the ritual. Goldman differentiates between more generic *orixás* which are like forces of nature and gender-free, and individual *orixás* that are often – but not always – gendered and only created during the initial possession. He writes that the outcome of an initiation is that "a more or less undifferentiated individual... becomes a structured person and a generic *orixá*... is actualized as an individual *orixá*" (2007: 112). Initiation means therefore, "the ritual production of two individualized entities out of two generic substrates" (Goldman, 2007: 112).

At this point I turn back to Hallowell's concept of persons, human and other-than-human to reflect on the nature of the *orixás*. As Harvey points out, Hallowell "was not privileging humanity or saying that what makes something a person is its likeness to humans", and consequently, a person "is not defined by human characteristics or behaviour" (Harvey, 2010: 21). What makes entities persons is communication and relationships. "All beings communicate intentionally and act towards others relationally: this makes them 'persons'" (Harvey, 2010: 21). The differentiation between generic and individualised *orixás* does not really matter; both fall under the category of persons that communicate with other persons – humans and other-than-humans – in various ways such as hand gestures and other body movements. In this sense what happens in these events I described in the ethnographic *intermezzi* above are cross-species communications and the establishment of new relationships across species boundaries.

Reflection of Spirit Possession and Trance as Humpty Dumpty Words

In Chapter 6 of *Through the Looking Glass*, Alice meets Humpty Dumpty, who asks her name and business. However, when she tells him her name, he interrupts with another question, "what does it mean?", to which Alice replies "*Must* a name mean something?" "'Of course it must,' Humpty Dumpty said with a short laugh: '*my* name means the shape I am – and a good handsome shape it is too. With a name like yours, you might be any shape, almost'" (Carroll, 2018 [1872]). What follows is a long and sometimes rather bizarre conversation about the meaning of words. While Alice is sceptical that Humpty Dumpty can make up the meaning of words, he insists that deciding the meaning of words shows "which is to be master".

It seems to me that this is exactly what we do in academia when applying academic labels. As Ann Taves points out, we often forget that terms carry associations "that may be at odds with, and thus distort, the experience of our historical subjects" (1999: 8). Scholars run the risk, she continues, of "obscure[ing] the subjective experience of the native actor" (Taves, 1999: 9). This divide between academic categories and lived experiences as reflected in the ethnographic *intermezzi* above is nowhere so visible as when it comes to the means of communication between the human and the spiritual world. "Spirit possession" is still the commonly used academic category, though it disguises the meaning of the lived experience, while the people experiencing it reject the term categorically. Following Taves I wrote elsewhere that "labelling something creates an unequal power relationship between the scholar and the person experiencing it" (Schmidt, 2016: 5). Why is it then still in the title of my monograph and other publications? When struggling with challenging categories in the past, I tried to suggest alternative labels, but with little success as the little engagement with the phrase "polyphonic bricolage" shows (Schmidt, 2008). This time I decided on a different route by putting forward "spirit possession" as a deictic term whose meaning depends on the context, historical, cultural and social. Consequently, "spirit possession" became my Humpty Dumpty word, which was perceived differently in every context. By using it with such a range of definitions, spirit possession "worked hard" and indeed in eccentric ways (Harvey, 2010: 32). But is it enough to acknowledge the lived religion? In this chapter I followed Graham's lead further than before and applied his definition of "possession" to what I encountered in Brazil. Whatever label we give this lived experience – mediumship, incorporation or indeed spirit possession – common features were communication between persons, humans and other-than-human, and relationships across different species. I ended up therefore going even further than Graham. Led by a reflection on Hallowell's concept of "persons, humans and other than human" and Graham's "adjusted styles of communication" I decided to rethink the use of the term "spirit possession". While it was indeed made to work hard over the last decades, as the growing number of publications show (e.g., Espírito Santo and Shapiro, 2022; Pócs and Zempléni, 2022), it might be time to retire it.

References

Carroll, L. 2021 [1872]. *Through the Looking Glass, and what Alice found there*. A Project Gutenberg eBook. Available at: www.gutenberg.org/cache/epub/12/pg12-images.html (accessed 17 March 2023).

Eliade, M. 1964. *Shamanism: Archaic Technique of Ecstasy*. New York: Pantheon.

Espírito Santo, D. and Shapiro, M. (eds) 2022. *The Dynamic Cosmos: Movement, Paradox, and Experimentation in the Anthropology of Spirit Possession*. London: Bloomsbury.

Evans-Pritchard, E.E. 1965. *Theories of Primitive Religion*. Oxford: Clarendon.

Goldman, M. 1985. "A construção ritual da pessoa: a possessão no Candomblé", *Religião e Sociedade* 12(1): 22–55.

Goldman, M. 2007. "How to learn in an Afro-Brazilian spirit possession religion: Ontology and multiplicity in Candomblé", in Berliner, D. and Sarró, R. (eds), *Learning Religion: Anthropological Approaches*. New York and Oxford: Berghahn Books, pp. 103–119.

Harvey, G. 2003. "Guesthood as ethical decolonising research method", *Numen* 50(2): 125–146.

Harvey, G. 2010. "Animism rather than shamanism: New approaches to what shamans do (for other animists)", in Schmidt, B. and Huskinson, L. (eds), *Spirit Possession and Trance: New Interdisciplinary Perspectives*. London: Continuum. pp. 14–34.

Harvey, G. 2013. "Introduction", in Harvey, G. (ed.) *The Handbook of Contemporary Animism*. Durham: Acumen, 1–12.

Harvey, G. (ed.) 2013. *The Handbook of Contemporary Animism*. Durham: Acumen.

Hallowell, A.I. 1960. "Ojibwa ontology, behavior, and world view", in Diamond, S (ed.), *Culture in History*. New York: Columbia University Press, pp. 19–52.

Hogan, L. 2013. "We call it tradition", in Harvey, G. (ed.), *The Handbook of Contemporary Animism*. Durham: Acumen, pp. 17–26.

Ingold, T. 2000. *The Perception of the Environment: Essays on Livelihood, Dwelling and Skill*. London: Routledge.

Johnson, P. 2011. "An Atlantic genealogy of 'spirit possession'", *Comparative Studies in Society and History* 53(2): 393–425.

Klass, M. 2003. *Mind over Mind: The Anthropology and Psychology of Spirit Possession*. Lanham, MA: Rowman & Littlefield.

Kohn, E. 2013. *How Forests Think: Toward an Anthropology Beyond the Human*. Berkeley, CA: University of California Press.

Pócs, É. and Zempléni, A. (eds) 2022 *Spirit Possession: Multidisciplinary Approaches to a Worldwide Phenomenon*. Budapest, Vienna, New York: Central European University Press.

Rodríquez Vázquez, E. 1994. *El espiritismo on Puerto Rico es una inmensa telefónica metafísica*. Rio Piedra: III. Simposio Internacional: Afroamérica y su cultura religiosa.

Schmidt, B.E. 2008. *Caribbean Diaspora in the USA: Diversity of Caribbean Religions in New York City*. Aldershot: Ashgate.

Schmidt, B.E. 2013. "The spirit white feather in São Paulo: The resilience of indigenous spirits in Brazil", in Cox, J. (ed.), *Critical Reflections on Indigenous Religions* (Vitality of Indigenous Religions series). London: Ashgate, pp. 123–141.

Schmidt, B.E. 2015. "Spirit mediumship in Brazil: The controversy about semi-conscious mediums", *DISKUS: The Journal of the British Association for the Study of Religions* 17(2): 38–53.
Schmidt, B.E. 2016. *Spirits and Trance in Brazil: Anthropology of Religious Experiences*. London: Bloomsbury.
Schmidt, B.E. 2022. "'Incorporation does not exist': The Brazilian rejection of the term 'possession' and why it exists nonetheless", in Pócs, É. and Zempléni, A. (eds), *Spirit Possession: Multidisciplinary Approaches to a Worldwide Phenomenon*. Budapest, Vienna, New York: Central European University Press. pp. 75–92.
Schmidt, B.E. and Engler, S. (eds) 2016. *Handbook of Contemporary Brazilian Religions*. Leiden: Brill.
Schmidt, B.E. and Leonardi, J. (eds) 2020. *Spirituality and Wellbeing: Interdisciplinary Approaches to the Study of Religious Experience and Health*. Sheffield: Equinox.
Schmidt, B.E. and Huskinson, L. (eds) 2010. *Spirit Possession and Trance: New Interdisciplinary Perspectives* (Continuum Advances in Religious Studies series). London: Continuum.
Strong, P.T. 2017. "A. Irving Hallowell and the ontological turn", *Hau: Journal of Ethnographic Theory* 7(1): 461–488.
Taves, A. 1999. *Fits, Trances, & Visions: Experiencing Religion and Explaining Experience from Wesley to James*. Princeton, NJ: Princeton University Press.
Tylor, E.B. 1913 [1871]. *Primitive Culture*. London: John Murray.

About the Author

Bettina E. Schmidt is Professor in Study of Religions and Anthropology of Religion at the Centre for Humanities and Social Science, University of Wales Trinity Saint David, UK and the Director of the Alister Hardy Religious Experience Research Centre. Previously she worked at Marburg University, Oxford University and Bangor University. She was also visiting professor at the City University of New York and visiting scholar at the Pontifícia Universidade Católica de São Paulo. She served as President of the British Association for the Study of Religions (2018--2021). She has published extensively on Caribbean and Latin American religions. Her academic interests include anthropology of religion, diaspora identity, religious experience, spirituality and wellbeing, and gender. Her main fieldworks were conducted in Mexico, Puerto Rico, Ecuador, New York City, and in São Paulo, Brazil. She is the author of *Spirit and Trance in Brazil: An Anthropology of Religious Experiences* (2016, Bloomsbury) and other monographs as well as co-editor of the *Handbook of Contemporary Brazilian Religions* (2016, Brill) and *Spirituality and Wellbeing: Interdisciplinary Approaches to the Study of Religious Experience and Health* (2020, Equinox) among others.

7   Plants and People/Plants as People: Plants and Their Medicinal and Ritual Uses in Mesoamerica and South America and Religions in the Caribbean

Christina Welch

Introduction

This chapter will explore the notion of plants as people taking inspiration from the work on animism by Graham Harvey, and the central role that plants have played as medicines and during rituals with a focus on firstly, Mesoamerica and South America, and secondly, the Caribbean. This is a part of the world influenced by diverse Mesoamerica and South American ways of thinking, and also the plant-ways of enslaved Africans who were forcibly brought to labour on plantations during the era of transatlantic chattel slavery. Academic work around plant use in indigenous ritual, and through the lens of plants as persons has been carried out in a number of colonialised countries, notably Aotearoa/New Zealand, Australia, North America, and Mesoamerica and South America, but the Caribbean remains a somewhat marginalised area of study, especially with regard to plants used in religion.

In terms of exploring plants as people in Mesoamerica and South America, this chapter expands the aspects of Harvey's work in *Animism: Respecting the Living World* (2005) and *Food, Sex and Strangers: Understanding Religion as Everyday Life* (2013), which both touch on human–plant relations in various contexts. In *Animism* Harvey notes that "Yekuana [people] 'bring out' new yucca plants with [the] …greeting and protective songs sung to newborn babies and to girls becoming women at first menstruation" (2005: 106),[1] and that whilst the Achuar men "socially relate to game animals as affines, Achuar women sustain consanguineal relationships with the plants they cultivate" (Rival in Harvey, 2005: 106). In *Food, Sex and Strangers* he notes that for the

---

1   For more detailed accounts of the Yukuana people, see Guss (1989).

Shuar people, again from Amazonia, everyone "is encouraged or enabled to… [ingest] vision-granting plants to know the future and (importantly) the rules for proper, respectful and healthy communal living" (Harvey, 2013: 31). Here we see that for these South American Amazonia peoples, intimate human–plant relations is normative.

In this chapter, however, the focus is on the South American Shipino and Jotï peoples, and the Mesoamerican Taíno, and explores the relationships each has with various plants. The use of plants in these case studies includes ingestion for specific purposes, including for communication with spirit guides, and for reproductive health. As such this chapter also draws on Harvey's work concerning religions and the senses, as human–plant relationships are best understood as a "sensual, corporeal and worldly" exchange between human bodies and plant bodies (2018: ix).

In terms of the Caribbean, this chapter focuses on rituals that use plants, and examples where plants are understood as teachers communicating and passing on their plant knowledge. In *Food, Sex and Strangers*, Harvey draws on Debbie Rose's work on Aboriginal Australian human–plant relationships, which focuses around co-dwelling; this is where humans and plants are members of the same community and together "look after the well-being of the community which is formed by their being and relating" (Harvey, 2018: 88). This chapter draws on a form of human–plant co-dwelling in three African-derived "religions" in the Caribbean: Obeah, which flourished in the Anglo-islands, and Haitian Vodôu and Cuban Regla de Ochá from the Spanish colonial islands. It also draws on archival material to explore the relationships between plants, and indigenous and enslaved African peoples in colonial St Vincent, to consider how human–plant co-dwelling can be understood as geographically unboundaried.

Plants and People/Plants as People: Context

The notion that plants are sentient, communicate and live in relationship to non-plant species is by no means recent, although by and large it is a relatively recent addition to the world of academia. Much of the academic work on plants has been in the fields of ethnobotany, ethnobiology and ethnomedicine, which are in effect the study of how people in a particular culture make use of plants local to them (Martinez et al., 2019). Although ritual, and indigenous "religions", have featured in these fields, writing often has a distinct traditional Western philosophical bias, using complex, contested and imposed terms such as religious, sacred, deities, taboos and supernatural. Perhaps an over-simplification and homogenisation of these fields, but the idea that plants can be understood as being in meaningful and international relations/relationships with the non-plant world, and thus having enmeshed agency, is largely missing (Hall, 2011; van der Veen, 2014; Lawrence, 2022). However, as van der Veen notes, because individual plants are unable to physically move locations, plants have "developed strategies to get others to help them" deal with enemies, and with reproduction (2014: 799–800). That some of the strategies can harm non-plants means that human-peoples have long developed strategies to work with certain plants, farming them, eating and excreting them, understanding them as kin and utilising them in ritual (Hall, 2011: 101–18).

A kinship relationship with plants is largely absent in the contemporary Westernised urbanised world. David Abrahams in his 1996 book *The Spell of the Sensuous* brought to the fore the distinction between this indigenous way of relating to plants and the normative Western one. He argued that many indigenous communities perceive plants as active participants in a wider-than-human world, whereas the Aristotelian-influenced Western notion is typically one where plants are understood to only have a vegetal soul and thus cannot feel as individual beings that can physically relocate. Nor do they know or have intellect (Abrahams, 1996: 38, 43); intellect here being a property unique to adult non-intellectually disabled humans (Stainton, 2001). However, very recent work in science has begun to unpick the notion that plants are unable to feel. The *National Geographic* ran an article entitled "Plants can talk. Yes, really. Here's how" (Yang, 2023), evidencing the surprise of the Western scientific world that plants are more than Aristotle's vegetal soul. However, this knowledge, which has long been held by indigenous peoples, is also not a surprise to academics working in the field of new animism. By exploring the relationships between humans and other than humans in a more-than-human world (Harvey, 2022; van Dooren and Chrulew, 2022), this inter- and multidisciplinary perspective reflects on the relational aspects of interactions between plants and non-plant species.

Terminology

At this point it is worth noting that from here on the term "wider-than-human" as opposed to "other-than-human" will be used when referring to non-humans; the latter, despite featuring more frequently in academic writing, can be understood as divorcing humans from the integrated whole that is the ecosystem of planet earth. Further, as Paul Gilroy has noted, people of colour and especially enslaved Africans were widely associated with non-humans in the colonial mindset (2014, 24). As such the term "other-than-humans" could inadvertently feed into perceptions that are not only inaccurate but continue to play into right-wing colonial tropes (Walcott, 2014). The term "wider-than-human" (w-t-h) is, however, not unproblematic but it largely avoids the linguistic othering, and generally places the human-world within its broader context. It is also important to note that the terms "religion/religious tradition" and "spiritual tradition/lifeways" will be used interchangeably. All these terms are problematic and the three Caribbean "religions" which are the focus of this paper are predominantly non-dogmatic orally transmitted ways of connecting to the wider-than-human world. In some academic publications they are listed as religions (e.g. Taylor and Case, 2013) or religious traditions (Oggunbemi, 2015), and in others as spiritual practices (Díaz, 2023). Further, historically some, such as Obeah, were once understood as witchcraft (O'Neal, 2020) whilst more recently this has shifted to a designation as a religion (Paton and Forde, 2012). The nomenclature is bound up with imperialism, colonialism and neo-colonialism, and unpacking it is beyond the scope of this chapter. The colonial tendency to other by italicising non-English terms is also problematic and, in this chapter, only Latin (a dead language) will be italicised, along with italicised words in quotes.

As noted, this chapter will explore ritual plant use in the Caribbean region and will highlight the role of plants as ritual agents in the w-t-h world. Extending Sørensen's argument that "an agent is characterised by his or her ability to influence the world by means of action" (2007, 282), this chapter unpacks the active role that plants are understood to play in ritual. Plants here are not explored in relation to their gender or their reproductive parts, although note will be made where parts of plants are traditionally considered to have a gendered relationality to humans (Frazão-Moreira and Carvalho, 2021).

Plants and People/Plants as People: Background Studies

There have been studies on indigenous plant use covering the various colonialised countries and regions of the world. Of these, contexts such as Aotearoa/New Zealand (e.g. Taiepa, 2004), Australia (e.g. Rodd, 2004), Asia (e.g. Sharma and Pegu, 2011) and North America (e.g. Uprety et al., 2012) provide some comparative background for this chapter. However, traditional Caribbean plant use reflects the migration of indigenous peoples of Mesoamerica and the transatlantic chattel slavery that transported enslaved Africans to various areas of the so-called New World, and so the main focus here is plant use in South American (e.g. Voeks, 1997; Torres-Avilez et al., 2015; van Andel et al., 2015) and African contexts (e.g. Quiroz and van Andel,

2015; Boakye et al., 2022), as well as plant use by enslaved Africans in the Americas (e.g. McClure, 1982; Fett, 2002: Schiebinger and Swan, 2005; Voeks and Rashford, 2013). Some enslaved Africans managed to escape bondage and relocate, thus taking plants and plant knowledge from one island to another, or from one part of an island to another, as was the case in Jamaica with the Maroons. Because the lot of an enslaved person was rarely to stay on one plantation (if they survived the journey from Africa and the first few years of enslavement), for as chattels they were bought and sold as goods, meaning enforced relocation usually within the Caribbean and/or South America, plants did sometimes move with enslaved peoples to areas inside the language group of those who claimed ownership over them; for example those who were enslaved to British people typically remained on British colonised islands, and it is the Anglo-Caribbean as well as two Spanish colonised islands that inform this chapter.

The African-derived religious traditions in Cuba, practitioners of Regla de Ochá or Lucumí (also termed Santería), use plants in healing rituals, whilst in Haitian Vodôu, plants are used in order to release the souls of the dead; both of these islands were colonised by the Spanish and the dominant settler religion was Roman Catholicism. Meanwhile in the Anglican British colonialised islands Obeah flourished, and here plants healed, but were also used to hurt. Although the Caribbean is largely known for the African-derived religious traditions brought by and adapted by the millions of African people trafficked by (most notably) the British and the Spanish, some islands were also home to indigenous peoples who had migrated from Mesoamerica into the Caribbean. Indigenous peoples of the region have a long history of plant use, hardly surprising given that what the land provided was their food store and medicine cupboard. The descendants of the indigenous Arawak-speaking peoples are today known as Kalinago or Taíno people in the Caribbean. The Kalinago people were once termed Caribs, hence Caribbean, and traded with various Arawak-speaking peoples, some of whom now identify as Taíno, such as those in the Dominican Republic; in Dominica, however, the indigenous population identify as Kalinago-Taíno (UNHCR, 2023).

One island in the Anglo-Caribbean is St Vincent. Although small it was one of the colonised islands where there were not only settlers and enslaved African peoples, but a population of the then-called Caribs. It also was home to the first Botanical Garden in the Western hemisphere, opened in 1765. Recent research by this author has discovered that a number of abortifacients grew in this Garden which most likely would have aided enslaved pregnant females to miscarry, preventing their children being birthed into enslavement. Some of these plants were well known to the Caribs (today known as Kalinago and Garifuna peoples). This type of plant knowledge, although reported in colonial times, has only recently become more prominent in academic writing, for example in the work of Londa Schiebinger (2004).

Whilst there can be a difference with the use of plants as medicines and in "religious" ritual, which is unpacked in the three Caribbean case studies, both types of interactions with plants include dealings with plants that have power. In terms of ritual, sometimes offerings are made to powerful plants, and sometimes powerful plants are the offering. In terms of medicinal plants, many times this power is curative or helps neutralise a disease or dis-ease, although sometimes that power is used to harm. But regardless of the use, the relationship between plant and human is clear; the plant has certain powers, and some people know which plant has what powers, where they grow, and when (and how) to harvest the plant to make the best use of the powers (Hogan, 2014: 21). However, where this knowledge came from originally lies in the realm of myth or is lost to history. But regardless, globally, some plants are "treated as individuals" having a distinct personality (Gundaker, 2014: 243), and acting knowledgeably (Harvey, 2014: 5).

Plants and People/Plants as People: Mesoamerica and South America

Before moving onto the three Caribbean religious traditions/spiritual lifeways, Obeah, Vodôu and Regla de Ochá, a brief overview of individual plants (who in many ways are themselves individuals) and their Mesoamerican and South American uses will help set the scene. For the South American Jívaro people of northern Peru and Equador, the manioc[2] is considered to "suck in through its leaves the blood of those who brush by them, but it mainly attacks the women who cultivate it and also their young children… [and] women have to sing special ancient incantations to this plant, in an attempt to switch its thirst for blood toward other[s]". Manioc is understood as a child who needs to be nourished by the women in order to thrive, and thus provide food for the community, especially the young children whose "sole nourishment for several years" is manioc porridge. But the relationship is complex as this is a plant who will take the blood of young children even unto their death (Descola, 2013: 343). It is notable that there are many names for the

---

2   Manioc has the accepted botanical name, *Manihot esculenta* Cranz. Where known, in this article botanical nomenclature is provided. This comprises an italicised genus and species, followed by the non-italicised abbreviated authority name; see 'Plant and Gardening FAQ' on the New York Botanical Garden website for information on botanical naming https://libanswers.nybg.org/faq/223266.

various varieties of manioc and the names of each are only learned through a direct interaction with the plants, although information about their various curative powers is shared between Jívaro women rather than being gained directly from the plants (Boster, 1986: 430). Here we see that this plant acts as a type of person, a somewhat needy vampiric person with a penchant for the blood of the young, and the women who tend the manioc gardens have to work with the plant to ensure both its survival, and the survival of their own human offspring, for both rely on them, their manual labour and their horticultural and social knowledge.

In terms of healing in South America, Monica Gagliano notes the crucial importance of plants for the Amazonian Shipino indigenous people of the Amazon rainforest of Peru. Don M., a Shipino plant shaman, informed her that "each plant has its own song and its own language to sing it" (2018: 56). The spirits of plants are believed to be gifted shamans, who through medicine songs (icaros) which are whistled or sung during ceremonial or healing rituals, "deliver the required medicine" to each patient. These songs are "tangible gestures of a plant's fondness to communicate and relate to the human through kinship" (2018: 56), and knowledge from the plant comes via ingestion.

This particular type of relationship (via ingestion) has been explored by Attala, again in an Amazonian context, where she understands the act of eating as a "co-productive relationship" where bodies "profoundly *engage with each other* (sic)". She argues that it is through the act of digestion where plants communicate, and this is done through the use of chemical signals (2019: 48, 52). *Banisteriopsis caapi*,[3] a hallucinogenic vine often called Soul Vine, is, according to Attala, "particularly communicative" and uses its hallucinogenic properties to bring about an intimate relationship with its ingestors, who value its "social, spiritual and medicinal" powers, and understand it as a friend and living guide (2019: 65–67). This relationship has to be sustained, however, with the plant actively nurtured (fed, cultivated, protected) for the relationship (chemical interchange) to be established and maintained.

Gagliono connected with (ingested) the spirit of Brazilian tobacco,[4] who gifted her "*icaro de ayuda*, a medicine song to call for his assistance whenever it was required" (2018: 246–47). The gendering of plant spirit guides is not unusual. Estévez notes that for the indigenous Taíno people of Americas, the peyote spirit guide is male, whilst the ayahuasca spirit guide is female. However, the gender can depend on which part of a plant is used. If roots,

---

3   *Banisteriopsis caapi* has the accepted botanical name of *Banisteriopsis caapi* (Spruce ex Griseb.) C.V.Morton.
4   Brazilian Tobacco has the accepted botanical name of *Nicotiana rustica* L.

bark or branches are used to make a preparation, the spirit guide is male, whilst seeds and leaves have a female spirit guide (2023: 174); it is notable that the male plant parts are tougher and more permanent than the female plant parts in this context. For the Taíno, their intimate relationship with plants is central to their identity. Estévez's mother, Doña Patria, states, "being Indian is knowing all properties of the plants. An Indian can kill you with one plant or cure you with two" (in Estévez, 2023: 184).

For the Jotï people of Venezuelan Guayana, plants also play a "prominent within all aspects of" their life, and are understood to have "multiple characters, acting contextually, and locationally as hypostatic beings, tricksters, predators, immanent beings...that potentially perpetuate or end life dynamics". Some plants, but by no means all, are considered to be persons having the "same social organization and dynamics as the Jotï...even being direct kin to people" (Zent, 2009: 9, 12). In their creation myths, the Jotï are born from trees, and wild plants are attributed with agency as they are widely believed of as originally being human (Zent, 2009: 18, 27). Further, plants are central to many rituals that help ensure wellness (Zent, 2009: 20–25) but as well as being understood to guarantee "life and its continuation", certain plants can "avoid, and terminate pregnancy" (Zent, 2009: 32).

The use of plants in women's reproductive health was particularly important for indigenous people in the era of colonialism (Schiebinger, 2004: 326), and for enslaved African women trafficked into chattel slavery. Schiebinger has noted the low fertility rate amongst enslaved African women with "one Jamaican planter estimat[ing] that in 1794 and 1795 only half of his 240 resident female slaves...ever became pregnant" (2017: 143). Domestic as opposed to field workers had the highest rates of reproduction (Morgan, 2006: 238) speaking to the toll that sugar production took on women's health, but also on their life expectancy and reproductive rates. On the Mesopotamia sugar estate in Jamaica in 1762, statistics show that the mean age of death for men and women was 30 years; women would still have been fertile, yet births were low in number (Forster and Smith, 2011: 909, 916). One explanation posited is that like the Jotï, they were using abortifacients to control reproduction. As Schiebinger notes in her work exploring lost fertility control, there is "overwhelming evidence...that women in the colonies, especially slave women and free women of color, practiced abortion" (2004: 142). One notable abortifacient was the plant commonly known as Peacock Flower, also known as Barbados Pride, and Red Bird of Paradise,[5] a plant species we will come back to again shortly.

---

5   The Peacock Flower has the accepted botanical name of *Caesalpinia pulcherrima* (L.) Sw.

Another notable abortifacient was the Savin tree or Savin Juniper,[6] which was widely used in Europe in connection with women's reproductive health (Schiebinger, 2004: 126–128), and also as a medicine used to treat gastric conditions and wounds (Bias et al., 2014). The plant has a long history of ritual use too, commonly used for "sacramental cleansing" (Kujawska et al., 2015; Tahir, 2016: 86), including by the indigenous peoples of the Americas (Vogel, 1970: 186), for whom the "spirit of the plants… is believed to have the therapeutic effect" (Borchers et al., 2000). Interestingly, Lesley-Gail Atkinson has noted that the ethnobotanical use of the Savin tree in Jamaica has been influenced by the indigenous American Taíno people (2010), and although there is no written record of it being used for abortions in that context, it would be naïve to think otherwise. Lauren Derby has argued there is a definite Taíno ethnobotanic legacy on Hispaniola today (2021: 23) and a 1541 report about the treatment of the Taíno on the island of Hispaniola noted that their treatment by the Spanish caused "the women, with the juices of some plants, [to] interrupt…their pregnancies, so as not to give birth" (Benzoni in Schiebinger, 2004: 129). That this knowledge of plants was indigenous to the region and people can be seen from a 1799–1804 account of young Amerindian women of the Orinoco River area who did not yet wish to become mothers and prevented "pregnancy by the use of deleterious herbs" (von Humboldt in Schiebinger, 2004: 129). However, other Juniper species also have abortifacient properties, notably red cedar[7] (Ivanova et al., 2021). Research into the species growing in the Botanical Garden in St Vincent has found this tree listed in the 1806 catalogue of plant species (it does not appear in previous extant catalogues of March 1791, December 1792 and June 1794). Given the Garden was worked by enslaved African labour, the tree may have been used, as Schiebinger notes, by enslaved African women on the island to prevent children being born into enslavement; enslavement was legal in the Anglo-Caribbean until 1 August 1834.

Abortifacients can be understood as an example of human–plant co-dwelling although not in the Aboriginal Australian context of direct kinship. Harvey in *Food, Sex and Strangers* draws on Debbie Rose's work on plants and "totemism" (2018: 88). In a conference paper delivered in 1998, Rose notes in an Aboriginal Australian context that there are human–plant relations where people and certain plant species are bound together (1998: 11). Extending this into the context of colonised and enslaved women in the Caribbean, given that specific plants were used as abortifacients specifically to avoid children being born into slavery, there is an argument to be made

---

6   Savin Juniper has the accepted botanical name *Juniperus communis* L.
7   Red cedar has the accepted botanical name *Juniperus virginiana* L.

that certain plants became increasingly bound to indigenous and enslaved African/African-descent people. In a form of decolonial co-dwelling, indigenous and enslaved African/African-descent gardeners ensured these plants thrived despite colonial encroachments, whilst the plants ensured that unwanted pregnancies did not.

Plants and People/Plants as People: Caribbean

The Mesoamerican case studies noted above relate directly to indigenous Caribbean relationships with plants, and one important plant for the now-called Kalinago-Taíno people of Dominica is *Bixa orellana* L., known in the region as Roucou. In 1938 Douglas Taylor recorded it having been used as a form of body preservation for the dead, and as a body paint to protect against the Caribbean sun and insects with seeds providing a red colour (1938, 121, 136). The writings of Alexander Anderson, who was the superintendent of the St Vincent Botanical Garden from 1785 to 1811, noted a similar use among the then-called Island or Red/Yellow Caribs (now Kalinago) of St Vincent. In a late eighteenth-century manuscript (Linnsoc MS606) Anderson notes the use of *Bixa orellana*,[8] stating all "yellow Carribes" had the plant near their homes, and it was used on "Their skins as well as all their household furniture & ornaments [which were] stained red with annotto or Racou/ *Bixa orellana*". *Bixa orellana* was and remains a noted dye with a long history and both decorative and protective uses (Donkin, 1974: 41). Daniela de Araújo Vilar et al. have noted that amongst the protective uses are the leaves from snakebites, and seeds as an insect repellent, with it having a range of medical uses including for dysentery, gonorrhoea, malaria, worms and as a diuretic (2014: 3–4). The plant was listed by Anderson as growing "in abundance" in the Botanic Garden in March 1791 under his Commercial and Medicinal Uses (uncatalogued Kew Archive: Anderson letters). In his c.1800 plant catalogue (LinnSoc MS 607) he notes that it is "native of S. America, introduced & cultivated by the aborigenes". He further notes the names "Annatto, Rocou, Caribb dye" for the plant. Earlier extant plant catalogues by Anderson to this have not survived, but Annatto appears in the 1773 list of plants in the Botanical Garden by John Ellis when it was in the hands of the previous superintendent, George Young (in Howard, 1996: 2). That the plant was growing so soon after the Botanic Garden was established in 1765

---

8   *Bixa orellana* has the accepted botanical name *Bixa orellana* L. I would like to thank Kristina Patmore and Tizianan Cossu from The Royal Botanical Gardens, Kew for their work on Anderson's plant nomenclature.

suggests that it was valuable commercially and medicinally and given that Young had been instructed to obtain information about medicinal plants from indigenous peoples on the island (Howard, 1996: 1) suggests that information about its healing properties were obtained from the now-called Kalinago people of the island.

Anderson obtained information about other medicinal plants from the now-called Kalinago people. For instance, he states in his c.1800 plant catalogue for *Gardenia genissa*[9] that "a Carrib chief in St. Vincent told me the green fruit roasted or baked in an Iron pot, and applied was an effectual remedy for that disgusting & infectious disease the yaws." A further late eighteenth-century manuscript of his, "Medical Observations and for Catalogue" (Linnsoc MS 606), adds that the fruit needs to be bruised, and the boiled roots "cures the Gonorrherea". The plant first appears in Anderson's March 1791 plant catalogue as a "fruit for the yaw", with *Verbena indica*[10] and *Verbena jamaicensis*[11] also listed as cures for yaws, specifically "decoction & juice". Interestingly, both Verbenas are also listed as good for "obstructions", and the latter is known to have "abortive effects" (Liew and Yong, 2016: 2), as are other members of the *Stachytarpheta* family (Chowdhury et al., 2004). Amongst the several abortifacients growing in the Botanic Garden during Anderson's time was the aforementioned Peacock Flower/Barbados Pride, which appears in a list of the plants in the Garden when Anderson took over his appointment in 1785; it is noted as its synonym *Poincina pulcherrima*[12] and listed as medicinal. It appears again as a medicine on his c.1800 plant catalogue as *Poinciana pulcherrima* Lin. and Anderson notes it as a plant native to South America. He provides no specific medicinal use for this plant, but its use as an abortifacient was widely known by the indigenous peoples in Mesoamerica and South America, and thus by their Caribbean descendants.

Anderson also drew on the medicinal plant knowledge of enslaved Africans. As Robert Dirks has noted, enslaved Africans with medical knowledge, known as "hot-house doctors", often had a greater chance of curing a patient than a colonial physician. Although largely condemned due to their skin colour with their treatments understood as know-how rather than knowledge, the skills of "hot-house doctors" were regularly sought out (1987: 41). As such, it is perhaps no surprise that Anderson was asked to continue Young's task of seeking out the plant skills of enslaved Africans. In terms of medicinal

---

9 *Gardenia genissa* has the accepted botanical name accepted name *Genipa americana* L.; Anderson also lists the plant as *Genissa americana Linn.*
10 *Verbena indica* has the accepted botanical name *Stachytarpheta indica* (L.) Vahl.
11 *Verbena jamaicensis* has the accepted botanical name *Stachytarpheta jamaicensis* (L.) Vahl.
12 *Poincina pulcherrima* has the accepted botanical name *Poinciana pulcherrima* L.

cures, Anderson noted several plants in his c.1800 plant catalogue with information gained directly from enslaved Africans. Of *Andropogon insulae* (known as Lemon Grass[13]), he notes that the plant when bruised can be applied to sores and ulcers, and that the leaves of *Cassia bicapsularis* (known as Day Bush[14]) when "mixed with a little rum" (or mushed up in water) cure the itch when rubbed on the skin two or three times. Of *Cissus cordiofolius* (known as Princess vine[15]), he notes that the young leaves applied to the skin heal sores (and says he has seen it used "to good effect") but the juice given internally is poisonous, whilst the powdered root of *Eryngium focticlum* (known as Stink Weed[16]) is used for epileptic fits and the "Hystericks". The milky decoction of the leaves of *Huia crepitans* (known as Sandbox tree[17]) he writes are used "to heal sores" with one or two seeds proving a "violent emetic & Cathartic", and a decoction of *Jatropha gossypifolia* (known as Belly-ache bush[18]) is "a sovereign remedy for the dry belly ach in some of the Islands and generally given to Hores [horses] in the Belly ach and for them is probably a more congenial medicine than to man".

However, several others also appear in his "Medicinal Observations". *Convolvulus brasiliensis*[19] is noted as having been used in decoction form for "obstructions of the viscera", and a decoction of the leaves and tops of *Cytisus cajan*[20] was a remedy for sores and ulcers. The ripe berries of *Solanum bahamense*,[21] known as bitterberry, were eaten as a purgative by the enslaved Africans in Barbados, whilst a decoction of Guavas and the bark of *Anacurdii occidentatis*,[22] the cashew nut, was an enslaved African cure for dysentery. That Anderson explicitly notes ten medicinal plant species growing in the Botanical Garden directly connected to enslaved African botanical knowledge demonstrates that importance of this information to his own grasp of ethnobotanic cures.

Although the examples above do not provide detail on ritual plant use, they demonstrate clearly how Western colonial science benefitted from

---

13 *Andropogon insulae* has the accepted botanical name *Digitaria insularis* (L.) Mez ex Ekman.
14 *Cassia bicapsularis* has the accepted botanical name *Senna bicapsularis* (L.) Roxb.
15 *Cissus cordiofolius* has the accepted botanical name *Cissus verticillata* subsp. Verticillate.
16 *Eryngium focticlum* has the accepted botanical name *Eryngium aquaticum* var. aquaticum.
17 *Huia crepitans* has the accepted botanical name *Hura crepitans* L.
18 *Jatropha gossypifolia* has the accepted botanical name *Jatropha gossypiifolia* L.
19 *Convolvulus brasiliensis* has the accepted botanical name *Convolvulus brasiliensis* L.
20 *Cytisus cajan* has the accepted botanical name *Cajanus cajan* (L.) Huth.
21 *Solanum bahamense* has the accepted botanical name *Solanum bahamense* L.
22 *Anacurdii occidentatis* has the accepted name *Anacardium occidentale* L.

indigenous and enslaved African knowledge of plants. Anderson specifies plants in the garden that were introduced by, and used by indigenous peoples, and also plants used by enslaved African peoples; a couple he states were introduced to St Vincent from Africa through the so-called Middle Passage, notably *Amomum Zingiber* (known as ginger[23]). And from here, we move to exploring the ritual use of plants in African-derived religions/spiritual lifeways; Obeah, which was prominent in Barbados and Jamaica during the colonial era, and Haitian Vodôu, and Cuban Regla de Ochá which continue to the present day.

Obeah once flourished in the Anglo-Caribbean, causing concerns of the colonial authorities where it was widely understood as a form of witchcraft, and legislated against (Bilby and Handler, 2004: 167–172). However, in reality, Obeah men and women were specialists in plant medicines (Bilby and Handler, 2004: 154, 158), and the name given to Obeah practitioners by the French, "poisoner", speaks to the centrality of their plant knowledge (Schiebinger, 2017: 117). As well as working with plants, Obeah wo/men were "believed to be able to manipulate unseen forces… [including working] the spirits…and practice[ing] healing" (Chireau, 2006: 21) and Jamaican anti-Obeah Acts prohibited explicitly the use of "materials relative to the practice of witchcraft" (Schiebinger, 2017: 128). Noted Obeah plants included camphor, myrrh and frankincense (Williams, 1934: 102) and these were, and continue to be, used to keep evil spirits away. A belief in duppies, the evil spirits of the dead, is central to Obeah. A duppy comes about from not carrying out the appropriate death rituals; coming together to celebrate the deceased with friends (food and alcohol) in the ritual known as Nine Nights (Hume, 2018: 121–33). Today camphor is considered especially important in banishing duppies (Morgan-Lindo, 2022).

Other plants directly linked to Obeah include *Abrus precatorius* L., known as rosary pea, which was used for divination, and for making curses; they could be worn as beads on a necklace for good luck. *Ricinus communis* L., the castor oil plant, was used as a poison for revenge (McClure, 1982: 295–98) and famously the leader of the Windward Jamaican Maroons (descendants of Africans who had freed themselves) known as Queen Nanny (c.1686-c.1733) "reputedly used her mastery of medicinal herbs to kill soldiers sent to re-enslave fugitive blacks" (Carney, 2003: 171). Plants with medicinal and protective functions were also used as decorative markers, but may also have acted as a mnemonic, reminding the enslaved (dead and alive) of their African botanical heritage (Matternes and Richey, 2014: 271). Notably, plants were not, and are not today, considered as w-t-h persons, but Obeah wo/

---

23 *Amomum Zingiber* has the accepted botanical name *Zingiber officinale* Roscoe.

men were and continue to ritually tap into the powers inherent in the plant to command spirits in the w-t-h world; Obeah was a hidden presence in St Vincent in colonial times (Haines, 1972), and Obeah wo/men in the country do not widely publicise their work today (Jones, 2017).

The w-t-h spirit world in Obeah, included the afterlife and as after death, African-Caribbeans believed they return (go home) to Africa. This belief led to a number of suicides during the era of enslavement. In response, planters dug up the bodies of enslaved peoples who they believed had taken their own lives, and to show they had not gone back to Africa, either placed decapitated heads on poles by roadways, or put the body in a gibbet; these acts were intended as a physical statement against the return-to-Africa belief, especially as a beheaded body was believed to be unable to find its way home (in Epstein, 2012: 246). In response some enslaved people found non-obvious ways to take their own lives dying by such as geophagy, also known as dirt-eating (Gadpaille, 2014), and through food poisoning.

There may be an example of deliberate death by food poisoning in the Anderson manuscripts. In his entry for *Jatropha Manihot*[24] he notes there are two varieties, *Manihot rubra* (bitter cassava, also known as French manioc), and *Manihot alba* (sweet cassava). He states, "the only discrimination between the two is in the colour. The bitter cassava being of a red colour and the other white but so vague & incertain is this mark that [enslaved Africans] are often deceived and use the poisonous kind for the other, and Death is generally the consequence." Visually the two varieties are similar (although Anderson specifically notes the abla is whiter in colour) and even today, there have been deaths from consumption of incorrectly processed bitter cassava (Harkup, 2017). However, the plant was introduced into the Gulf of Guinea (the principal source of enslaved Africans) towards the end of the sixteenth century (Cooper, 2012) and as such it is unlikely that enslaved Africans working in the Caribbean in the eighteenth century would have been unfamiliar with this esculent. As such, it is entirely possible that whilst there may have been some accidental deaths through consuming bitter cassava instead of sweet cassava, enslaved Africans may have deliberately used it to enable them to escape the misery of chattel slavery, hiding their considered action behind the mask of an error.

Shifting from enslaved African plant use, and plant use by their African-Caribbean descendants, in the Anglo-Caribbean islands to those colonised by the Spanish, this chapter next considers Haitian Vodôu and Cuban Regla de Ochá. In terms of Vodôu and plants rituals there are overlaps with Regla de Ochá. Further, in both, there are strong Roman Catholic elements as

---

24 *Jatropha Manihot* has the accepted botanical name *Manihot esculenta* Crantz.

well as a complex pantheon of spirits that broadly map onto the Orishás (intermediary deities who are venerated and operate to assist humans in this world) of the Yorùbá people of West Africa. In Vodôu, however, this is only a very broad mapping as the Orishás, "as well as symbols and the actual spaces of…worship, may change and new spirits may appear and be welcomed on a local basis" (Coates, 2006: 184). Despite regional variabilities, one constant in Vodôu is that everything is believed to share the same "chemical, physical, and/or genetic properties" and because life is sacred, everything is sacred; life here is "not so much…the *thing* as…the *spirit* of the thing". Thus, plant life or rather the spirit of each plant is sacred, although there is no separation between the sacred and the profane in any Durkheimian sense of these terms (Bellegarde-Smith, 2004: 24).

In Vodôu all things (or more accurately the spirits of all things) have importance to the whole of life and are potent, although the level of their spiritual potency varies according to their use. Forest plants in particular are known to have particular powers that can help those who "find them" and ask in the appropriate way for assistance. Landry argues that by exploring the Fon people of Benin's understanding of forest and the azizà (forest-spirits), the Vodún concept of forest plants acting as teachers can be understood. He notes that the forest/azizà can choose to tell a person to "combine this leaf with that feather…even give you the power to talk to animals, so you could ask the birds for their feathers without killing them" (2022: 237, 253). This argument is reinforced when considering Harvey's assertion that "it is a mistake to think of…plants…as merely instinctive or mechanically responsive… [they] make choices", stressing that non-human-persons "do not always benefit every individual" (Harvey, 2018: 89). Landry highlights this choice noting that the forest/azizà assist (share their power with) fewer humans today that they ever have before because they no longer trust humans, as humans have embraced capitalism (Landry, 2022: 233–38). There are a number of initiatives around the Caribbean exploring indigenous plant knowledge in an effort to decolonise with in effect, traditional human–plant relations acting as a symbol of African/African-descendant cultural resistance. Here then we see plants not only as w-t-h persons with powers and knowledges, able to exercise choice in whether to pass these to humans, but as w-t-h persons connecting with pre-colonial lifeways. However, there are levels of potency embedded in these plant-people, with some more potent than others.

Medicinal plants are particularly important in Vodôu, and have more potency than non-medicinal plants. For Haitian Vodôu practitioners, because there is a co-dependence between "men, women, plants, animals, and the spirits", when someone is sick, the spirits in specific plants are used to heal. Most illnesses in Haiti are believed to be caused by too much heat, and cooling plants (either taken as food or as drinks) are needed to restore the balance of the body. This understanding has, as Pierre Minn notes, similarities with the concept of humorism. Cooling food include okra, cucumber, banana and melon, as well as cassava bread, which is made from the manioc plant, whilst drinks including coconut milk, and beverages made from hibiscus, orange or soursop (2006: 138–39). One women informed Minn during his fieldwork in Bèlans on Haiti's north coast, that if one needs to cool, after eating a banana, it should be tied to the forehead, where after 15–20 minutes it will have drawn out the excess body heat, and that is evident from the "almost dry" peel (Minn, 2006: 140). For Haitians, vernacular medicine is crucial, not only because of the country's poor health services but as a connection to ancestral knowledge, and the power of the spirit of the plants. It is important to note here that being Haitian is synonymous with Vodôu: "if you ask a Haitian what [their] religion is, [they] will most likely say 'I'm Catholic', In fact a running joke in Haiti says the country is 90% Catholic, 10% Protestant…and 100% Vodou!" (Tann, 2021: 14).

One particularly important plant in Haitian Vodôu is the gourd. This is the hard-shell of particular members of the *Cucurbitaceae* family, and once dried and hollowed, it forms the basis of an asson (or ason), which is a crucial symbol of Vodôu priesthood. The gourd is "covered with a mesh of glass-beads and snake vertebrae" which make a rattling sound. This sound summons and sends away the lwa, the Vodôu spirits. The lwa are dependent on the living for food and a hungry lwa is disorderly; the asson helps to control them. One way of doing this is by using the asson to affect the "key changes in the drum rhythms in a Vodôu service". The drums help heat up the crowd and until the crowd has worked up sufficient energy, the lwa will not appear and "mount" the priest/ess. The asson is also used when a Vodôu priest or priestess becomes a healer; at this level of initiation the asson provides "some measure of leverage in the spirit realm". The asson is gifted by the spirits to enable a member of the priesthood to communicate and interact with them (Brown, 2006: 12–13,15); without the gourd, this is not possible. From medicines to calling and controlling lwa, plants, and rituals using plants, are vital w-t-h persons in Vodôu lifeways.

Cuban Regla de Ochá also has a wealth of connections with plants as medicines (Brandon, 1991; Oggunbemi, 2015) and in rituals (de la Torre, 2004: 131). Plants and the parts of plants (roots, bark, flowers, seeds etc.) used in Regla de Ochá are termed Ewe, and each plant belongs specifically to one or two Orishá, with Santeros (Santería practitioners) needing to be botanically literate to ensure they do not offend an Orishá by using an incorrect plant (Gonzalez-Wippler, 1991: 133). Each Orishá also has specific colours associated with them, and favours certain foods, drinks and animals used in sacrifice (Menéndez, 2012: 920). For instance, Changó (the Orishá of thunder, lightning, and traditional masculinity) likes cornmeal with okra, banana, apple and sweet cornmeal as food offerings, and red wine as a drink, whilst Yemayá (the ocean mother) enjoys fried fish, green plantain slices and watermelon as offerings, along with molasses and sweet potato sweets. Her favoured drink is eau-de-vie (a colourless brandy); notably both Orishá welcome rams, and guinea hens as animal sacrifices and neither have specific plants associated with them. However, Obatalá (son/daughter of Olodumare, the creator deity) is associated with the cotton plant, and enjoys food offerings of roasted yam, soursop and custard apple. Plants in the form of vegetal offerings are normative here but the association of an Orishá with a specific plant is less usual.

Trees and plants (including weeds) in Regla de Ochá are believed to be ensouled and have intelligence and have the power "to help human beings lead healthful and abundant lives" (Brandon, 1991: 58). This is made possible through aché (divine power), and their power and intelligence (their plant knowledge), they pass to a Santeros, with "plant knowing yielding associated spiritual knowledge" (Daniel, 2005: 72); in this way plants act as teachers to Regla de Ochá practitioners. All vegetation belongs to Osain (known as Loko in Vodôu) and he knows all the secrets of the herbs and plants. All vegetation is understood to have personalities, some are shy, some easily frightened, others have an explosive temperament and "require the utmost in etiquette and respect before they are picked" (Brandon, 1991: 58). Like humans, the power of plants fluctuates during the day, and they rest at night. Wild rather than cultivated plants are the most potent, and their main use is in ritual; although as noted they are used as cures and offerings.

The two main types of ritual in Regla de Ochá that use plants are Ozains, and Omieros which are cleansing rites that prepare objects and people for contact with an Orishá, or a Santeros. An Ozain is purely a cleanser, but making it requires the presence of a master who knows the songs of the Orishá, several Santeros and an ozainista, a Santeros particularly knowledgeable about plants and their personalities. Making an Ozain is a long process and complex as each form of vegetation associated with a particular Orishá must be correctly prepared. Once prepared the plants (usually herbs) are placed in a container of water which will be used for the cleansing ceremony, and discarded once the ritual is complete. The Omieros, however, whilst also an empowering cleanser identical to the Ozain, gains and retains power from the particular rituals it is used in and is not discarded; it is kept until it is used up. The Omieros cleanses only the most important things; the bead necklace that a new Regla de Ochá practioner wears, the head of a practitioner when preparing for spirit possession by an Orishá, and washing the knives used in animal sacrifice, which are very powerful rituals and done only occasionally (Brandon, 1991: 61). Plants are central to these and other rituals and, as with Vodôu are used as medicines, and act as teachers passing on specific plant knowledge. In both Vodôu as with Regla de Ochá, plants are w-t-h persons in every sense of the word.

Conclusion

This chapter, in drawing on Harvey's work on animism and human–plant relations, has explored the central role that plants have as medicines and in rituals. In providing a background to plant use in three African-derived Caribbean case study "religions", it has drawn on plant use in Mesoamerica and South America where plants, or sometimes only specific plants, are widely understood to be w-t-h people with distinct personalities. It has also provided evidence for colonial plant knowledge and a form of human–plant co-dwelling, drawn explicitly from Caribbean indigenous peoples, descendants of Mesoamericans who crossed to the various Caribbean islands, and enslaved Africans who were trafficked to the Caribbean in the era of transatlantic chattel slavery. In the Anglophone Caribbean island of St Vincent, indigenous and enslaved African peoples intermingled (SVG UN, undated) with knowledge passing between them as well as being collected by the superintendent of the islands colonial Botanic Garden.

In terms of the three Caribbean case studies and the role of plants, not all plants are understood as having personalities and being people. In Obeah, an African-derived religious tradition that flourished in the Anglo-Caribbean, plants are not considered as w-t-h persons, but Obeah wo/men were able to, and secretly continue to, tap into the powers inherent in the plant through rituals to command spirits in the w-t-h world, notably in relation to duppies. In the islands colonised by the Spanish, in both Haitian Vodôu and Cuban Regla de Ochá, plants are understood to be ensouled or enspirited and have intelligence. In Vodôu, all plants are considered important w-t-h persons, although they have varying levels of potency. And as with Regla de Ochá, individual plant species have distinct personalities and are used in medicinal and ritual ways with wild plants being more powerful and thus more used, than cultivated ones. Also, in both religious traditions, trees, and plants (including weeds) are believed belong to a specific Orishá, although the produce from various plants is widely used as offerings to other Orishá.

Although this chapter focuses on a specific part of the world geographically, globally as Harvey has noted in his various works on animism, plants are understood to be very powerful; they can heal and they can harm, and they can be used in rituals that prevent or cause disease/dis-ease; the humans who have been taught to work with plants, however that comes about, are powerful too. With the prevalence of Western scientific ways of understanding and relating to plants and plant knowledge, the information that these powerful humans have has largely been marginalised. For all colonised peoples, unlearning colonised ways of thinking about plants is vital to assist indigenous people, and the descendants of enslaved African peoples, in their struggle to decolonise, and also to reclaim globally the potency of plants to be our teachers. In our w-t-h world, some plants are understood by some humans as a useful form of vegetal life, but for many others, notably including Harvey, plants are conceived of as people; intelligent, communicative and even gendered.

References

Abrahams, D. 1996. *The Spell of the Sensuous*. New York: Pantheon Books.
Atkinson, L. 2010. "Taíno influence on Jamaican folk traditions", *Jamaican National Heritage Trust*. Available at: www.jnht.com/download/influence.pdf.
Attala, L. 2019. "'I am Apple': Relationships of the flesh. Exploring the corporeal entanglements of eating plants in the Amazon", in Attala L. and Steels, L. (eds), *Body Matters: Exploring the Materiality of the Body*. Cardiff: University of Wales Press. pp. 48–78.
Bellegarde-Smith, P. 2004. *Haiti: The Breached Citadel* (Revised and Updated Edition). Toronto: Canadian Scholars Press Inc.
Bias, S., Gill, N.S., Rana, N. and Shandil, S. 2014. "A phytopharmacological review on a medicinal plant: Juniperus communis", *International Scholarly Research Notices*, 11 November. Available at: https://pubmed.ncbi.nlm.nih.gov/27419205/.
Bilby K.M. and Handler, J. 2004. "Obeah: Healing and protection in West Indian slave life", *Journal of Caribbean History* 38(2): 153–183.
Boakye, M.K., Agyemang, A.O., Turkson, B.K., Waife, E.D., Baidoo, M.F. and Bayor, M.T. 2022. "Ethnobotanical inventory and therapeutic applications of plants traded in the Ho Central Market, Ghana", *Ethnobotany Research and Application* 23: 1–20.
Borchers, A.T., Keen, C.L., Stern, J.S. and Gershwin, M.E. 2000. "Inflammation and Native American Medicine: The role of botanicals", *American Journal for Clinical Nutrition* 72: 339–347.
Boster, J.S. 1986. "Exchange of varieties and information between Aguaruna Manioc cultivators", *American Anthropologist* 88(2): 428–436.
Brandon, G. 1991. "The uses of plants in healing in an Afro-Cuban religion, Santeria", *Journal of Black Studies* 22(1): 55–76.
Brown, K.M. 2006. "Afro-Caribbean spirituality: A Haitian case-study", in Michel, C. and Bellegarde-Smith, P. (eds), *Invisible Powers: Vodou in Haitian Life and Culture*. New York: Palgrave Macmillan. pp. 1–26.

Carney, J.A. 2003. "African traditional plant knowledge in the Circum-Caribbean region", *Journal of Ethnobiology* 32(2): 167–185.
Chireau, Y. 2006. *Black Magic: Religion and the African-American Conjuring Tradition*. Berkeley, CA: University of California Press.
Chowdhury, R., Ur Rashis, M., Khan, O.F. and Hasan, C. 2004. "Bioactivity of extractives from *Stachytarpheta urticaefolia*", *Pharmaceutical Biology* 42(3): 262–267.
Coates, C.F. 2006. "Vodou in Haitian Literature", in Michel, C. and Bellegarde-Smith, P. (eds), *Invisible Powers: Vodou in Haitian Life and Culture*. New York: Palgrave Macmillan. pp. 181–198.
Cooper, T. 2012. Manihot glaziovii & Manihot esculat – two shrubs with history. *Tropical Biodoversity blog; University of Reading*, 17 December. Available at: https://blogs.reading.ac.uk/tropical-biodiversity/2012/12/manihot-glaziovii-manihot-esculenta-two-shrubs-with-history/.
Daniel, Y. 2005. *Dancing Wisdom: Embodied Knowledge in Haitian Vodou, Cuban Yoruba, and Bahian Candomblé*. Urbana, IL: University of Illinois Press.
de Araújo Vilar, D., de Araújo Vilar, M.S., de Lima e Moura, T.F., Raffin, F.M. de Oliverira, M.R., de Oliverira Franco, C.F., de Athayde-Filho, P.F., Melo Diniz, M. de F.F. and Barbosa-Filho, J.M. 2014. "Traditional uses, chemical constituents, and biological activities of *Bixa orellana* L.: A review", *Scientific World Journal* 1–11. www.ncbi.nlm.nih.gov/pmc/articles/PMC4094728/pdf/TSWJ2014-857292.pdf.
de la Torre, M.A. 2004. *Santería: The Beliefs and Rituals of a Growing Religion in America*. Grand Rapids, MI: Wm. B. Eerdmans Publishing.
Derby, L. 2021. "Zemis and zombies: Amerindian healing legacies on Hispaniola", in Smith, S.M. and Willoughby, C.D.E. (eds), *Medicine and Healing in the Age of Slavery*. Baton Rouge, LA: Louisiana State University. pp. 21–44.
Descola, P. (translated by Lloyd, J.). 2013. *Beyond Nature and Culture*. Chicago, IL: University of Chicago Press.
Díaz, R. (ed.) 2023. *Decolonizing Paradise: A Radical Ethnography of Environmental Stewardship in the Caribbean*. New York: Peter Lang.
Dirks, R. 1987. *The Black Saturnalia: Conflict and its Ritual Expression on British West Indian Slave Plantations*. Gainsville, FL: University of Florida Press.
Donkin, A.A. 1974. "*Bixa orellana*: 'The eternal shrub'", *Anthropos* 69(1/2): 33–56.
Epstein, J. 2012. *Scandal of Colonial Rule: Power and Subversion in the British Atlantic during the Age of Revolution*. Cambridge: Cambridge University Press.
Estévez, J.B. 2023. "Sacred plants, stones, and the art of dreaming", in Díaz, R. (ed.), *Decolonizing Paradise: A Radical Ethnography of Environmental Stewardship in the Caribbean*. New York: Peter Lang. pp. 171–186.
Fett, S.M. 2002. *Working Cures: Healing, Health and Power on Southern Slave Plantations*. Chapel Hill, NC: University of North Carolina Press.
Forster, M. and Smith, S.D. 2011. "Surviving slavery: Mortality at Mesopotamia, a Jamaican sugar estate, 1762–1832", *Journal of the Royal Statistical Society* 174(4): 907–929.
Frazão-Moreira, A. and Carvalho, A.M. 2021. "Gendered plants and plant categorization by gender: Classificatory and "storied" knowledge in Trás-os-Montes, Portugal", *Ethnobotany Research and Applications* 21: 1–20.
Gadpaille, M. 2014. "Eating dirt, being dirt: Backgrounds to the story of slavery", *AAA: Arbeiten aus Anglistik und Amerikanistik* 39(1): 3–210.

Gagliano, M. 2018. *Thus Spoke the Plant: A Remarkable Journey of Groundbreaking Scientific Discoveries and Personal Encounters with Plants*. Berkeley, CA: North Atlantic Books.

Gilroy, P. 2014. Lecture I. Suffering and Infrahumanity, Lecture II. Humanities and a New Humanism. The Tanner Lectures on Human Values, 21 February. Available at: https://tannerlectures.utah.edu/_resources/documents/a-to-z/g/Gilroy%20manuscript%20PDF.pdf.

Gonzalez-Wippler, M. 1991. *The Complete Book of Amulets & Talismans*. Woodbury, Min: Llewellyn Worldwide.

Gundaker, G. 2014. "Ritualized figuration in special African American yards", in Ogundiran, A. and Saunders, P. (eds), *Materialities of Ritual in the Black Atlantic*. Bloomington, IN: Indiana University Press. pp. 236–257.

Guss, D.M. 1989. *To Weave and Sing: Art, Symbol and Narrative in the South American Rain Forest*. Berkeley, CA: University of California Press.

Haines, L. 1972, "Obeah is a fact of life, and afterlife, in the Caribbean", *New York Times*, 10 September. Available at: www.nytimes.com/1972/09/10/archives/obeah-is-a-fact-of-life-and-afterlife-in-the-caribbean-obeah-a-fact.html.

Hall, M. 2011. *Plants and Persons: A Philosophical Botany*. Albany, NY: State University of New York.

Harkup, K. 2017. "Cassava crisis: The deadly food that doubles as a vital Venezuelan crop", *The Guardian*, 22 June. Available at: www.theguardian.com/science/blog/2017/jun/22/cassava-deadly-food-venezuela.

Harvey, G. 2005. *Animism: Respecting the Living World*. New York: Columbia University Press.

Harvey, G. 2013. *Food, Sex and Strangers: Understanding Religion as Everyday Life*. Abingdon: Routledge.

Harvey, G. 2014. "Introduction", in Harvey, G. (ed.), *The Handbook of Contemporary Animism*. London: Routledge. pp. 1–16.

Harvey, G. 2018. "Series Foreword", in Harvey, G. and Hughes, J. (eds), *Sensual Religion: Religion and the Five Senses*. Sheffield: Equinox. pp. vii–ix.

Harvey, G. 2022. "Animism and ecology: Participating in the world community", *2022 Taiwan Art Biennial*. Available at: https://2022taiwanbiennial.ntmofa.gov.tw/essays-02-en.html.

Hogan, L. 2014. "We call it tradition", in Harvey, G. (ed.), *The Handbook of Contemporary Animism*. London: Routledge. pp. 17–26.

Howard, R.A. 1996. "The St. Vincent Botanical Garden: The early years", *Harvard Paper in Botany* 1(8): 1–6.

Hume, Y. 2018. "Death and the construction of social space: Land, kinship, and identity in the Jamaican mortuary cycle", in Forde, M. and Hume, Y. (eds), *Passages and Afterworlds: Anthropological Perspectives on Death in the Caribbean*. Durham: Duke University Press. pp. 109–138.

Ivanova, D.I., Nedialkov, P.T., Tashev, A.N., Olech, M., Nowak, R., Llieve, Y.E., Kokanova-Nedialkova, Z.K, Atanasova, T.N., Angelov, G. and Najdenski, H.N. 2021. "Junipers of various origins as potential sources of the anticancer drug precursor podophyllotoxin", *Molecules* 26(17): 5179.

Jones, S. 2017. "The mysteriousness of Obeah in SVG", *Searchlight VC*. 5 December. Available at: www.searchlight.vc/features/2017/12/05/the-mysteriousness-of-obeah-in-svg/.

Kujawska, M., Łuczaj, Ł. and Typek, J. 2015. "Fischer's *Lexicon of Slavic Beliefs and Customs*: A previously unknown contribution to the ethnobotany of Ukraine and Poland", *Journal of Ethnobiology and Ethnomedicine* 11: 85.

Landry, T.R. 2022. "Spirited forests and the West African forest complex", in Montgomery, E.J., Landry, T.R. and Vannier C.N. (eds), *Spirit Service: Vodún and Vodou in the African Atlantic World*. Bloomington, IN: Indiana University Press. pp. 230–258.

Lawrence, A.M. 2022. "Listening to plants: Conversations between critical plant studies and vegetal geography", *Progress on Human Geography* 46(2): 629–651.

Liew, P.M. and Yong, Y.K. 2016. "*Stachytarpheta jamaicensis* (L.) Vahl: From traditional usage to pharmacological evidence", *Evidence-based Complementary and Alternative Medicine* 7842340: 1–7.

Martinez, J.L., Muñoz-Acevedo, A. and Rai, M. (eds) 2019. *Ethnobotany: Local Knowledge and Traditions*. Baton Rouge, FL: CRC Press.

Matternes, H.B. and Richey, S. 2014. "I cry 'I am' for all to hear me: The informal cemetery in central Georgia", in Ogundiran, A. and Saunders, P. (eds), *Materialities of Ritual in the Black Atlantic*. Bloomington, IN: Indiana University Press. pp. 258–279.

McClure, S.A. 1982. "Parallel usage of medicinal plants by Africans and their Caribbean descendants", *Economic Botany* 36(3): 291–301.

Menéndez, L. 2012. "Santería", in Taylor, P. and Case, F.I. (eds), *The Encyclopedia of Caribbean Religions* Vol.2 M–Z. Urbana, IL: University of Illinois Press. pp. 916–923.

Minn, P. 2006. "Water in their eyes, dust on their lands: Heat and illness in a Haitain town", in Michel, C. and Bellegarde-Smith, P. (eds), *Invisible Powers: Vodou in Haitian Life and Culture*. New York: Palgrave Macmillan. pp. 135–154.

Morgan, K. 2006. "Slave women and reproduction in Jamaica, c.1776–1834", *History* 91(2): 231–253.

Morgan-Lindo, S. 2022. "'Olive oil and frankincense barely a work again' – Obeah man says nowadays ghosts are too bad for traditional tool. *Jamaica Star*, 21 September. Available at: http://jamaica-star.com/article/news/20220921/'olive-oil-and-frankincense-barely-work-again'-obeah-man-says-nowadays-ghosts.

Oggunbemi, M. 2015. *Ritual Use of Plants in the Lucumí Tradition*, 3rd edn. Milton Keynes: Lightening UK.

O'Neal, E. 2020. *Obeah, Race and Racism: Caribbean Witchcraft in the English Imagination*. Kingston, Jamaica: University of West Indies Press.

Quiroz, D. and van Andel, T. 2015. "Evidence of a link between taboos and sacrifices and resource scarcity of ritual plants", *Journal of Ethnobiology and Ethnomedicine* 11(5): 1–10.

Paton, D. and Foorde, M. (eds) 2012. *Obeah and Other Powers: The Politics of Caribbean Religion and Healing*. Durham, NC: Duke University Press.

Rodd, R. 2004. *The Biocultural Ecology of Piaroa Shamanic Practice*. PhD thesis, University of Western Australia, June 2004. Available at: https://research-repository.uwa.edu.au/files/3219238/Rodd_Robin_2004.pdf.

Rose, D.B. 1998. "Totemism, regions, and co-management in Aboriginal Australia (draft)", *Crossing Boundaries, the Seventh Biennial Conference of the International Association for the Study of Common Property*, 10–14 June. Available at: https://dlc.dlib.indiana.edu/dlc/bitstream/handle/10535/1187/rose.pdf.

Schiebinger, L. 2004. *Plants and Empire: Colonial Bioprospecting in the Atlantic World*. Cambridge, MA: Harvard University Press.

Schiebinger, L. 2017. *Secret Cures of Slaves: People, Plants, and Medicine in the Eighteenth-century Atlantic World*. Stanford, CA: Stanford University Press.

Schiebinger, L. and Swan, C. (eds) 2005. *Colonial Botany: Science, Commerce, and Politics in the Early Modern World*. Philadelphia, PA: University of Pennsylvania Press.

Sharma, U.K. and Pegu, S. 2011. "Ethnobotany of religious and supernatural beliefs of the missing tribes of Assam with special reference to the 'Dobur Uie'", *Journal of Ethnobiology and Ethnomedicine* 7(16): 1–13.

Sørensen, J. 2007. "Acts that work: A cognitive approach to ritual agency", *Method and Theory in the Study of Religion* 19: 281–300.

Stainton, T. 2001. "Reason and value: The thought of Plato and Aristotle and the construction of intellectual disability", *Mental Retardation* 39(6): 452–460.

SVG UN. Undated. *Permanent Mission of Saint Vincent and the Grenadines to the United Nations*. Available at: http://svg-un.org/who-we-are.

Tahir, A., Jilani, M.I., Khera, R.A. and Nadeem, F. 2016. "*Juniperus communis*: Biological activities and therapeutic potentials of a medicinal plant – a comprehensive study", *International Journal of Chemical and Biochemical Sciences* 9: 85–91.

Taiepa, T. 2004. "Weaving our stories worldwide: An indigenous approach to global economics and ecology", *Ethnobotany Research and Application* 2: 93–99.

Tann, M.C. 2021. *Haitian Vodou: An Introduction to Haiti's Indigenous Spiritual Tradition*. Woodbury, MI: Llewllyn Press.

Taylor, D. 1938. "The Caribs of Dominica", *Smithsonian Institution Bureau of American Ethnology Bulletin* 119(3): 109–159.

Taylor, P. and Case, F.I. (eds) 2013. *The Encyclopedia of Caribbean Religions*. Urbana, IL: University of Illinois Press.

Torres-Avilez, W., Méndez-González, M., Durán-García, R., Boulogne, I. and Germosén-Robineau, L. 2015. "Medicinal plant knowledge in Caribbean Basin: A comparative study of Afrocaribbean, Amerindian and Mestizo communities", *Journal of Ethnobiology and Ethnomedicine* 11(18): 1–11.

UNHCR. 2023. World Directory of Minorities and Indigenous Peoples – Dominica. *UNHRC Refworld*. Available at: www.refworld.org/docid/4954ce32c.html.

Uprety, Y., Asselin, H., Dhakal, A. and Julien, N. 2012. "Traditional use of medicinal plants in the boreal forest of Canada: Review and perspectives", *Journal of Ethnobiology and Ethnomedicine* 8(7): 1–14.

van Andel, T., Ruysschaert, S., Boven, K. and Daly, L. 2015. "The use of Amerindian charm plants in the Guianas", *Journal of Ethnobiology and Ethnomedicine* 11(66): 1–12.

van der Veen, M. 2014. "The materiality of plants: Plant-people entanglements", *World Archaeology* 46(5): 799–812.

van Dooren, T. and Chrulew, M. (eds) 2022. *Kin: Thinking with Deborah Bird Rose*. Durham, NC: Duke University Press.

Voeks, R.A. 1997. *Sacred Leaves of Candomblé: African Magic, Medicine, and Religion in Brazil*. Austin, TX: University of Texas Press.

Voeks, R. and Rashford, J. (eds) 2013. *African Ethnobotany in the Americas*. New York: Springer.

Vogel, V.J. 1970. *American Indian Medicine*. Norman, OK: Oklahoma University Press.
Walcott, R. 2014. "The problem of the human: Black ontologies and 'the Coloniality of Our Being'", in Broeck, S. and Junker, C. (eds), *Postcoloniality – Decoloniality – Black Critique: Joints and Fissures*. Frankfurt; Campus Verlag. pp. 93–105.
Williams, J. 1934. *The Psychic Phenomena of Jamaica*. New York: Dial Press.
Yang, A. 2023. "Plants can talk. Yes, really. Here's how", *National Geographic* 12 April. Available at: www.nationalgeographic.com/science/article/plants-can-talk-yes-really-heres-how.
Zent, E.L. 2009. "'We come from trees': The poetics of plants among the *Jotï* of the Venezuelan Guayana", *Journal for the Study of Religion, Nature and Culture* 3(1): 9–35.

About the Author

Christina Welch is a neurodivergent interdisciplinary scholar desperately trying to hold onto her sanity and job.

8 The Animacy of Fire and Personhood of Plants in Indigenous-led Land Restoration[1]

Sarah M. Pike

One Friday a few days after Summer Solstice 2021, volunteers arrived at the Mechoopda tribe's native plant restoration site, Verbena Fields, in northern California, to find a scene of destruction. As I and other volunteers walked into our usual summer *c'ipa*/willow processing gathering place near a shady oak tree, Ali Meders-Knight, our Mechoopda Traditional Ecological Knowledge (T.E.K.) teacher, noticed some small trees in the channel had been cut down.[2] They had been roughly hacked at with an axe by vandals and it felt like a desecration. One tree I sat under a few weeks ago while stripping *c'ipa*/willow had deep gashes in it. A young *t'at'am c'a*/alder was one of the victims. Meders-Knight had seen this one grow from a baby. It was for her in that moment, a "twelve-year-old friend that died…before its time." I had learned earlier from Meders-Knight that *t'at'am c'a* is an important actor on the landscape and has cultural and medicinal benefits as well: it brings the

---

1 I am extremely grateful to Ali Meders-Knight (Mechoopda) for the amazing work she has done at Verbena Fields, her willingness to share her knowledge and passion, the extensive community of land-tenders she helped create and her permission to write about her work in this chapter. A big thank you as well to Meleiza Figueroa and Raphael DiGenova for their support of Ali's work, their wild-tending skills and their intense dedication to Verbena Fields and decolonising the landscape.

2 This essay is informed by participation and observation as a volunteer from 2021 to 2023 at Verbena Fields and other land restoration sites in the northern California foothills and Sacramento River valley. Verbena Fields is situated in Mechoopda ancestral homelands in the Sacramento River valley and lower foothills of the Sierra Nevada, north of the Feather River and east of the Sacramento. The Mechoopda are a federally recognised tribe and a sub-division of the Northwestern or Konkow Maidu. Maidu is the basic term for "human beings" and was not what they called themselves before contact with Europeans. The name refers to related language groups and peoples in adjacent areas, designations first given them by linguists and anthropologists. Where possible I continue Ali Meders-Knight's practice by giving the Konkow Maidu names I have learned from her word list, rather than Latin ones.

water table up and helps other plants, its bark has antibiotic qualities and an orange dye used for basket designs. We inspected the riparian area and found more damage. We were all upset about our friends that had been needlessly damaged. What could be done to heal and repair the despoiled site? What did the trees require?

The following week, a large group of volunteers assembled where the vandalism happened and paid homage to the fallen trees. Meleiza Figueroa, a geographer who worked with Meders-Knight at Chico Traditional Ecological Stewardship Program and California Open Lands, lent me a knife to peel t'at'am c'a/alder bark. "We honor the t'at'am c'a/alder" by putting it to use, Mel said. Everyone was working with hand tools and chatting about life, local politics, jobs. The village was doing healing work for its plant community and for each other.

Meders-Knight, who is the Executive Director of California Open Lands, a restoration organisation, founded the Chico Traditional Ecological Stewardship Program. In addition to holding weekly volunteer work hours at Verbena Fields, Meders-Knight has run a number of T.E.K. workshops for both Native and non-Native participants at Verbena Fields and in other locations across the state of California (https://californiaopenlands.org/).[3] She encourages volunteers to approach tending plants at Verbena Fields as practices of decolonisation in the larger context of a history of genocide and ecocide carried out by colonial settlers and state and federal governments (Madley, 2016). For Meders-Knight, to un-invade is to decolonise. Reversing invasion includes supporting Indigenous-led land-tending by planting and caring for local native seeds and plants while removing non-native invasive plants. Re-seeding a landscape that was occupied by settlers during and after the Gold Rush when Indigenous people were removed from the area or massacred, supports a reoccupation by native plants and local Indigenous knowledge. This work remakes the world after disaster by reviving relationships of kinship, reciprocity, respect and gratitude with other species that were common across what is now California before European colonisation.

Meders-Knight's project and similar initiatives in northern California are spreading ancient ways of approaching the living world around us based on Native Californian traditions that see the world as full of other

---

3   At an online panel on T.E.K. and fire sponsored by the Middletown Art Center in March 2022 (Ali Meders-Knight was one of the panelists, along with moderator Corine Pearce (Redwood Valley Little River Band of Pomo) and Meyo Marrufo (Eastern Pomo), I learned that T.E.K. is essentially the "intellectual property of a tribe" (Meders-Knight), "place based knowledge" (Marrufo) or "place based science" (Pearce), not a one-size-fits-all practice frozen in the past, but distinctively local and dynamic. For more information on Meders-Knight's work see Meders-Knight (2021).

beings deserving care and respect. In his reconsideration of the concept of "animism," *Animism, Respecting the Living World* (2005), Graham Harvey distinguishes between "old" and "new" animisms. The old animism of E. B. Tylor (1913) and others saw the attribution of personhood to plants, rocks and other non-human entities as "primitive thinking", or a confused mistake. Instead of dismissing animism as a mistake, Harvey points us to the "new animism", drawing on the work of anthropologists like Irving Hallowell (1960) and Nurit Bird-David (1999), as well as his own observations from fieldwork with Indigenous people such as the Māori and contemporary Pagans. For Harvey, "animists live a theory of personhood and selfhood that radically challenges the dominant point of view which is that of modernity" (Harvey, 2005: xviii). As Ali Meders-Knight explained it in an interview, "place-based knowledge of what plants can do" is not "primitive, the way we treat forests now is primitive" (Moody, 2020).

The work of Indigenous peoples tending the land across northern California inscribes Indigenous views of personhood and respect for the other-than-human world over the colonised landscape using fire, seeds, and other local, land-based practices to decolonise the land. As Potawatomi scholar Kyle Powys Whyte puts it: "settler ecologies have to be inscribed into indigenous ecologies" (Reed, 2020: 39). Restoration at Verbena Fields is one of numerous examples of the work California tribes and their allies are doing in the twentieth-first century to bring Indigenous knowledge and practices back to the landscape that animate the world around us and offer a way forward during this time of climate crises.

Plant Relations

"Mechoopda" means "when the snow melts, the land gets wet." Getting and keeping the land wet is one of the goals at Verbena Fields, both to nourish native plants and reduce fire danger. The tribe's name ties it to this particular valley and foothills where snowmelt is essential to restore waterways and wetlands. The Mechoopda have a moral claim of belonging here, expressed through stories. In *World-Making Stories: Maidu Language and Community Renewal on a Shared California Landscape*, linguistic anthropologist M. Eleanor Nevins remarks that stories work to establish "a prior indigenous moral claim to land" because ancestors, including humans, plants and animals, originate there (2017: 4). Such moral claims of belonging to particular places are at the core of Meders-Knight's work at Verbena Fields, in ancestral lands where her people's creation story establishes a Mechoopda homeland. In many Maidu stories, plants are clearly treated as persons, often described as kin, that play important roles in the origins of humans and the landscape around us.

At the heart of Verbena Fields is a gathering circle and ceramic tile display of a Mechoopda creation story created in 2009 by Meders-Knight and a group of Native youth. In the art piece, Earth Maker and Turtle appear, as does an oak tree bearing acorns. Meders-Knight explained that Turtle helped Earth Maker by diving down under the waters and bringing up dirt in its claws. Earth Maker shaped the dirt into the Earth and used *c'ipa* (willow) sticks to create humans. Acorns became trees and rocks became mountains. Earth Maker gave the people songs and observances, many of them for plants and animals. In these ways, the more-than-human world, including beings such as willow and acorn, are closely related to humans. In *Tending the Wild: Native American Knowledge and the Management of California's Natural Resources*, M. Kat Anderson explains that such stories "instruct humans that plants and people are from the same source and are related" (2013: 249). These relationships of kinship necessitate tending so that humans and all the species they are related to can thrive.

Oak trees, and especially their acorns, are among the many plants that appear in stories about human–plant relationships of tending and care. When we shook branches and collected fallen acorns from one of the *ló:wi*/valley oaks at Verbena Fields, we were engaging in an ancient practice, gathering this once essential food. In another local creation story told by Konkow Maidu artist Frank Day to Donald Jewett, author of *Indians of the Feather River*, Earth Maker tells Coyote that humans' food will come from "grass and the seeds of the grass and the root bulb in the earth". A slightly different Konkow Maidu story, recounted by Damon B. Akins and William J. Bauer Jr. (Round Valley Indian Tribes) in *We Are the Land: A History of Native California*, tells us that after Earth Maker made the stars, he created a tree with twelve different kinds of acorns. Weary from his work making the world, he sat down to rest under the world's first oak tree (2021: 17). In a Konkow Maidu acorn song that journalist Stephen Powers learned in the early 1870s, both human and acorn speak, expressing their responsibilities to each other:

> Hu'-tim yo'-ki[dash over i]m koi-o-di'.
> The acorns come down from heaven.
> Wi'-hi yan'-ning koi-o-di'.
> I plant the short acorns in the valley.
> Lo'-whi yan'-ning koi-o-di'.
> I plant the long acorns in the valley.
> Yo-ho' nai-ni', hal-u'-dom yo nai, yo ho' nai-nim'.
> I sprout, I, the black-acorn acorn, sprout, I sprout (Powers, 1976: 308).

These stories suggest a long history of human relationships with oak trees, native grasses, *waji* (California blue dick and other "Indian potatoes"), and *c'ipa*/willow, all of which are among the plants volunteers are tending at Verbena Fields. Stories like these remind humans of the ways that plants fit into a larger world of relationships and teach younger generations appropriate wild-tending practices.

In addition to carefully evolved techniques of burning, planting, nourishing and harvesting, other rituals of gratitude and reciprocity were practised in Mechoopda villages pre-colonisation in order to receive the gifts of plants. Dances in semi-submerged round houses ensured the world stayed in balance by honouring and giving thanks to the many beings that sustained the people. The Mechoopda ceremonial cycle of dances began in October and ended in June according to Mechoopda elder Henry Azbill, who was interviewed in Chico in the 1960s (Azbill, 1966). The tile art piece created by Ali and Native youth at Verbena Fields references the Aki dance, an important event on the ceremonial calendar. According to Azbill, the Aki dance was held in Spring, at the time of "the awakening of the sleep of the Earth mother", when "the grasses begin to ripen and the seeds and acorns show form again". Performed by a women's society, the Aki was a "prayer of thanksgiving" and one of the three most sacred dances. Azbill noted that dancers "asked the spirits to bring rain when needed, nourish the earth, assure a bountiful supply of food, and ward off sickness, floods, earthquakes, and other evils" (Azbill, 1966). Acorn dances that included praying for a good crop of acorns took place during winter (Loeb, 1933: 171). Like dances in other California Native communities, these ceremonies nurtured ongoing relationships with the more-than-human world that included giving thanks and requesting help.

Appropriate relationships with plants, then, involved ceremonial expressions of care, respect, gratitude and need, as well as careful tending for plant and human flourishing. In *How a Mountain Was Made*, Greg Sarris describes how villagers in coastal Miwok and southern Pomo lands (near the coast and over the mountains to the west of Mechoopda lands) paid tribute to plants and trees through a Spring ceremony. During this ceremony every tree and plant was named and celebrated. As Sarris tells it, "If any one tree or plant is forgotten, it is said that the plant or tree will forget the people. It will leave the people and may not be found again for a long time, or ever again" (2017: 53). Basket-weaver Mabel McKay insisted that plants need to be used: "If they're not gathered from, or talked to and cared about, they'll die" (Ortiz, 1993: 199).

In what is now the state of California, colonisation resulted in genocide and ecocide: the destruction of peoples and their ecosystems went hand in hand (Akins and Bauer, 2021; Reed, 2020). For example, our current fire crisis in California – really a fire *deficit* – began with the Spanish, who were the first to banish fire, in the late 1700s, as they established missions throughout California, though missions never reached the far northern part of the state (Lewis, 1993: 82). When European explorers first arrived on the west coast, an estimated 310,000 people lived in what is now California. By the 1850s, Indigenous populations in California had dwindled to a shocking 30,000 (Blackburn and Anderson, 1993, 18). This tragic decline, exacerbated by Christian missions and secular forces, shaped ecological history in California. After European colonisation, everywhere in California, fire was excluded through fire suppression policies and the absence on the land of Native people who had a relationship with fire (Hankins, 2021). Fire exclusion dramatically altered plant communities and entire ecosystems and at the same time was a "vehicle for Native dispossession" according to Kari Marie Norgaard (Worl and Norgaard, 2019: 11).

That dispossession and its human and ecological results were devastating to California tribes. In the 1850s and 1860s northern California tribes were removed or killed with the support of state and federal governments, documented in horrific detail in Benjamin Madley's *An American Genocide: The United States and the California Indian Catastrophe, 1846–1873* (2016). Relocations and the ruthless killing of Mechoopda and other tribes culminated in the Konkow Trail of Tears in which local Natives were forced to march to Round Valley, over 100 miles away. In Chico, some Mechoopda stayed on John Bidwell's ranch where his Presbyterian wife Annie subjected them to aggressive missionising, but where they were somewhat protected from bounty hunters and other settler violence (Jacobs, 1997).[4] When Mechoopda were killed, relocated or converted, relationships with plants and animals, including those involving ceremonial relationships with fire, disappeared (Margolin, 2017: 178–179). Henry Azbill described how dances died out because there was no initiation of younger generations, no society to sponsor dances and no sweathouse to purify dancers (Azbill, 1966). At an Indigenous-led restoration workshop I attended, one speaker noted that: "When song, ceremony, and dance stop, so does the earth."

---

4 The Bidwells' relationship to local Natives is complicated. Annie Bidwell was in the Women's Temperance Union, a suffragette and a devout Presbyterian. Both Bidwells were concerned with the rights of Native people, compared to others in their communities, but within the cause of "civilizing" them. Because they had political and economic power, they were able to offer some protection, but on their own conditions, which resulted in the loss of many aspects of Mechoopda culture (Jacobs, 1997; Hill, 1978).

Meders-Knight and volunteers at Verbena Fields are helping plants remember their human tenders and letting plants guide the way to restoring the ecosystem. In Indigenous-led restoration work, plants are often seen as teachers and guides: they will let you know what they need, you just have to follow their lead. "They're my best teachers," explained Raphael DiGenova, a native plant expert who propagates native plants for Verbena Fields and often leads plant walks and volunteer work, alongside Meders-Knight, during a seed workshop in May 2023. For DiGenova working at Verbena Fields became a therapeutic response to grief about what was lost, as well as something to do in the face of impending climate change. Verbena Fields offers this therapeutic experience to anyone who wants to come out and work, DiGenova explained to me: "Nothing special about me, I just recognised that if I came here, I could have a taste of being more fully human." Being more fully human came about because of DiGenova's connection to the land that they used to grieve, that they thought was gone, but that was coming back to life. Being fully human meant, in part, being in a relationship of tending and care with plants and the land, restoring kinship relationships to plants as important "elders".

Restoring our relationships to native plants as teachers and kin helps to transpose certain aspects of the past onto the present as plants remind us what they need. On a *c'ipa*/willow work day in early summer at Verbena Fields I was sitting on the ground, alongside other volunteers, while we stripped bark from *c'ipa*/willow shoots. Meders-Knight observed how alike we were to ancient villages where people gathered to do this work. Two hundred years ago, perhaps a group of Mechoopda basket weavers were sitting in this very spot, stripping *c'ipa*/willow and wrapping their foreheads to fend off summer heat. *C'ipa* was used for baskets and headaches, as well as to make women's skirts. Willow is referred to as *c'ipa* when it is cut and *c'ipoo* when it is still part of a tree, reflecting its animate nature and the transformation it goes through in human hands.

Like humans, plants have different personalities or attributes that shape what they give to humans in return for human tending. At Verbena Fields plants offer medicine, food, and fiber for baskets. *Múnmuni*/mugwort is a common example of a plant medicine at Verbena Fields. Verbena Fields featured a year-round creek before colonisation. *C'ipa*/willow and *múnmuni*/mugwort grew on its banks, tended and harvested by the Mechoopda and their neighbours. With help from human tenders both are now thriving at Verbena Fields. One week when I was working there, volunteers collected *múnmuni* into bundles, tied with bark that had been stripped off *c'ipa* branches. I took a bundle home with me and placed it near my bed, inhaling its pungent, sweet smell before going to sleep. Meders-Knight explained to visitors on one plant walk around Verbena Fields that *múnmuni* was also for dreams and broken hearts. *Múnmuni* has many medicinal uses according to Josephine Peters (Karuk/Shasta/Abenaki tribal affiliations). It can serve as a liver tonic, tick repellent and medicine for sore throats and colds. It can also be made into poultices for sprains and bruises and used to treat poison oak, skin cancer and various skin ailments (Peters and Ortiz, 2010: 192–194).

From a T.E.K. perspective, tending plants requires learning about their likes and dislikes as well as what they offer. On work days and plant walks, Meders-Knight told volunteers about plants' personalities and spirits, their preferences, and who their friends are. We learned that *l'yli* (Western redbud) does not like to be alone, so it should be planted with others of its kind. Without friends, says Meders-Knight, "they die of a broken heart." We learned that *c'awk'awi*/blue oak and *tó:ni*/gray pine like to be planted together. "They are best friends," says Meders-Knight, because they grow well together and help each other thrive. Being aware of their relationships with each other, as well as ours with them, is important for helping them thrive. *Tó:ni*'s long needles are acidic and break down nutrients in the soil. *C'awk'awi* is specialised to live in hot, dry climates and can grow on lava cap, where valley oak cannot. It has deep roots and holds water well, sometimes in small cavities where chorus frogs might over-summer. Even though it helps other plants and animals, *c'awk'awi* needs help, too, when it is growing. It is one of many seeds and seedlings we learned to plant with "nurse plants" that provide a little shade from the relentless summer sun. *Múnmuni* offers medicine, *c'awk'awi* and *tó:ni* offer food, but plants at Verbena Fields are also important for basketry.

Meders-Knight is a basket maker and tends plants at Verbena Fields for other cultural uses such as basket-weaving, as well as for food and medicine. Baskets once played, and continue to play, crucial roles, both practical and ceremonial, in many Native California cultures (Hill, 1978). *C'ipa*/willow, sedges, *l'yli*/redbud and many other plants restored to Verbena Fields were traditionally tended for basketry needs. Anthropologist Dorothy M. Hill's Mechoopda interviewees that she spoke with in the 1960s told her that one household might have twenty baskets of different sizes and shapes for gathering, winnowing, cooking, serving and storing food, carrying water, cradling babies, carrying materials and use in ceremonies such as burning objects for the dead (Hill, 1978: 45–47).

Collecting materials for these baskets and tending plants for basket-weaving have been sacred activities with complex social rules from pre-colonial times through the present (Anderson and Blackburn: 19; Ortiz, 1993: 196). Even sites used to gather plants for basketry may be "consecrated" (Anderson 2013, 36). Plants to be harvested should be approached with good intentions and thanked afterwards, according to Mabel McKay (1907–1993), a well-known Pomo basket-weaver (Ortiz, 1993: 199). Thus baskets, like the plant beings used to create them, are seen as animate. They have power and are treated respectfully. As Pomo basket-weaver Susan Billy puts it, "For me, basketry always has been a spiritual process…I don't consider it a craft. We have to pray, and ask the plants if they want to be in a basket" (Taylor, 2022). Specific practices of respect, such as asking plants what they want, praying and making offerings to give thanks for the help of the plant, create relationships of reciprocity and gratitude.

At workshops and land-tending days, Meders-Knight teaches what Potawatomi botanist Robin Wall Kimmerer calls Indigenous people's "grammar of animacy" that "immigrants", such as myself, must learn to speak (Kimmerer, 2015: 58). Learning this grammar means nurturing personal relationships of reciprocity with plants that we invite back to the land, what Kimmerer calls a "moral covenant of reciprocity" (2015: 384). In the months I worked at Verbena Fields, Meders-Knight taught us practices of reciprocity and gratitude. On one work day we made offerings before harvesting seeds from California poppies that filled the park's large meadow. As Meders-Knight explained to volunteers, "you have to have your own symbiotic relationship with plants." I put down a strand of my hair (it offers nitrogen to the soil) and silently thanked the poppies for their seeds. Through such practices of gratitude and respect for plants, relationships of reciprocity return to the land and work towards healing it.

In 1972, Vine Deloria, Jr. (1933–2005), Standing Rock Sioux theologian and lawyer, called for "a radical reversal of our attitudes toward nature" given the ecological crisis. He stated that it was time "for the people to gather and perform their old ceremonies and make a final effort to renew the earth and its peoples – hoofed, winged, and others" (Deloria, 1973: 2–3). Ceremonies that honour and thank plants, that honour and engage with fire are part of a larger call by Indigenous authors and tribal leaders to restore more broadly across the landscape reciprocal and symbiotic relationships between humans and other species that their cultures have always practised. As Robin Wall Kimmerer explains it, "ceremony is a vehicle of belonging, to a family, to a people, to the land." Kimmerer recognises Native people's sense of loss and settler people's shame, but she argues, "It is not enough to weep for our lost landscapes; we have to put our hands in the earth to make ourselves whole again" (Kimmerer, 2015: 327). Putting their hands in the earth to tend to unhealthy and neglected lands allows Indigenous people and their restoration allies to assert and make visible their belonging to the landscape.

T.E.K. practitioners such as Meders-Knight are drawing on an Indigenous past and connecting with their ancestors to create a viable future for their children and grandchildren (Meders-Knight has five daughters and a granddaughter). These cultural practices involve ongoing human care of the land and the presence of Indigenous land stewards on a vibrant landscape of many species. That vibrant landscape has always been and continues to be, from a Traditional Ecological Knowledge perspective, in a close and intimate relationship with fire.

Bringing the Fire Back

On the morning of 8 November 2018, a black cloud of smoke from the Camp Fire in Paradise, California, ten miles from my home, blocked the sun for most of the day. Eighty-four people and incalculable plants and animals died in the fire and more than 14,000 homes and other buildings were destroyed. The Camp Fire, catastrophic as it was, also created new and rekindled older relationships between humans and the devastated land, facilitated by restoration practices involving fungi, native plants, earthworks and prescribed cultural fire.[5]

In response to the Camp Fire and other disastrous wildfires, California has witnessed a broader movement to return to the landscape cultural fires set ceremonially by local tribes, including the Mechoopda tribe, whose ancestral homelands are in the Camp Fire burn scar and the land my university was built on (Hankins, 2021; von Kaenel, 2019). Cultural fires, such as those intended to create optimum basket materials, are a type of prescribed fire that restores and continues earlier close relationships between Indigenous people, plants and fire. What is at stake in these practices around fire includes contested moral and spiritual meanings of the landscape, our deepest relationships with its various non-human agencies, and especially our understandings of what it means to live with fire in the context of climate change.

Before the arrival of Europeans, fires, many of them intentionally set, burned constantly throughout California (Kelsey, 2020; Anderson, 2013: 136). These often low-intensity prescribed fires, "creeping" fires, were usually not the mega-fires that are common in the twenty-first century. Native communities treated fire as an ally to increase biodiversity, improve basket materials, control pests and diseases, enhance the growth of grasses and bulbs, germinate seeds, encourage mushroom growth and reduce the chances of high-intensity fires (Anderson, 2013: 144–184; Cagle, 2019). Fire was also seen (and continues to be seen) as a practice of healing land and its

---

5   Not all prescribed (intentionally set) fires are "cultural fires." Cultural fires are connected to tribal communities and have cultural (basket-making materials, for example) as well as ecological goals.

peoples. As Karuk fire and fuels researcher Frank K. Lake, a U.S. Forest Service research ecologist, puts it, "The Karuk Tribe, among others, sees fire as medicine, and as such views traditional burning as a human service for ecosystems." Places where fire has been excluded, he said, "are sick, as are the people who live there, from a tribal perspective" (Worl and Norgaard, 2019). From this perspective, the root of this sickness of land and people is European colonisation that destroyed ancient relationships between people and fire.

This is the deeper history that Verbena Fields provides a window onto. Like other twenty-first century catastrophic fires in California, the Camp Fire revealed cultural histories as well as ecological ones. The fire crisis is, in a sense, also a spiritual crisis, not just the absence of a management technique, but the absence of ceremonial practices that approach fire as an animate relation deserving respect and care. As Leaf Hillman, a Karuk ceremonial leader, explains it, "We are closely related to fire. Fire takes care of us and we take care of fire" (Norgaard, 2019: 88). When Indigenous ceremonies were outlawed in California, suppression of religion and suppression of fire went hand in hand. During the Amah Mutsun Land Trust Fire Symposium that brought together tribal leaders and fire scientists, Amah Mutsun tribal chair Valentin Lopez explained that his people made a "sacred covenant" with fire that needs to be upheld by bringing fire back to Amah Mutsun ancestral lands (Lopez, 2020). As another cultural fire practitioner, North Fork Mono tribal chairman Ron Goode explains it in a film on cultural burning in the series *Tending the Wild*, "fire has spirit, this land has spirit, and when we're burning, they come alive." Fire is a "gift from Creator", Valentin Lopez told the Symposium audience. The absence of Native people tending native plants, especially regular burning with low-intensity fires, and their many seasonal ceremonies, created the conditions for vulnerability to climate change. Reversing these trends necessitates the return of cultural fire.

In an interview about her work in response to the Camp Fire, Meders-Knight emphasised the importance of bringing fire back: "Each tribe around here has a fire story, and there's always a bird or animal that takes the fire back, because fire is power… That's us. We are helping the community steal the fire back" (von Kaenel, 2019). Cultural fire returned to Verbena Fields in March 2022, for the first time in about 150 years. Meders-Knight began the cultural burn by lighting a clump of deergrass (*Ósoko sáwi*), a prized basket-weaving material. As the grass burned, some sandhill cranes flew overhead and she commented on their presence: "So we have the cranes above us who love fire, who are watching us – I think the birds are really excited today – and the crows were here earlier talking to us. So I think not only the humans are excited to see the change, the paradigm shift that's happened here" (Bohannon, 2022). In a video about the 2022 cultural burn at Verbena Fields, pyrogeographer and cultural fire practitioner Don Hankins (Plains Miwok) described Meders-Knight's stewardship work putting plants back in the ground at the site, but noted that now "the real connection is having that relationship with fire back in this place…every single plant I see out here has some relationship with fire. Culturally…these plants have that connection to us." He explained that for cultural reasons, such as basketry, the burn will stimulate new growth in the deergrass and make it healthier, but that it's not just for baskets that they burn: "critters need the plants to flourish too…it's also our responsibility to our relations" (TEK Chico, n.d.). Like Indigenous relationships with plants, relationships with fire also entail respect, reciprocity, and responsibility to the larger ecosystem.

Because so many of California's native plants are fire-adapted, fire exclusion has had a devastating effect on them (Anderson, 1993: 156–170). Like humans, native plants co-evolved with fire (Hankins, 2021). Mountain Maidu elder Tom Young/Hánc'ibyjim describes the effects on certain plants of setting fires or allowing them to burn in an interview from the 1920s: "Then the countryside caught fire/seeming to be everywhere, sweeping over the land, and Milkweed person says 'I, when it has passed, shall be what is left standing'" (Nevins, 2017: 189). Milkweed and many other plants we worked with in the Camp Fire burn scar and at Verbena Fields in Chico are fire-resilient or even fire-dependent. After the Camp Fire, in a burned-over area around Butte Creek that Meders-Knight had tended, *nokomhyni*/elderberry and *l'yli*/redbud survived, as did some *c'awk'awi*/blue oak and sedges. Bringing back fire is an important strategy for bringing back native plants to local ecosystems and thus creating more fire-resilient landscapes as well restoring healthy plant–human–fire relationships.

Decolonising California's Wildfire Zone

On a plant walk at Verbena Fields in 2023, Meders-Knight and DiGenova, who lead monthly tours of the park together, pointed out a flourishing patch of *wedakdaka*/Indian lettuce (otherwise known as "miners' lettuce") where a year ago there had been far less. *Waji*/blue dick that they planted a couple of years earlier was pushing through the soil in tiny shoots. Deergrass that was burned earlier that year was visible thriving, in contrast to other deergrass that had not been burned. Meders-Knight, DiGenova and community volunteers are working a reversal, returning Verbena Fields to something like it looked for millennia before this very recent (170 years ago) period of colonisation. The land remembers human tending as *c'ipa*/willow and its companion plants at Verbena Fields respond to being regularly cared for once again. As DiGenova suggested, if so much can change in 170 years, reversing it in the context of a thousands of years long human-land relationship in this place should not be impossible.

Rituals of repair and relationship around fire and plants in Indigenous-led restoration work both express and constitute relationships between humans and the more-than-human world. They offer healing because they link the health of plants and people. As Native American Studies scholar Kaitlyn Reed (Yurok, Hupa, Oneida) puts it, "to heal a people from genocide, you also need to heal the land – because we are a part of the land and the land is us" (Reed, 2020: 30). These practices express the continued resilience and revival of earlier relationships between people and the land they lived in as well as constituting hoped for relationships that could come to characterise the future, returning relationships of care and reciprocity to the land. By claiming land with native seeds and Native plant names, knowledge and burning practices, T.E.K. practitioners such as Meders-Knight are inscribing an Indigenous past and future onto the landscape.

For non-Native participants such as myself, restoration work is a way of furthering these relationships and contributing to post-fire land regeneration, as well as restoring Indigenous peoples' place as stewards of the land that was devastated by colonisation and its effects. In these ways, our restoration practices also function as rituals of *reparation* for a colonial past that had terrible consequences for both the Indigenous people of California and the animal and plant communities they were closely related to. As Meders-Knight put it during one work day, "Giving back to the plants is like giving reparations to the tribe."

Decolonising land and making it fire-resilient means supporting Indigenous land management, removing invasive species and invaders' ways of relating to land, and nurturing native species. Mel Figueroa reminded the audience at a workshop on "Listening to the Land Together. Weaving Connections Among Indigenous Wisdom Keepers and Ecosystem Restoration Allies" that "All plants are political." Thus it is essential to address California Indian history and the effects of colonisation that impacted plant and human communities. Returning lands to Indigenous land-tending, encouraging cultural fire and prescribed burning – these are responses to tragic disasters like the Camp Fire that imagine a different future. Fire-shaped California landscapes before European colonisation and fire are essential for decolonisation. Traditional ecological land-tending furthers the "de-colonial environmental policy" called for by Beth Rose Middleton Manning, who heads the Native American Studies program at University of California, Davis. As Middleton Manning sees it, "By not highlighting Indigenous homelands and Indigenous stewardship in the study of environmental science, policy, and management, we are disregarding millennia of Indigenous scientific knowledge and practice, and perpetuating a colonial process that disregards Indigenous knowledge, Indigenous struggle, Indigenous survivance, and Indigenous leadership in land and water planning and stewardship" (Middleton Manning, 2021).

This kind of decolonisation is not just political, it is also about moral values, worldviews, ecology and spirituality. It means re-establishing sacred relationships with the land and fire that disappeared when Native people were removed, killed or Christianised. Such sacred relationships are at the heart of Graham Harvey's work and the reconsideration of animism that he has advocated (Harvey, 2006, 2015). As catastrophic wildfires reveal intertwined cultural and ecological histories of colonisation, they also necessitate rethinking what ecological and ritual practices might reinstate a healthier relationship to fire. But such restoration work is a long game. Land restoration and decolonisation are not quick fixes. Meders-Knights says she wants to "create restorative places and ecosystems for the next 100 years." Until then it will be hard to know the full fruits of her labour. As she put it in an interview on the radio show "Cultivating Place", "I will be visiting and tending these places in a spirit form."

References

Akins, D.B. and Bauer Jr., W.J. 2021. *We Are the Land: A History of Native California*. Oakland, CA: University of California Press.

Anderson, M.K. 1993. "Native Californians as ancient and contemporary cultivators", in Blackburn, T.C. and Anderson, K. (eds), *Before the Wilderness: Environmental Management by Native Californians*. Menlo Park, CA: Ballena Press. pp. 151–174.

Anderson, M.K. 2013. *Tending the Wild: Native American Knowledge and the Management of California's Natural Resources*. Oakland, CA: University of California Press.

Azbill, H. 1966. *Some Aspects of Mechoopda Indian Culture*. Chico, CA: Dorothy Hill Collection. Interview by Jim Neider, CSU, Chico Oral History Program.

Bird-David, N. 1999. "'Animism' revisited: Personhood, environment, and relational epistemology", *Current Anthropology* 40(S1): S67–S91.

Blackburn, T.C. and Anderson, K. 1993. "Introduction: Managing the domestic environment", in Blackburn, T.C. and Anderson, K. (eds), *Before the Wilderness: Environmental Management by Native Californians*. Menlo Park, CA: Ballena Press. pp. 15–25.

Bohannon, S. 2022. "Fire returned: Making cultural fire history in Chico", *North State Public Radio*. Available at: www.mynspr.org/2022-05-13/fire-returned-mechoopda-tribe-members-make-history-at-verbena-fields (accessed 10 October 2023).

Cagle, S. 2019. "Fire is medicine: The tribes burning California forests to save them", *The Guardian*. 21 November. Available at: www.theguardian.com/us-news/2019/nov/21/wildfire-prescribed-burns-california-native-americans (accessed 20 May 2020).
Deloria, V. 1973. *God Is Red: A Native View of Religion*. New York: Grosset & Dunlap.
Hallowell, A.I. 1960. "Ojibwa ontology, behavior, and world view", in Diamond, S (ed.), *Culture in History*. New York: Columbia University Press. pp. 19–52.
Hankins, D. 2021. "Reading the landscape for fire", *Bay Nature*. Available at: https://baynature.org/article/reading-the-landscape-for-fire/ (accessed 10 April 2022).
Harvey, G. 2005. *Animism: Respecting the Living World*. New York: Columbia University Press.
Harvey, G. 2015. *The Handbook of Contemporary Animism*. London: Routledge.
Hill, D.J. 1978. *The Indians of Chico Rancheria*. Chico, CA: KaCa Ma Press.
Jacobs, M.D. 1997. "Resistance to rescue: The Indians of Bahapki and Mrs. Annie E.K. Bidwell", in University of Nebraska – Lincoln, Faculty Publications, Department of History 16. Available at: https://digitalcommons.unl.edu/cgi/viewcontent.cgi?&article=1015&context=historyfacpub (accessed 10 April 2022).
Kelsey, R. 2020. "Wildfires and forest resilience: The case for ecological forestry in the Sierra Nevada", *Fremontia: Journal of the California Native Plant Society*, 47(2): 8–17.
Kimmerer, R.W. 2015. *Braiding Sweetgrass: Indigenous Wisdom, Scientific Knowledge, and the Teachings of Plants*. Minneapolis, MN: Milkweed.
Lewis, H.T. 1993. "Patterns of Indian burning in California: Ecology and ethnohistory", in Blackburn, T.C. and Anderson, K. (eds), *Before the Wilderness: Environmental Management by Native Californians*. Menlo Park, CA: Ballena Press.
Loeb, E.M. 1933. "The Eastern Kuksu Cult", *University of California Publications in American Archeology and Ethnology* 33(2): 139–232.
Lopez, V. 2020. *Amah Mutsun Tribal Band's Land Stewardship Traditions. Amah Mutsun Land Trust, Fire Symposium*. 19 November. Available at: www.amahmutsunlandtrust.org/events/2020/11/19/amlt-fire-symposium.
Madley, B. 2016. *An American Genocide: The United States and the California Indian Catastrophe, 1846–1873*. New Haven, CT: Yale University Press.
Margolin. M. (ed.) 2017. *The Way We Lived: California Indian Stories and Reminiscences*. Berkeley, CA: Heyday Books.
Meders-Knight, A. 2021. "Climate change adaptation: What we can learn from traditional ecological knowledge", *California Native Plant Society*. Available at: www.cnps.org/event/climate-change-adaptation-what-we-can-learn-from-traditional-ecological-knowledge.
Middleton Manning, B.R. 2021. "Trust in the land: New directions in legal and policy approaches to protecting indigenous lifeways and homelands", *California Institute for Indigenous Studies, Religion and Ecology Summit: Indigenous Lifeways, Cosmologies, and Ecology*. 15 March. Available at: www.ciis.edu/academics/graduate-programs/ecology-spirituality-and-religion/religion-and-ecology-summit/religion-and-ecology-summit-2021.
Moody, K. 2020. "Wild Tending" series, interview with Ali Meders-Knight. *Ground Shots*. Available at: www.ofsedgeandsalt.com/podcastblog/alimedersknight.

Nevins, M.E. (ed.) 2017. *World-Making Stories: Maidu Language and Community Renewal on a Shared California Landscape*. Lincoln, NE and London: University of Nebraska Press.
Norgaard, K.M. 2019. *Salmon and Acorns Feed Our People: Nature, Colonialism and Social Action*. Rutgers, NJ: Rutgers University Press.
Ortiz, B. 1993. "Contemporary California Indian basketweavers and the environment", in Blackburn, T.C. and Anderson, K. (eds), *Before the Wilderness: Environmental Management by Native Californians*. Menlo Park, CA: Ballena Press. pp. 195–211.
Peters, J. and Ortiz, B. 2010. *After the First Full Moon in April: A Sourcebook of Herbal Medicine from a California Indian Elder*. London and New York: Routledge.
Powers, S. 1976. *Tribes of California*. Oakland, CA: University of California Press.
Reed, K. 2020. "We are a part of the land and the land is us: Settler colonialism, genocide & healing in California", *Humboldt Journal of Social Relations* 1(42): 27–49.
Risling Baldy, C. 2021. "#LandBack: What good is a land acknowledgment?" Keynote talk. NorCal Resilience Network. Listening to the Land Together. Weaving Connections Among Indigenous Wisdom Keepers and Ecosystem Restoration Allies. *Native Land Digital*. 27 February. Available at: www.native-land.ca (accessed 27 February 2021).
Sarris, G. 2017. *How A Mountain Was Made: Stories*. Berkeley, CA: Heyday Books.
Taylor, D. 2022. "Preserving the ancient tradition of basket weaving in Sonoma County", *Sonoma Magazine* September. Available at: www.sonomamag.com/preserving-the-ancient-tradition-of-basket-weaving-in-sonoma-county/ (accessed 10 October 2023).
TEK Chico. (n.d.) "The Meaning of Cultural Burning." Available at: https://tekchico.org/cultural-burning-in-chico) (accessed 2 March 2024).
Tylor, E.B. 1913 [1871]. *Primitive Culture*. London: John Murray.
Von Kaenel, C. 2019. "'We are helping the community steal the fire back': Tribe-driven stewardship of Butte County forests gains traction", *Chico Enterprise-Record*. 7 December. Available at: www.chicoer.com/2019/12/07/we-are-helping-the-community-steal-the-fire-back-tribe-driven-stewardship-of-butte-county-forests-gains-traction/ (accessed 21 February 2023).
Worl, S. and Norgaard, K.M. 2019. "What Western states can learn from Native American wildfire management strategies", *GreenBiz*. November 1. Available at: www.greenbiz.com/article/what-western-states-can-learn-native-american-wildfire-management-strategies (accessed 10 October 2023).

About the Author

Dr Sarah M. Pike is Professor of Comparative Religion at California State University, Chico in the U.S. She has written numerous books, articles and book chapters on contemporary Paganism, ritual, the New Age movement, Burning Man, festivals, spiritual dance, environmentalism, the ancestral skills movement, climate protests and youth culture. Her most recent book is *For the Wild: Ritual and Commitment in Radical Eco-Activism.* Her current research focuses on ritual, spirituality and ecology in several different contexts, including a project on ritualised and restorative relationships with landscapes after wildfires.

9 Gaian Animism: Ritual Innovation and Nature Spirituality in Radical Environmentalism and the Global Environmental Milieu

Bron Taylor

Introduction

Professor Graham Harvey, whom we honour with this volume, has played a major role in illuminating social phenomena that he has termed Neo-Animism. He has not, of course, advanced such study alone but he has been drawing on and engaging with a growing chorus of scholars who are also looking at such phenomena, in different times and places, and with increasingly diverse interpretive lenses. Like Harvey, most of those analysing such phenomena have had personal experiences that have led to their scholarly interest and feelings of affinity with such spiritualties and concomitant values and practices.

Harvey is aware, of course, that E.B. Tylor's use of the term "Animism" was entangled with colonial and racist assumptions, and corresponding arguments that scholars should, therefore, eschew the term's usage, apart from critiquing its putatively pernicious origins (Chidester, 2014, 2005a, 2011).

But for Harvey, Animism has become a useful term that need not be understood pejoratively (Harvey, 2005). This is clear in part because increasing numbers of people use the term self-referentially. This is also the case, he avers, because Animism need not involve nor refer to supernatural or invisible spirits. Rather, for Harvey, contemporary Animism is best understood to refer to perceptions that the world is replete with diverse life forms and forces with whom humans are related and to whom they have moral obligations that enjoin respect, and even reverence, when these beings are perceived as divine or holy (Harvey, 2006).

In ways similar to Harvey due in part to my own idiosyncratic experiences (Taylor, 2019a, 2019b), I have been drawn to study the natural dimension of religion, including social phenomena that Harvey and increasing numbers of others now call Animism. What I have found through my wanderings is that within the global environmental milieu (by which I mean the wildly diverse cultural spaces around the world where individuals and groups wrestle with, and over, their environment-related perceptions, values and behaviours) many people have had experiences that lead them to express what, at least from an etic perspective, we can aptly call Animism.

Like Harvey, I also recognise that many forms of Animism have nothing to do with perceptions of non-material beings or forces, but instead they are rooted in personal experiences with non-human organisms, within environmental systems, and derived from scientific understandings. In *Dark Green Religion* (Taylor, 2008, 2010a) I called those whose perceptions included invisible spiritual beings or forces Spiritual Animists.[1] Naturalistic Animists, in contrast, I construed as those who base their perceptions either on their relationships with and observations of animals, or on ethology, the science of animal consciousness and behaviour, a science that, in its own ways, makes it possible to surmise many things about what non-human animals think, feel and communicate.

I have not only analysed Animism's diverse, contemporary forms, but also the ways it combines with an ancient perception commonly known as Organicism, which more recently has been dubbed Gaia, after the Greek Mother Earth goddess.[2] And while Organicism involved beliefs that the universe is animated by one or more superordinate divine intelligence, a phenomena I call Gaian Spirituality, Gaian Naturalism, as I construed the term, stands for those who base their views on scientific understandings about interactions and mutual dependence of diverse organisms within the biosphere. During the 1970s, for example, James Lovelock and Lynn Margulis advanced the Gaia Hypothesis, which spread quickly and has become the most prominent example of such a worldview (Primavesi, 2003; Harding, 2006, 2022; Ruse, 2013, Tyrrell, 2013; Latour, 2017; Jabr, 2019). They argued that Earth's biota functions in ways that maintain the conditions necessary for complex, multi-cellular life to exist and flourish (Lovelock, 1972, 1979; Margulis, 1981; Margulis and Sagan, 1986; Lovelock, 2005). I have also noted

---

1 Most of the material presented here is new, but since my analysis includes some reflection on earlier work that is relevant to Professor Harvey's work, I have reused some words and phrases from previous analyses, as, e.g., in Taylor (2013, 2017). For simplicity's sake, I have not put such words and phrases within quotation marks.
2 James Lovelock, of course, through his Gaia Hypothesis, has been the one most responsible for the increasing popularity of Gaia as a shorthand way to express the ultimately Organicist notion that the living things and processes within the biosphere function like an organism to create and maintain the conditions necessary for the continuance of life on Earth (Lovelock, 1972, 1979).

that in the belief systems of many, there is an unclear and permeable line between the more spiritual and naturalistic forms of both animistic and organicist spiritualities.

Herein, I will use the neologism Gaian Animism as shorthand for these entangled spiritual and naturalistic spiritualities.

To illuminate the complexities and ambiguities involved in the spread of Gaian Animism, in the following analysis I will explore examples of it within the North American radical environmental movement, before briefly reviewing some of the evidence of the growing cultural traction of such spirituality.

Discovering Gaian Animism

During the summer of 1991, more than 100 Earth First! activists gathered in a clearing of a National Forest in the State of Vermont in the Northeastern United States. It was the first full day of the gathering they called the "Round River Rendezvous", which was named for a beloved essay penned generations earlier by the wildlands ecologist, and philosopher, Aldo Leopold. The encircled activists listened to organisers explaining camp rules and workshop organisers describing their plans. Toward the end of the announcements, Jim O'Connor, a bearded man who appeared to be in his 40s, indicated that he would lead a day-long Council of All Beings, and after a brief explanation of what it involved, invited those interested to listen for and follow the sound of a drum, which will begin soon after the end of the morning meeting.

Earth First!, which was then the most high-profile manifestation of a wider radical environmental movement, had been founded in 1980 by a group of wildlands advocates who, in various ways, considered ecological systems and non-human organisms to have intrinsic value. They also believed that humans were precipitating a massive and accelerating extinction episode, and that governments, corporations and Western, capitalist-friendly legal systems were most responsible for it, and mainstream environmental groups were often complicit – far too willing to compromise, sometimes for self-interested, careerist reasons.

These perceptions led to their conclusion that reform-focused politics (electoral politics and grassroots lobbing), had not and would not halt anthropogenic extinctions and consequently, illegal resistance was both morally permissible and strategically necessary. Despite considerable diversity, the moral sentiment these activists shared – that all life has value apart from its usefulness to human beings – was typically rooted in nature-based perceptions and experiences that most of them, in some way, considered to be religious or, for those uncomfortable with that term, spiritual. This was the case as well for those among them who drew foremost on the sciences for their understandings of the human place in the universe and biosphere. Some of these were avowed atheists.

Like most of those drawn to this gathering, by reading *Earth First!*, the movement's nationally distributed tabloid, I had been learning about the movement and its spiritual, ecological and political perceptions. I had seen how, from its very beginning, its writers and activists considered Western, monotheistic religions and philosophies to undergird a pernicious anthropocentrism and even an ideology of human supremacy. In contrast, Earth First!ers typically considered indigenous and Pagan traditions, and religions originating in Asia (especially Buddhism and Daoism), to be more naturally eco-friendly. These spiritualities were also typically lauded as a way to connect to other species; they were also, often, understood to be forms of Animism.

Some movement writers argued that shamanic practices indebted to indigenous societies were especially effective in awakening participants to the value, agency and personhood of non-human organisms and the possibility of communication and communion with them.

Meanwhile, other writers drew on scientific understandings, especially physics and ecology, to advance notions of the interconnections and interdependencies within Earth's living systems. The Gaia Hypothesis, especially, precipitated a wave of spiritual enthusiasm, a development that bemused Lovelock, who commented that he appreciates and shares the impulse to have respect and reverence for the Gaian system (Lovelock, 2005). And influenced by Lovelock and Margulis, as well as by his studies of indigenous sorcerers, philosopher David Abram fused shamanism and Animism with the Gaia Hypothesis, arguing in *Earth First!* that such spiritualities are "no supernatural thing" but rather, they simply involve cultivating an ability to hear "the myriad voices of Earth" (Abram, 1988; cf. Abram 1989).

The contributors to *Earth First!* were thus advancing an innovative spiritual worldview, which can indeed be called Gaian Animism. Through its journal the movement drew activists to it who shared its typical ecological, political and spiritual perceptions, as well as its moral sentiments, thereby setting the stage for the day's Council of All Beings ritual.

Gaian Animism and the *Council of All Beings*

John Seed, an Australian Buddhist, Deep Ecologist and activist who had founded the Rainforest Information Centre, and Johanna Macy, an American scholar of Buddhism and prominent anti-nuclear activist who had developed "despair and empowerment workshops" to help activists stay with the struggle, invented the Council. They sought to fuse deep ecology's ecocentric spirituality with Macy's efforts to overcome despair among activists. Their stated intention expressed Gaian Animism; they quoted the Vietnamese Zen Buddhist Thich Nhat Hanh when explaining that they designed the Council to help people "hear within themselves the sounds of the earth crying" (Seed et al., 1988: 7) and to enable them to "let other life forms speak" through them.[3]

By following Jim O'Connor and those he led into the Council during that 1991 Earth First! rendezvous, we can see how this ritual evokes and reinforces animistic perceptions.

Soon after the conclusion of the morning announcements that morning in Vermont, O'Connor began beating a drum in a slow, solemn, cadence. As he wove through the camp, activists fell in behind him. Eventually, well away from the hubbub of the camp, O'Connor arrived at a meadow and asked his followers to form a circle. Several who were unsure whether they wanted to participate, or who arrived late, remained on the periphery as observers.

When the Council is conducted over a three-day weekend, which is common, it typically begins with trust exercises to build community with the assembly. This may involve participants being asked to close their eyes, after which their partner leads them around, positioning them in various ways, then tapping the partner with closed eyes, who then, only for a moment, blinks their eyes open and closes them again. This exercise not only requires trust that one's sighted partner will not cause them injury as they lead them, but it is designed to draw attention to the wonders of nature that people, in their everyday lives, tend to ignore. Animistic perception typically involves cultivating alertness to the liveliness of the world, and this simple ritual seems designed to awaken or reinforce such alertness.

On this occasion, O'Connor began by explaining the intentions behind the ritual: to help us work through our despair over the destruction of the world we love; to more deeply understand that the evolutionary process is a sacred one to which we belong; and to listen to other-than-human voices. He added that their common goal was to empower their resistance to the forces of destruction. Then, drawing on an invocation written by John Seed (Seed et al., 1988: 2–3), he asked for "the spirit of the presence of Gaia" to guide the process so the denizens of the Earth would come and speak freely.

After that, O'Conner took a metre-long fallen branch from a tree and placed it in the centre of the circle, which he called a "cairn of mourning". In a

---

3   For more information about the religious sources Macy and Seed drew upon for the ritual, see Taylor (1994: 190–192).

way that drew on Macy's despair and empowerment workshops, he explained that the pain we feel in our personal and activist lives can lead us to become paralysed by grief, and it is important to express such feelings. Handing out a pebble, he invited whoever wished to, to come forward, place a stone on the cairn and express those feelings.

One young woman described her pain at the recent death of her mother, but given the framing, most of the others mourned the loss of a forested childhood playground that had been destroyed by loggers for some human development, or expressed pain about some newly extinct species. One young man wept when describing a time when as a child he killed a bird with a slingshot, immediately and deeply regretting what he had done when he observed its beautiful but lifeless body. This experience led directly to his life of radical vegan activism; he would eventually spend several years in prison after he participated with a small group of Earth Liberation Front activists in the arson of a facility used to corral and slaughter wild horses.

After the mourning ritual, O'Connor led the group in a guided "Gaia Meditation" and a process of "evolutionary remembering" (Seed et al. 198: 41–51; 57–65). Beginning with the Big Bang, followed by the eventual formation of the Earth, the emergence and diversification of life, the emphasis was on how all life emerged from a common ancestor. This demonstrated that all living things arrived here in exactly the same way, and they are kin, they are, quite literally, biologically related. As part of this process, O'Conner asked the participants to view with one another features of their own bodies, and to contemplate their own profound connections as members of the same species. The emphasis was on the wonder of the unfolding universe and how all living things *are* Gaia.

To set up the main event, the Council of All Beings, O'Connor instructed participants to go into the forest with an open heart, alert and sensitive to an entity in nature who wished to speak through them. He emphasised that the participants should not choose those for whom they would speak but to wait until some non-human entity or life form chose them. This emphasis seemed designed to acknowledge the agency and personhood of non-human organisms and entities, and thus, to break through enculturated anthropocentrism.

After participants spent more than an hour in the forest, O'Conner used his drum to call them back. They returned to find materials were ready for them to craft a mask representative of the entity they would soon represent. Then, assembled in a circle, the Council of All Beings began.

Representing diverse organisms, as well as entities and natural forces such as swamp, mountain, wind and ocean, voices spoke of their anger, pain and frustration, at the way humans were harming them, and their diverse beloved relations, and Gaia as a whole. One of the participants rose to speak, and after a few moments, closed his eyes, and for a few moments, his entire body shook. Then, partially re-opening his eyes and gazing upward, he began to speak words supposedly from his spirit animal, in a voice entirely unlike his own. His demeanor in this was akin to those in the New Age movement who purport to provide a "channel" for the spirits of ancestors or other, earlier, human beings, or less commonly, of non-human spirits. Afterward, he told me he did not remember anything he had said, thus suggesting that a spirit of a non-human other had indeed used his body as a channel for its voice.

On this occasion participants were well acquainted with a host of environmental issues and threats to ecosystems and species. From what they spoke, it seemed to me that few if any of the others thought they were actually channeling the spirit of some natural being, force or entity. Rather, they seemed to be engaged in a kind of animistic performance art. There is, of course, typically a performative dimension to ritual. The Council of All Beings is no exception.

After this, the first part of the council during which these entities spoke to one another, was over, O'Connor asked three of those gathered to re-assume their human identities and come to the centre of the circle and sit back-to-back, facing those encircling them. Then, he asked those still in their other-than-human identities to speak directly to the humans at the centre of the circle. As they did, the emotional intensity grew, as, for example, when non-human animals expressed rage toward the humans for destroying their homes and killing their relatives, even for driving them toward extinction. But there were also expressions of fondness and a corresponding confusion toward the human representatives, about how their species could be so callous and indifferent to their sufferings.

After this part of the process, O'Connor noted that all of the humans there were working to protect life on Earth and that they faced long odds, and he invited the non-human members of the assembly to consider giving to the assembled humans their special gifts, to empower them for the ongoing struggle for life on Earth.

Once again, with creative imagination, in response, nature's voices gave their special powers to the humans: water and ice's ability to break through concrete; eagle's ability to see clearly from great heights; owl's night vision and penguin's sense of direction; mushroom's ability to turn death and decay into new life, including by awakening in humankind proper perceptions of the beauty and kinship of all life.

The intention of the ritual was in plain view: to help participants overcome their psychic pain, deepen their sympathies for the non-human world and empower them in the struggle to defend earthly life. For many of the participants, the council also functioned as rituals typically do, to bind a spiritual community together in its sacred mission. Indeed, the vulnerability these activists shared with one another created a kind of empathetic intimacy that, in some cases, led to enduring friendships.

The ritual varies significantly in different times and places, and it has taken place on nearly every continent since its invention during the late 1980s. Council facilitators often weave in evocative prose and poetry from animistic writers, including indigenous ones. Indeed, the original book explaining the ritual and how to conduct a council suggested having participants listen to and reflect on words from a speech attributed to Chief Sealth, a nineteenth-century leader of the Salish people of the Puget Sound region of what is now Washington State with the city of Seattle as its cultural centre, in the Northwestern United States. The Salish Nation has come to refer to Sealth as Chief Seattle and holds "Chief Seattle Days" celebrations annually, which is how I will refer to him here.[4]

Gaian Animism and the Mythic Chief Seattle Speech

According to an 1887 newspaper account, Chief Seattle's 1854 oration took place at a time when the U.S. government was pushing him and his people, under the threat of continued violent suppression, to agree to the sale of their traditional lands, in order to relocate them to a reservation, in exchange for a promise of protection from settlers and retention of certain livelihood rights. Seattle's oration provided inspiration for the speech that has come to bear his name. The versions that became well known, however, which was the one that the Council of All Beings inventors printed in their primer, bore little resemblance to the original oration by the Salish chief. Complicating the record further, what the chief originally said is uncertain because Henry Smith, the white physician who wrote the newspaper account, based his account upon notes (now lost to history) that he had taken during the speech more than three decades earlier.

Nevertheless, the 1887 newspaper account likely reflects the chief's 1854 sentiments (Bierwert, 1998; Kaiser, 1987; Furtwangler, 1997), which included bitterness about the deracination of his people from their lands, efforts to explain why young warriors had so long and violently resisted the white

---

4 The Salish Nation uses his better-known name. Notwithstanding this annual celebration, according to Salish anthropologist Crisca Bierwert, some Northwestern Indians considered Sealth to be a traitor who converted to Christianity and too easily accepted white hegemony (Bierwert, 1998).

invaders (presumably in part to excuse them), and his hopes "that the hostilities between us may never return".[5]

This part of the speech did not appear in what became the "Chief Seattle speech," the most widely disseminated version of which Edward "Ted" Perry, a screenwriter, crafted in 1970 for an Earth Day event.[6] Quite obviously, Perry drew on and was promoting contemporary environmental concerns and themes (Kaiser, 1987; Gifford, 2015). Although he was inspired by Seattle's speech, Perry knew, since the originally-recorded speech was really little more than a muse for his own creative prose, that what he had written ought not be called Chief Seattle's speech, and he objected to this labelling (Kaiser, 1987; Bierwert, 1998; Gifford, 2015).

There were several passages from the 1854 speech that Smith recalled, however, that likely did inspire Perry's pro-environmental version as, for example, when the chief asserted, "We are two distinct races with separate origins and separate destinies. There is little in common between us"; and, unlike the white settlers, he reportedly claimed, his people and their ancestors had a more intimate connection and love for "this beautiful world" and its "verdant valleys, its murmuring rivers, its magnificent mountains, sequestered vales and verdant lined lakes and bays" (Smith, 1887). According to Smith, Seattle also proclaimed,

> Every part of this soil is sacred in the estimation of my people. Every hillside, every valley, every plain and grove, has been hallowed by some sad or happy event in days long vanished. Even the rocks, which seem to be dumb and dead as they swelter in the sun along the silent shore, thrill with memories of stirring events connected with the lives of my people, and the very dust upon which you now stand responds more lovingly to their footsteps than yours, because it is rich with the blood of our ancestors, and our bare feet are conscious of the sympathetic touch. Our departed braves, fond mothers, glad, happy hearted maidens, and even the little children who lived here and rejoiced here for a brief season, will love these somber solitudes and at eventide they greet shadowy returning spirits (Smith, 1887).

Despite the stark contrast Seattle apparently drew between his own people and ever more numerous white settlers, Smith also recorded him as saying

---

5   The 1887 newspaper version is available at the Salish Nation website at https://suquamish.nsn.us/home/about-us/chief-seattle-speech/. Henry Smith's account was published as "The Speech of Chief Seattle" in Seattle's *Sunday Star* newspaper on 29 October 1887.
6   In his history of the various versions of the speech, Rudolf Kaiser also provided the versions in appendices (Kaiser, 1987; cf. Gifford, 2015).

that someday they might realise a "common destiny" and perhaps, "We may be brothers after all."

Although what Seattle said will remain uncertain – Salish anthropologist Crisca Bierwert concluded that the statement about the sacredness of the soil is probably authentic (Bierwert, 1998) – what is clear is that Perry's 1970 version has proven evocative and influential within the global environmental milieu. Among the most commonly cited passages from this version, for example, which appeared in the Council of All Beings primer, are those that express kinship between humans and the entire living world, and a spirituality of belonging and connection to nature, which is an affective underpinning of much contemporary environmentalism (Taylor, 2001b, 2001a, 2010a):

> The perfumed flowers
> are our sisters;
> the deer, the horse, the great eagle,
> these are our brothers.
> The rocky crests,
> the juices in the meadows,
> the body heat of the pony, and man –
> all belong to the same family…
> The Rivers are our Brothers…
> The air is precious…
>
> What is man without the beasts? If all the beasts were gone, man would die from a great loneliness of the spirit. For whatever happens to the beasts, soon happens to man. All things are connected…
>
> Whatever befalls the Earth befalls the sons of the Earth. Man did not weave the web of life; he is merely a strand in it. Whatever he does to the web he does to himself…
>
> The Earth does not belong to man – man belongs to the Earth. All things are connected.
>
> Even the white man cannot be exempt from the common destiny. We may be brothers after all. We shall see.

Rudolf Kaiser (1987) provided diverse examples of how, between 1970 and 1986, many religious texts and environmentally oriented journals reprinted such passages from Seattle's supposed speech in America and Europe, striking fertile cultural ground as environmental concerns quickened. A version that was "exhibited in the U.S. pavilion at the 1974 World Fair in Spokane, Washington" deleted the passages in which Seattle criticised white hegemony and worldviews, thereby making the tone of the speech more universal, and as Kaiser noted, "wholly ecological and nature-related in its outlook" (Kaiser 1987, 511).

The more evocative and poetic passages, especially, continued to be cited as the speech spread and became internationally influential. In 1988, for example, a year after the United Nations World Commission on Environment and Development issued its now famous study defining and promoting sustainable development, *Our Common Future* (Development) (1987), UNESCO published *Man Belongs to the Earth* (UNESCO and MAB, 1988). It took its title and its lead epigraph from the 1970 Chief Seattle speech. It thereby exemplified the sense of belonging and connection to nature so common in contemporary nature spiritualities.

Not to be outdone, the Bagels and Beans coffeeshop chain in the Netherlands printed excerpts from the World Fair version of the speech on its napkins. It included statements that "we are part of the earth" and that expressed kinship with the flowers, bear, deer, eagle and the pony (along with images of them), because "all belong to the same family". I first noticed this text in 2005 and it was still on those napkins when I returned to the Netherlands in 2020.

Although the speech from 1970, as well as subsequent versions, cannot be attributed to the Salish chief, as Kaiser concluded, the versions that were passed down did represent an authentic expression of "the mind of a sensitive Euro-American, worried about our ecological situation and the general dualism in our culture" (Kaiser, 1987: 517), who was keen to convey the idea that the entire living world is sacred.

In the decades after its invention, the Chief Seattle speech spread as rapidly as communicative technologies allowed at those times. It provides another example of Gaian Animism and how such spirituality has spread, especially since Western countercultures grew rapidly during the 1960s.[7]

The Council of All Beings was one ritual that helped to spread its influence. Rituals that survive well past their invention work for enough people who participate in them that those who value them decide to repeat and spread them. This was the case with the Council of All Beings. Seed, Macy and many others spread the ritual to many areas around the world.

The Council itself continues to be held, but from what I can tell by searching Google Trends and otherwise searching online for evidence of such events, it does not seem to be a ritual that is growing significantly in the

---

7   When considered authentic the speech exemplifies what David Chidester has called "authentic fakes", religious inventions involving false claims to authentic and authoritative sources, but that nevertheless function in the ways that religions typically do, such as providing meaning, values and assuaging existential anxieties (Chidester, 2005b).

twenty-first century. Although there are trained facilitators, those who elect to participate in the ritual must set aside considerable time to do it. In short, it is difficult to scale up. Moreover, it is not like a sacrament in some traditions, which demands repetition and that devotees are obligated to support financially. Although it is a powerful and even transformative ritual for some people, for these reasons, it does not seem to have great growth potential.

Even within a spiritual community, of course, rituals do not work for everyone. During the 1990s I attended the ritual several times and there were usually some individuals who confided to me afterward that they could not get into it, found it contrived, or said it reminded them of the religions of their upbringing from which they had fled.

Woo Woo and Ambivalence in Animistic Ritualising

Although some people invited into such processes do not find collective rituals comfortable or compelling, and few who participate in the Council end up facilitating or participating regularly in it, that does not mean, however, that those who have participated do not have affinities with an animistic worldview. During a wide-ranging conversation in 1993 with several of those who had just participated in a Wildlands Project board meeting near Tucson, Arizona, which included discussion of Animism, for example, Dave Foreman, the most charismatic of Earth First!'s founders, exclaimed, "I would rather die than go to a Council of All Beings."[8]

Foreman was not alone. Many in the movement have been critical of, and even ridiculed, some forms of explicit "woo woo", movement parlance for nature ritualising orchestrated by hippies and Pagans who had been drawn to the movement. Foreman's distaste for such ritualising, however, was more due to his personality as a private person than because he was dismissive of animistic or Gaian Spirituality.

Indeed, as the Editor of *Earth First!* during the 1980s, Foreman decided to publish the journal according to a pagan calendar and to discuss Paganism in its pages, defending these decisions and even calling himself "an out-and-out-howling-at-the-moon pantheist" (Foreman, 1982: 2). And he fervently

---

8   This conversation took place at Dave Foreman's home in Tucson, Arizona, on 24 February 1993, after a Wildlands Project board meeting that was previously held in the desert near there. Foreman died during his 75th year on 19 September 2022. For my reflections on his life, which were published in a book focusing on his influences on individuals, the environment, and culture generally, see Taylor (2023b).

believed that for humans to slow and halt the extinction crisis they must "resacralize" their perceptions of the Earth (Foreman, 1987: 22).

This perspective helps to explain why, before he withdrew from Earth First! and relinquished control of the movement's journal, he published many articles promoting animistic, Gaian, indigenous, shamanic, pagan, Daoist and Buddhist worldviews. While critical of aspects of them, he valued them to the extent that he thought they promoted the idea that nature is sacred and in need of reverent defence (Devall, 1987; Drengson, 1988; Faulstich, 1989; Frisk, 1993; Haenke, 1986; Hawkins, 1984; LaChapelle, 1986, 1989a, 1989b; LaRue, 1982; Lewis, 1989).

Foreman even praised the Wiccan author and activist Starhawk for writing, in *The Spiral Dance* (1979), what he declared was "the best religious book since the burning times" (Foreman, 1988: 35). Most of the movement's prominent leaders have expressed affinity with American Indian peoples, based on an understanding that Amerindian worldviews value the natural world more deeply than do people rooted in Western worldviews. For more than two years, for example, Foreman lived at a Zuni Pueblo in New Mexico. He later reported, "at Zuni ceremonials I learned more than I had in all the Sundays I spent in church as a kid" (Foreman, 1991: 174). During my 1990 interview with him, Foreman made a similar statement, "You know, I agree with Edward Abbey when asked what his religion and politics are. He said, 'Paiute,' referring to scores of Native American communities that before the arrival of Europeans were widely scattered around what is now the western United States."

After this, Foreman explained that his views had been shaped by scholars including Paul Shepard, who lauded foraging societies and their animistic worldviews as the ones in which people and the rest of the living world can flourish.[9]

Foreman revealed his animistic sensibilities on other occasions, such as when in 1986, after he and others were arrested in Yellowstone National Park for illegally protesting the destruction of grizzly bear habitat for a new campground, he and his fellow prisoners, while being transported in a law enforcement van, saw what they all took to be a positive omen from nature herself: a rare sighting of a "Mama Griz and two cubs". Despite feeling "silly" for considering what many would consider to be a coincidence, he wrote, "rationality be dammed. The ecstatic pagans in that bus had just received a sign from the wild!" (Foreman, 1986: 2).

---

9   Foreman specifically mentioned an influential early book by Shepard (1973), but the best starting point for Shepard's perspective is his last and posthumously published book (Shepard, 1998).

It is easy to understand why Foreman, who was a well-read environmental historian who took science seriously, might have felt silly when considering the possibility of natural entities speaking to alert and sympathetic humans. Nevertheless, he had uncanny experiences that made him reject the idea that science was the only path to knowledge. During the aforementioned group conversation in 1993, for example, after acknowledging that he was critical of and prone to ridicule much of the "woo woo" in the movement, he confided, "I do talk to trees. I think they're telling me that it's all connected." He added that he has also had "auditory hallucinations, now and then. Several times, when camping, I felt a place was telling me not to camp here. Several times that happened."[10]

During this conversation others spoke about how everything in nature has energy, and discussion followed about how the sciences are providing evidence about plant sentience and their communicative abilities. After first making clear that she is not at all woo woo, Nancy Morton, Foreman's wife and fellow activist, said that she thinks trees experience fear as the loggers approach. Then she mentioned a book by Peter Tompkins and Christopher Bird, *The Secret Life of Plants* (Tompkins and Bird, 1973), which argued that plants are sentient organisms who can communicate with other species.[11] Others then present indicated that this made sense to them because of similar experiences they have had. In that conversation, one could hear these intellectual-activists working to reconcile their scientific understandings and sensory experiences, especially those they had while in wildland ecosystems.

The day before this conversation, I had asked Foreman about his claim that to reharmonise life on earth we need to resacralise our perception of it. He answered:

> It is very difficult in our society to discuss the notion of sacred apart from the supernatural. I think that's something that we need to work on, a non-supernatural concept of sacred. A non-theistic basis of sacred. When I say I'm a non-theistic pantheist it is a recognition that what's really important is the flow of life, the process of life... [So] the idea is not to protect ecosystems frozen in time...but [rather] the grand process... of evolution... We're just blips in this vast energy field... just temporary manifestations of this life force,

---

10 Conversation with Dave Foreman, Tucson, Arizona, on 24 February 1993.
11 By all accounts of those who knew them, Morton was an exceptionally strong woman who contributed significantly to the movement Foreman once led. Later in life, Morton learned she had ALS. As a nurse, she knew what the final stages of this disease entails, so she took her own life on 16 January 2021.

which is blind and non-teleological. And so, I guess what is sacred is what's in harmony with that flow.[12]

During the 1980s, Foreman periodically wrote as Chim Blea, a pseudonym that he used to express some of his more controversial and personal thoughts. In 1983 he confessed, "I go alone into the wilderness in quest of visions. I sit in high windy places and listen to the powers of the earth" (Blea, 1983). In 1987, he wrote an essay titled "Spirituality", explaining that when he was younger he had "flirted briefly with eastern religions before rejecting them for their anti-Earthly metaphysic". This led him to become an atheist, he explained:

> until I sensed something out there. Out there in the wilderness. So, I became a pagan, a pantheist, a witch, if you will. I offered prayers to the moon, performed secret rituals in the wildwood, did spells. I placated the spirits of that which I ate or used (remember, your firewood is alive, too.) For almost ten years, I've followed my individualistic shamanism (Blea, 1987).

After this, he made it clear that he does not enjoy group ritualising, which reminds him of the organised religion that he had rejected. He also expressed ambivalence about the pagan ritualising that had become prominent at movement gatherings because of his doubts that people need these to be connected to the Earth. (Presumably he felt that he, at least, did not need them to feel a part of nature.) Spirituality might even be "a fatal flaw" that leads people to abstract thinking and to feel disconnected from nature, he further speculated. But then he conceded, "Nonetheless, we do seem to have a spiritual sense and…ritual is that which attempts, albeit imperfectly, to reconnect us." He concluded, musing, "Maybe I'll talk to the moon tonight" (Blea, 1987).

That Foreman wrote these words under his pseudonym suggests not only that he was uncomfortable with communal ritualising, but that he was reluctant to discuss his animistic perceptions and experiences beyond of small group of confidants. This passage also suggests that he recognised that, for some people, ritual facilitates felt connections to nature. And likely in part due to his experiences of having been brought up in a conservative evangelical church, Foreman's own speeches, which he regularly gave to large audiences, had some resemblance to the preachers he heard in his youth, but in his case, they promoted a very different spirituality.[13]

---

12 Interview with Dave Foreman, Tucson Arizona, 23 February 1993.
13 During the 1980s Foreman became increasingly well-known through his writings, speeches and the growing infamy of the movement he co-founded. His own infamy

Foreman's typical speech involved a mix of alarming ecological facts and humorous stories, but the one he gave most often concluded with a recitation of ecologist Aldo Leopold's famous story about when, as a young forest service timber surveyor in 1909, Leopold and a friend shot and killed a female wolf, only to see the "green fire" die in her eyes.[14] Leopold wrote evocatively about this experience, depicting it as an epiphany that taught him an important lesson, that the mountain (a metaphor for the entire natural world, or in today's parlance, Gaia), did not share his anthropocentric view that the entire natural world was made only for human beings.

At the end of the speech, Foreman would urge the assembly to recognise their own wild nature and the value of wilderness. Then, little doubt inspired by the altar calls he experienced growing up, he asked the audience to howl with him, like a wolf, in symbolic identification with all things wild. Typically, majorities of those drawn to the speeches would raucously join in the chorus of howls.

For many environmentalists, Leopold's moral fable is a sacred story, and its written form is tantamount to a sacred text (Meine, 1988; Van Horn, 2011). And through it, the wolf lives on, preaching about the value and kinship of all life. Indeed, for example, a well-received documentary, and a collection of essays and a popular radio and podcast series expressing and promoting felt kinship between humans and other living things, have all prominently featured the story (Van Horn, Kimmerer, and Hausdoerffer, 2021; Paulson and Strainchamps, 2020; Strainchamps, 2020).[15]

From Radical Environmentalism to the Global Environmental Milieu

After encountering the complicated spiritual terrain within radical environmental subcultures, I began to notice that, within the global environmental milieu, there has been increasing attention to, sympathy for, and expressed

---

and crowd sizes increased after, in 1990, the Federal Bureau of Investigation arrested and accused him of inspiring and funding several high-profile acts of sabotage, that had been designed to halt what movement activists considered to be environmentally destructive, desecrating acts, in the Southwestern United States (Taylor, 1995).

14 Susan Flader (2012: 28–30) documented the detective work that led her and fellow historian Curt Meine to find compelling evidence that dated the now famous green fire killing to 19 September 1909.

15 Leopold biographer Curt Meine co-wrote and narrated a documentary about Leopold that exemplifies how the story has become sacred to many environmentalists; see Dunsky et al. (2011).

affinity with, the kind of animistic and organicist understandings I am calling Gaian Animism.

Over time, within this milieu, there has been increasing respect for indigenous peoples and their worldviews, which are typically understood to involve kinship feelings toward non-human organisms and processes, and understandings that when it comes to the flourishing of life on earth, everything is connected. This is especially true among radical environmentalists and other civil society actors (such as in the anti-globalisation movement, the World Social Forum, and more recently, Extinction Rebellion). Many within these subcultures have affinity with organicist and animistic worldviews, and in their advocacy, they have contributed to the spread of such worldviews beyond their own green, leftist and anarchist subcultures.

Over the years I have documented the diverse forms that these sorts of spiritualities take and the ways they spread. In *Dark Green Religion* (2010), for example, I showed that those involved with such spiritualities include environmentalists and scientists, politicians and diplomats, artists, writers, musicians, filmmakers, businesspeople, teachers and museum curators, as well as mountaineers, surfers, gardeners and many others. I noted that some of these actors believe in the existence of non-material divine beings while others do not. But regardless of their metaphysical beliefs, I argued, such spiritualities typically stress ecological interdependence and mutual dependence, involve deep feelings of belonging and connection to nature and express beliefs that the biosphere is a sacred, Gaia-like superorganism. I also contended that such spiritualities were exercising increasing social and political influence.

After the book's publication I have continued to illuminate culturally important phenomena where cultural creatives are promoting dark green, Gaian Animism, as for example, in the blockbuster Film *Avatar* (Taylor, 2013), under the United Nations umbrella (Taylor, 2016, 2017), in Walt Disney's cinematic productions and theme parks (Taylor, 2019c), in Art and Science museums around the world (Taylor, 2021, 2023a) and elsewhere (Taylor, 2020).

What this work demonstrates is that if we broaden our understanding of Animism to include the forms that are naturalistic, as Graham Harvey has also spotlighted, and recognise that Animism is also typically connected to some form of ecological holism along the lines of Gaian Spirituality or Gaian Naturalism, then it becomes clear that this sort of religious phenomena is growing more rapidly, and is more prevalent and culturally significant, than is commonly recognised. A growing body of research has been documenting such trends (Taylor et al., 2016, 2020).

Although we do not yet have a firm grasp on what proportion of human populations in different regions have affinity with Gaian Animism, what does seem to be clear is that these proportions are increasing, and they will likely continue to grow in adherents, cultural expressions and political influence. They might even prove that the possibility of an emerging, global civil earth religion, or Terrapolitan Earth Civilisation, is no mere ecotopian fantasy (Deudney, 1995, 1998; Deudney and Mendenhall, 2016; Taylor, 2010a, 2010b).

References

Abram, D. 1988. "Deep ecology and magic: notes of a sleight-of-hand sorcerer", *Earth First!* 8(3): 25, 27.
Abram, D. 1989. "The perceptual implications of Gaia", *Earth First!* 9(3): 24–25.
Bierwert, C. 1998. "Remembering Chief Seattle: reversing cultural studies of a vanishing Native American", *American Indian Quarterly* 22(3): 280–304.
Blea, C. 1983. "The arrogance of enlightenment", *Earth First!* 3(7): 13.
Blea, C. 1987. "Spirituality", *Earth First!* 7(7): 23.
Chidester, D. 2005a. "Animism", in Taylor, B. (ed.), *Encyclopedia of Religion and Nature*. London and New York: Continuum International. pp. 78–81.
Chidester, D. 2005b. *Authentic Fakes: Religion and Popular American Culture*. Berkeley and Los Angeles: University of California Press.
Chidester, D. 2011. "Darwin's dogs: animals, Animism, and the problem of religion", in Lloyd, V.W. and Ratzman, E. (eds), *Secular Faith*. Oregon: Cascade Books. pp. 76–101.
Chidester, D. 2014. *Empire of Religion: Imperialism and Comparative Religion*. Chicago, IL and London: University of Chicago Press.
Deudney, D. 1995. "In search of Gaian politics: Earth religion's challenge to modern Western Civilization", in Taylor B. (ed.), *Ecological Resistance Movements: The Global Emergence of Radical and Popular Environmentalism*. Albany, New York: State University of New York Press. pp. 282–299.
Deudney, D. 1998. "Global village sovereignty: intergenerational sovereign publics, federal-republican Earth constitutions, and planetary identities", in Litfin, K. (ed.), *The Greening of Sovereignty in World Politics*. Cambridge, MA: MIT Press. pp. 299–325.
Deudney, D., and Mendenhall, E. 2016. "Green earth: the emergence of planetary civilization", in Jinnah, S. and Nicholson, S. (eds), *New Earth Politics*. Cambridge, MA and London: MIT Press. pp. 43–72.
Devall, B. 1987. "Primal peoples and deep ecology", *Earth First!* 7(7): 26.
Drengson, A. 1988. "Paganism, nature, and deep ecology", *Earth First!* 8(5): 19–20.
Dunsky, A., Dunsky, S. and Steinke, D. 2011. Green Fire: Aldo Leopold and a Land Ethic for Our Time. Directed by Dunsky, A., Dunsky, S. and Steinke, D. The Aldo Leopold Foundation, Center for Humans and Nature, and U.S. Forest Service.
Faulstich, P. 1989. "Shaman – Ritual – Place", *Earth First!* 9(8): 26.

Flader, S. 2012. "Searching for Aldo Leopold's green fire", *Forest History Today* (Fall): 26–34.
Foreman, D. 1982. "Reply to Charlie Watson's letter", *Earth First! Newsletter* 2(5): 2.
Foreman, D. 1986. "Around the campfire", *Earth First!* 6(7): 2.
Foreman, D. 1987. "Reinhabitation, biocentrism, and self defense", *Earth First!* 7(7): 22.
Foreman, D. 1988. "Review of the spiral dance", *Earth First!* 9(1): 35.
Foreman, D. 1991. *Confessions of an Eco-warrior*. New York: Harmony Books.
Frisk, T. 1993. "The goddess awakens", *Earth First!* 13(3): 21.
Furtwangler, A. 1997. *Answering Chief Seattle*. Seattle, WA: University of Washington Press.
Gifford, E. 2015. *The Many Speeches of Chief Seattle (Seathl): The Manipulation of the Record on Behalf of Religious, Political and Environmental Causes*. North Charleston, SC: CreateSpace Independent Publishing Platform.
Haenke, D. 1986. "Bioregionalism and Earth First!" *Earth First!* 7(2): 28–29.
Harding, S. 2006. *Animate Earth: Science, Intuition and Gaia*. Totnes: Green Books.
Harding, S. 2022. *Gaia Alchemy: The Reuniting of Science, Psyche, and Soul*. Rochester, VT: Bear & Company.
Harvey, G. 2005. "Animism – a contemporary perspective", in Taylor, B. (ed.), *Encyclopedia of Religion and Nature*. London and New York: Bloomsbury Academic; originally Continuum International. pp. 81–83.
Harvey, G. 2005. *Animism: Respecting the Living World*. New York: Columbia University Press.
Hawkins, R. 1984. "North American Bioregional Congress convening", *Earth First!* 4(4): 8.
Jabr, F. 2019. "The Earth is just as alive as you are: Scientists once ridiculed the idea of a living planet. Not anymore", *The New York Times* 20 April, SR4. Available at: www.nytimes.com/2019/04/20/opinion/sunday/amazon-earth-rain-forest-environment.html.
Kaiser, R. 1987. "Chief Seattle's speech(es): American origins and European reception", in Swann, B. and Krupat, A. (eds), *Recovering the Word: Essays on Native American Literature*. Berkeley and Los Angeles, CA: University of California Press. pp. 497–536.
LaChapelle, D. 1986. "Random notes on February pagan festivals", *Earth First!* 6(3): 19.
LaChapelle, D. 1989a. "Play: Crossing the artificial boundary between human and nature", *Earth First!* 9(3): 29.
LaChapelle, D. 1989b. "Thoughts on Autumn Equinox about the importance of ritual", *Earth First!* 9(8): 30.
LaRue, C. 1982. "Earth religion: Happy new year", *Earth First!* 3(1): 7.
Latour, B. 2017. *Facing Gaia: Eight Lectures on the New Climatic Regime*. Translated by Porter, C. Cambridge; Medford, MA: Polity.
Lewis, M. 1989. "Shamanism: A link between two worlds", *Earth First!* 9(8): 27–28.
Lovelock, J. 1972. "Gaia as seen through the atmosphere (letter to the editors) ", *Atmospheric Environment* 6: 579–580.
Lovelock, J. 1979. *Gaia: A New Look at Life on Earth*. Oxford and New York: Oxford University Press.

Lovelock, J. 2005. "Gaian pilgrimage", in Taylor, B. (ed.), *Encyclopedia of Religion and Nature*. London and New York: Bloomsbury Academic; originally Continuum International. pp. 683–685.
Margulis, L. 1981. *Symbiosis in Cell Evolution: Life and Its Environment on the Early Earth*. San Francisco: W.H. Freeman.
Margulis, L. and Sagan, D. 1986. *Microcosmos: Four Billion Years of Evolution from our Microbial Ancestors*. New York: Summit Books.
Meine, C. 1988. *Aldo Leopold: His Life and Work*. Madison, WI: University of Wisconsin Press.
Paulson, S. and Strainchamps, A. 2020. "Eye-to-eye animal encounters", *To the Best of our Knowledge*. Available at: www.ttbook.org/show/eye-eye-animal-encounters.
Primavesi, A. 2003. *Gaia's Gift*. London and New York: Routledge.
Ruse, M. 2013. *The Gaia Hypothesis: Science on a Pagan Planet*. Chicago, IL: University of Chicago Press.
Seed, J., Macy, J., Fleming, P. and Naess, A. 1988. *Thinking Like a Mountain: Towards a Council of All Beings*. Philadelphia, PA: New Society.
Shepard, P. 1973. *The Tender Carnivore and the Sacred Game*. New York: Scribners.
Shepard, P. 1998. *Coming Home to the Pleistocene*. San Francisco, CA: Island Press.
Smith, H. 1887. "The Speech of Chief Seattle", *Sunday Star (Seattle)* 29 October 1887. Available at: https://suquamish.nsn.us/home/about-us/chief-seattle-speech/.
Starhawk. 1979. *The Spiral Dance: A Rebirth of the Ancient Religion of the Great Goddess*. 1st edn. San Francisco, CA: Harper & Row.
Strainchamps, A. 2020. "Sharing eye-to-eye epiphanies with the animal world", *To the Best of Our Knowledge*. Available at: www.ttbook.org/node/13356.
Taylor, B. 1994. "Earth First!'s religious radicalism", in Chapple, C.K. (ed.), *Ecological Prospects: Scientific, Religious, and Aesthetic Perspectives*. Albany, NY: State University of New York Press. pp. 185–209.
Taylor, B. 1995. "Resacralizing earth: Pagan environmentalism and the restoration of Turtle Island", in Chidester, D. and Linenthal, E.T. (eds), *American Sacred Space*. Bloomington, IN: Indiana University Press. pp. 97–151.
Taylor, B. 2001a. "Earth and nature-based spirituality (part one): From deep ecology to radical environmentalism", *Religion* 31(2): 175–193.
Taylor, B. 2001b. "Earth and nature-based spirituality (part two): From deep ecology and bioregionalism to scientific Paganism and the New Age", *Religion* 31(3): 225–245.
Taylor, B. 2008. "From the ground up: Dark green religion and the environmental future", in Swearer, D. (ed.), *Ecology and the Environment: Perspectives from the Humanities*. Cambridge, MA: Center for the Study of World Religions/Harvard University Press. pp. 89–107.
Taylor, B. 2010a. *Dark Green Religion: Nature Spirituality and the Planetary Future*. Berkeley and Los Angeles, CA: University of California Press.
Taylor, B. 2010b. "Civil earth religion versus religious nationalism", *The Immanent Frame*. Available at http://blogs.ssrc.org/tif/2010/07/30/civil-earth-religion/.
Taylor, B. 2013. *Avatar and Nature Spirituality*. Waterloo, Canada: Wilfrid Laurier University Press.
Taylor, B. 2016. "The United Nations (via religion and its affiliated agencies) to the rescue in the cause of conservation?" *Journal for the Study of Religion, Nature and Culture* 10(4): 485–490.

Taylor, B. 2017. "Cultural creativity and the quest for a planetary earth civilization", in *Proceedings of the Second International Seminar on Environment, Culture and Religion – Promoting Intercultural Dialogue for Sustainable Development*, UNESCO and UNEP. Tehran and Nairobi: UNESCO/UNEP. pp. 180–193.

Taylor, B. 2019a. "An ecocentric journey", *The Ecological Citizen* 2 (Supplement A): 6–10. Available at: https://bit.ly/Ecojourney.

Taylor, B. 2019b. "Animism, tree-consciousness, and the religion of life: reflections on Richard Powers' The Overstory", *Minding Nature* 12(1): 42–47. Available at: http://bit.ly/OverstoryBackstory.

Taylor, B. 2019c. "Rebels against the Anthropocene? Ideology, spirituality, popular culture, and human domination of the world within the Disney empire", *Journal for the Study of Religion, Nature and Culture* 13(4): 414–454.

Taylor, B. 2020. "Dark green religion: A decade later", *Journal for the Study of Religion, Nature, and Culture* 14(4): 496–510.

Taylor, B. 2021. "Kinship through the senses, arts, and sciences", in Van Horn, G., Kimmerer, R.W. and Hausdoerffer, J. (eds), *Kinship: Belonging in a World of Relations (Volume 1)*. Libertyville, IL: Center for Humans and Nature Press. pp. 30–47.

Taylor, B. 2023a. "Bounding paganism: Who and what is in and out, and what does this reveal about contemporary kinship-entangled nature spiritualities?" *Journal for the Study of Religion, Nature and Culture* 17(3): 330–358.

Taylor, B. 2023b. "Dave Foreman: Wise guy", in Morgan, S. and Miles, J.C. (eds), *Wildeor: The Wild Life and Living Legacy of Dave Foreman*. Essex, NY: Essex Editions. pp. 205–216.

Taylor, B., LeVasseur, T. and Wright, J. 2020. "Dark green humility: Religious, psychological, and affective attributes of proenvironmental behaviors", *Journal of Environmental Studies and Science* 10(1): 41–56.

Taylor, B., Van Wieren, G. and Zaleha, B.D. 2016. "The greening of religion hypothesis (part two): Assessing the data from Lynn White, Jr., to Pope Francis", *Journal for the Study of Religion, Nature and Culture* 10(3): 306–378.

Tompkins, P. and Bird, C. 1973. *The Secret Life of Plants*. 1st edn. New York: Harper & Row.

Tyrrell, T. 2013. *On Gaia: A Critical Investigation of the Relationship between Life and Earth*. Princeton, NJ: Princeton University Press.

UNESCO, and MAB. 1988. *Man Belongs to the Earth: International Cooperation in Environmental Research*. Paris: UNESCO-MAB.

Van Horn, G. 2011. "Fire on the mountain: ecology gets its narrative totem", *Journal for the Study of Religion, Nature and Culture* 5(4): 437–464.

Van Horn, G., Kimmerer, R.W. and Hausdoerffer, J. 2021. *Kinship: Belonging in a World of Relations (5 volumes)*. Libertyville, IL: Center for Humans and Nature Press.

WCED (World Commission on Environment and Development). 1987. *Our Common Future*. Available at www.un-documents.net/wced-ocf.htm. Paris: United Nations.

About the Author

Bron Taylor is Professor of Religion and Environmental Ethics at the University of Florida. An interdisciplinary environmental studies scholar, he explores through the lenses of the sciences and humanities the complex relationships and influences among worldviews, values, ideologies, and socioecological systems. His books include *Dark Green Religion: Nature Spirituality and the Planetary Future* (2010), *Avatar and Nature Spirituality* (2013) and *Ecological Resistance Movements* (1995). He is also editor of the award-winning *Encyclopedia of Religion and Nature* (2005) and in 2017 received a Lifetime Achievement award from the International Society for the Study of Religion, Nature and Culture. See also www.brontaylor.com and at Twitter/X @BronTaylor.

10 Rituals, Wood, Bone, and Stone: Material Approaches to Indigenous Religions

Amy R. Whitehead

Introduction

Academic attention to Indigenous religions has grown steadily since the 1990s in parallel with increased attention to the "lived" and material dimension of religions. These interrelated moves in scholarship have been powered by the foundational scholarship of Graham Harvey. By guiding attention toward the significance of the everyday relationships between things, places, bodies, food, peoples, languages, rituals and performances, Harvey's work has pushed the boundaries of our discipline in rich and exciting ways. In particular, Harvey's "new animism", and the ethical relationality it presupposes, offers a dynamic framework from which to draw out and re-imagine the lived, vernacular and quotidian as central to Religious Studies. Indeed, reflecting Harvey's work with Māori friends and colleagues in Aotearoa-New Zealand, his scholarship is now an established part of an academic *whakapapa* (a Māori concept indicating layers that are built upon, a heritage, or genealogy) that is useful to the advancement of scholarship about how we, as researchers, might behave, treat and operate respectfully toward the various inhabitants of the "living world" (including people, hedgehogs and things).

In the spirit of salutation and admiration for my teacher and dear friend Graham Harvey, this chapter demonstrates (1) how Harvey's research has inspired the development of a material approach to exploring Indigenous religions. This approach draws out the dynamic relationships between animism, material religion, the environment and Indigenous religions, and offers a set of working guidelines, possibilities and considerations from which to think/re-think and practically (and respectfully) approach Indigenous objects, many of whom are better understood as persons, or subjects, in the field. It (2) explores the ways in which a material approach articulates the nature of Indigenous material cultures (and the wood, stone and bone from whence they are crafted) and their positions within their wider cosmological networks of kinship relations. These networks are comprised of stories, narratives, genealogies and materials that have their own *whakapapa*, all of which offer lenses on different ontological perspectives. Consequently, ritual protocols and performances are addressed as the processual, visual and dynamic elements that put human and non-human relations in motion. Drawing primarily on my own experience living and working in Aotearoa-New Zealand, the chapter (3) argues that employing a material approach to learning about, and with, Indigenous religions affords a further step toward forming decolonising perspectives that can inspire new ways of ethnographic knowing for our field. Combining a material approach with Harvey's method of "guesthood" (2003) in the final section, the chapter offers a suite of suggestions for respectful researcher engagements with Indigenous peoples (listening, learning, reciprocity, being a "good guest"), and how we might approach the other-human-persons who inhabit a pluriverse of worlds.

Indigenous Material Religions

"Indigenous religions" as a category in the study of religions was pioneered in the 1990s by the work of both Graham Harvey and James Cox. Developed as a "…comparative term steadily replacing labels like 'primitive' or 'tribal'" (Harvey, 2022: 59), interest in Indigenous religions has grown exponentially. The concept of "Indigenous religions" is, however, contested – and rightly so. Both terms, "indigenous" and "religion", carry their own theoretical baggage, and each reflects an historical set of power relations that correspond with the enduring resonances of colonisation. Reflecting on the practical deployment of the term "Indigenous religions", Siv Ellen Kraft et al. ask:

> In what ways do discourses about indigenous religion (in the singular) impact articulations of indigenous religions (in the plural) and vice versa? Who speaks about indigenous religion, when, where, to whom, for which reasons, on which scales, and with what consequences? How are indigenous and religious registers – acts, words, gestures, material objects, or assemblages that somehow index indigeneity and religion – means through which people recognise each other, form alliances, and distinguish themselves from others? (2020: 1–2)

These questions can be broached in the first instance by critically unpacking the term "Indigenous". Indigenous refers to a vast range of diverse societies with distinct kinship systems, mythologies and cosmologies, and groups who are both identified as Indigenous, and who identify themselves as such, live in all corners of the globe (the Pacific/Australasia, Africa, Asia,

Europe, the Middle East, North, Central and South America). It is also a term that, as Sarah Byrne (et al.) tells us, "has come into common use only since the mid-1970s through the prominence of globalized indigenous rights movements and the work of the United Nations and associated groups that have championed the shared experiences of marginalized peoples" (2013: 9). Currently, however, Harvey tells us that the term "Indigenous" "links diverse nations and language groups (e.g. Evenki, Lakota, Māori, Sámi and Yorùbá) and is of increasing value in enabling collaborations between such communities, especially as they celebrate cultural vitality and affirm their sovereignty" (2022: 57). Indigenous, then, is complex. Not only is it used as a self and group identifier that "rests on articulations of historical experiences with colonialism, assimilation policies, and loss of territory and sovereignty" (Kraft et al., 2020: 3), but it is also a tool for empowerment, capable of both operationalising and unifying once marginalised voices.

Another contested terminological question concerns whether or not the term "religion", with its contested, colonial past and imposition on the cultures of "other", non-Western traditions, is even useful in relation to Indigenous traditions and lifeways (see Chryssides and Whitehead, 2022). This contestation is reflected in Malory Nye's suggestion that, apart from the ability of the term "religion" to "create a conceptual space for understanding particular discourses" (1999: 222), when used as a noun and treated as a static thing, religion does not reflect the wider, complex elements of human experience within which it (whatever it is) sits. Instead, Nye helpfully offers to shift the paradigm from "religion" (noun) to "religioning" (verb) as an alternative for capturing the lived dynamics of the processes involved in the work and play regarding how religion is done (Nye, 1999: 230).

Much like a chrysalis in a butterfly's pupal life stage, the notion of "Indigenous religions" is caught in a concurrent, creative and uncomfortable process of tension and disentanglement. These processes include a host of sensually engaged practices, rituals, concepts and possibilities that, if taken as social facts, can signal new ways of bridging perceived ontological disparities between, for example, European and Indigenous religionings. To this effect, taking the reins of the opportunities (and subsequent challenges) afforded by combining "Indigenous" with "religion", the terms are being met head on by Indigenous and non-Indigenous scholars alike (see Harvey, 2022). This is due, in part, to the commitment that some non-Indigenous scholars of religions have to decolonising their scholarship (Harvey, 2022: 59) combined with the emergence of Indigenous scholars and associated networks who are speaking up and about what these terms mean for themselves (Harvey, 2022). For example, Indigenous scholar Jace Weaver offers his definition of Indigenous religious traditions as:

(1) local as opposed to world religions; (2) tied to specific peoples or geographic locations, and thus not proselytizing; (3) based upon oral tradition rather than texts; and (4) wholly within the hands of the practitioners themselves to define (2015: 321–22).

Although the "World Religions" paradigm is also contested and problematised as not adequately reflecting the diversity of "lived" religions in their geographic locations (see Taira, 2022; Harvey, 2017: 74), Weaver's definition draws out how Indigenous worlds, lifeways and cosmologies place emphasis on belonging to specific places and communities. In many cases, such as in the Native American Church in the US, the Ratana religion in New Zealand, Cargo Cults of Papua New Guinea or the Regla de Ochá or Lucumí religion of Cuba, Indigenous religions can be visibly perceived as a mix of colonial and Indigenous, or diasporic influences. They can also be something altogether new, reflecting Bettina Schmidt's concept of "religious bricolage" (Schmidt, 2022: 129–130). Whatever form an Indigenous religion takes, the category appropriately demands not only attention, but approaches that skilfully and respectfully hold the future of scholarship in tension with an acknowledged difficult and colonial past. A material approach to Indigenous religions carries the potential of helping us navigate these complex and troubled waters.

As indicated, the 1990s was clearly a decade of shifting paradigms. In addition to the adoption of Indigenous Religions as a category, it also saw the material turn in the study of religions begin to take root. This turn to the stuff of cultures was both accompanied and informed by renewed interest in folklore studies, out of which came the study of lived or "vernacular religion" – a term coined by the late Leonard Primiano (1995). Primiano's objective to redress "a heritage of scholarly misrepresentation, in what I [Primiano] see as the necessary methodological reflexivity on the ethnographic process" (1995: 42) took hold. It seems the time was fertile for challenging the status quo upheld by historians, anthropologists, folklorists and scholars in the study of religions who had "consistently named religious people's beliefs in residualistic, derogatory ways as 'folk,' 'unofficial,' or 'popular' religion, and have then juxtaposed these terms on a two-tiered model with 'official religion'" (1995: 38). For Primiano, this juxtaposition implied "that religion somewhere exists as a pure element which is in some way transformed, even contaminated, by its exposure to human communities" (1995: 39). Advancing and clarifying Primiano's work, Marion Bowman writes:

> Vernacular Religion is closely associated with the study of folk religion but is *not* a synonym for folk religion; it's a new concept that builds upon the insights,

subject matter and methodologies of the folkloristic and fieldwork-based approach to the study of religion (2022: 43).

This series of turns and movements came together in the 1990s to form what might be considered a transformative *zeitgeist* of the time, which continued to grow through the 2000s and laid the ground for a paradigm shift. Here, scholars such as Bowman, Harvey, and others began demonstrating interest in the materialities through which religions were lived (handled, treated, used, spoken with) in both everyday and in more highly ritualised performances. For Harvey, alongside the PhD students his research inspired (myself included), religion was to be approached as a sensual, earthy, performative, tactile, material and embodied affair. Seeded during this fertile time, it is no wonder that one of the main influential factors currently "propelling attention toward Indigenous religions is the radical and exciting emphasis on lived religion and material religions [that are] giving new life to the academic Study of Religions" (Harvey and Whitehead, 2018: 1).

Relationality and Other-Than-Human Persons

Indigenous cosmologies are relational. Yet as a common feature they include the incorporation of place-related sites from which generative stories, analogies and metaphors (coded in cosmological narratives) inform culturally specific ontologies, or ways of being in the world (Cajete, 2000: 62). Writing about the breadth, shape and composition of Amazonian Tanimuka and Yukuna cosmologies, Elizabeth Reichel tells us that Indigenous cosmological dynamics, or "cosmo-dynamics", are "composed of horizontal linkages between peoples and habitats, and also of vertical linkages connecting peoples with the skies, world and underworlds through material and spiritual dynamics" (2012: 127). The material-spiritual, cosmo-dynamics presented in Amazonian and other Indigenous cosmologies are living, and work with, and transform the raw materials that are assembled to make up Indigenous material/spiritual worlds.

Sharing features with Amazonian and other Indigenous perspectives, and because I am currently writing from the context of Aotearoa New Zealand, the Māori world comprises a complex web of relations whereby the environment is experienced as a community of interconnected persons, only some of whom are human. All of these persons descend from the sky father, Ranginui, and earth mother, Papatūānuku (or Rangi and Papa), including a range of other *atua* (gods, spirits). Mentioned in the introduction, the Māori concept (knowledge, or philosophical construct) of *whakapapa* acknowledges that "all things have an origin (in the form of a primal ancestor from which they are descended), and that ontologically things come into being through the process of descent from an ancestor or ancestors" (Roberts, 2013: 93). From this we can see how the sky, the stars, trees, plants, animals, fish, the land, woodlands, oceans, spirits, gods, fellow humans, ancestors and rivers are all related, and that each has a special place in the cosmic family tree.

An example of how this cosmology directly relates to the creation of Māori material cultures can be seen in how the offcuts and chips of wood or stone that remain after a carving are respectfully returned to the earth. Because all things originate from Rangi and Papa, carving stone or wood is likened to the cutting of bone, or the body of the gods. The wood for a *whakairo* (carving) is part of Tāne (god of the forest), and the felling of trees such as the tōtara are accompanied by special rituals that if not undertaken correctly, could be taken as life-threatening (Neich, 2001: 162).

Similarly, the *pounamu* (New Zealand jade, or greenstone) for Māori is highly valued. It is *taonga* (treasure) and is found only in a small number of sites on the South Island. In the past it would have been used as a weapon, and some of its continued uses include that of tools, revealing authority and social status, adornment (pendant or earrings), or for making peace. Like the tōtara tree, it occupies a firm place in Māori cosmology (i.e. it has a creation story and is protected by a *taniwha*, or guardian), and it is playing a role in Māori cultural revitalisation efforts; making the decision to wear a *pounamu* is not to be taken lightly. The stone must always be gifted. Foods provide further examples of things with *whakapapa* that can also constitute forms of material religion. Vegetables grown from the earth can therefore be included as further sites for conversations about Indigenous religious material cultures.

Mere Roberts (2013) uses the example of the kūmara (*Ipomea batatas*, or sweet potato) as the ideal non-human who has *whakapapa*. Kūmara is a species valued by Māori. Like all things in the Māori world, the kūmara has a rich and complex migration story. Roberts writes:

> Māori knowledge concerning the origin and relationships of material things such as the kūmara is visualized as a network of time-space co-ordinates arranged upon a genealogical framework called whakapapa… The past (personified as ancestors) is still present and continues to impact on events today; so that each planting and harvest of the kūmara is a reenactment of the circumstances surrounding its origins… Relationships extend beyond the biological to material objects such as stars, as well as spiritual and historical things which are all perceived as somehow related in space-time (Roberts, 2013: 97).

In this inclusive cosmology, no thing is left out. Following Miguel Astor-Aguilera and Harvey's understanding that a "thing" "functions both as a reference to objects and also (drawing on historical Norse and Anglo-Saxon terminology) as a synonym for 'assemblies'" (2018: 2), Indigenous "things" such as the *Pou* carving illustrated in Figure 10.1 is not just a piece of wood.

Figure 10.1 *Pou*. Artist: Whiu Waata (Ngā Puhi). Carved from a tōtara log. Photo taken by Amy Whitehead, 2022.

Similar to the kūmara, it cannot be understood as "one thing" but as a relational assemblage of component parts that includes Māori understandings about time (where the past is still present and continues to impact on events today), stories, trees, its process of being crafted and the rituals undertaken by the carver to ensure safety. Ritual safety precautions are needed because when one deals in wood one is dealing directly with Tāne, god of the forest, which is dangerous business. More than art or artefact, then, such rich cosmological assemblages coalesce with an appreciation for, enhanced understanding and respectful treatment of the materials that occur naturally (wood, stone) and the food that is grown from the land to which the people, spirits, ancestors, and gods belong. Indeed, they are ensembles of different beings.

Indicated in his edited collection *Indigenizing Movements in Europe*, Harvey (2020) draws on Paul C. Johnson's notion of indigenising as another possibility for understanding aspects of Indigenous religions. In this collection, Harvey distinguishes "…Indigenous peoples from the European Pagan and other groups who *indigenize* [my emphasis] or extend their repertoires of ideas, practices and/or discourses" (2020: 1). This last reflects the processual nature of indigenising that be seen in some of the European movements that began to emerge in late twentieth and early twenty-first centuries, and includes traditions such as British Bear Feasts, Irish Paganism, Druidry, Powwows in the UK, the Glastonbury Goddess movement, and more (see Harvey, 2020). Whether or not European movements such as those outlined in Harvey's collection can, should, or could possibly be considered "Indigenous" continues to be an issue of rigorous debate. The types of indigenising discussed in the contributions to Harvey's edited collection accounts primarily for actions being taken by contemporary Pagan groups to re-direct attention toward the earth, and therefore establish more respectful, considered, animist relationships. In my own research among Glastonbury Goddess Pagans in the Southwest of England (Whitehead, 2019), I found that many of the efforts to indigenise were done primarily through a complex mix of the re-telling different stories about Avalon (Glastonbury's mythical counterpart) combined with creative and ad hoc ritualisation and the creation of their material cultures. For example, the material used to craft the Temple Goddess statues is willow that has been locally grown and sourced from the Glastonbury levels (the land surrounding the town) (Figure 10.2). Interviews with Goddess Temple members revealed how the willow is understood to be indigenous to Glastonbury, which gives it a special value and quality. This understanding reinforces their perspective that anything grown or born in Glastonbury comes from, and is therefore indigenous to, the body of the Goddess herself (Whitehead, 2020).

Figure 10.2 Glastonbury Goddess Temple, Willow Goddess statues. Photo taken by Amy Whitehead, 2013.

Indigenis-*ing* as a verb-like conceptual tool is helpful in these instances because, similarly to Nye's concept of "religioning", it is more a visible, active style of relating than a fixed label (such as "religion"). In the case of the Glastonbury Goddess religion, the Goddess both belongs to and forms part of the land. Her devotees are not indigenous to Glastonbury. Therefore, their creative material practices that use materials sourced from the land act as the prime medium through which this movement strategically indigenises and engages with more respectful engagements with the environment.

These relational cosmologies signal ontologically unique ways of being in the world. They are animist; and along with those individuals who

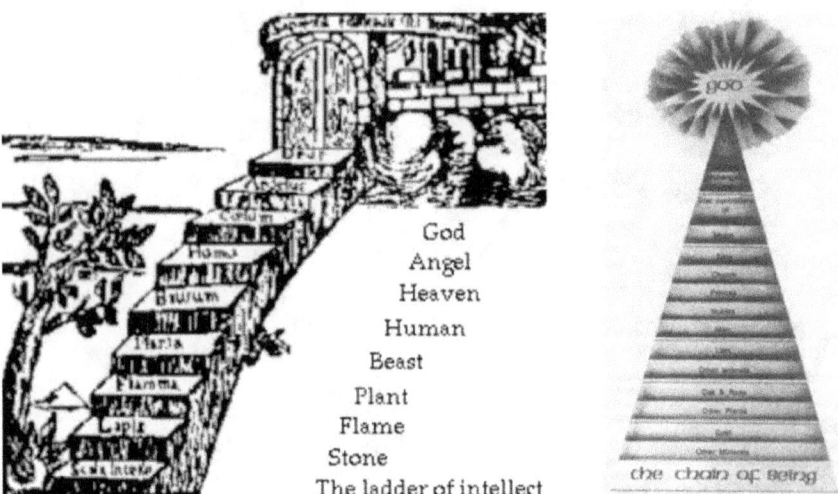

Figure 10.3 The Ladder of the Intellect.

self-identify as animists (the numbers of which have grown particularly since Harvey coined the term "new animism" in 2005), they perceive, know and understand the world as relational. This differs significantly from Christian and traditionally Western cosmological orientations which are mostly hierarchical and can be effectively illustrated using the visual of the Ancient Greek philosophical *Scala Naturae*, the Ladder of the Intellect and, later, the medieval Christian Great Chain of Being (Figure 10.3).

Here, stones, beasts, and plants are positioned on the bottom, above which beasts, humans, heaven, angels ascend before arriving at God. This illustration provides a visual indication of Christian cosmological understandings about, and consequent treatment of, both nature and matter. In the Māori cosmic family tree, a *pounamu*/greenstone would not occupy a lower rung on the ladder because the ladder does not exist.

Remnants of the *Scala Naturae*, however, remain structurally intact in modern (religious and academic) discourses and continue to be identifiable in Cartesian separations between subject and object, nature and culture, mind (or spirit) and matter, or tangible and intangible. Modern and Protestant biases against materiality have long tails in both the academy and in wider Western cultural discourses, and they have had an enduring impact on how the so-called "strange beliefs" and practices of putative "superstitious others" (suggesting "other-than-Christian") have been presented and framed (typically in contrast to scientific advancement, logic, linear time, progress and social evolution). As I have argued elsewhere, bias against materiality (and ritual) is intricately related to how "others" have been pejoratively labelled as superstitious (Whitehead, 2022: 125). These biases are even further challenged when faced, not only with the realities of Indigenous material cultures, but with the realities of how Europeans in different religious contexts live alongside, honour and treat the objects of their devotion. For example, evidence drawn from my ethnographic research among religious statues in Spain and England naturally segued into the understanding that some objects, in some instances, may be more accurately understood as subjects. Here, I built on Harvey's new animism research to argue that religious statues can have personhood that exists beyond human affordances (Whitehead, 2013). Sonia Hazard's work on the new materialism and the material turn in the study of religions is a further development in this move away from anthropocentrism in the study of religions and materiality (2013: 64).

Yet as Bruno Latour told us, even the most popular theories "are not sufficient to describe the many entanglements of humans and non-humans" (Latour, 2005: 84). The lack of being able to fully account for (and therefore continually grapple with) human and non-human engagements reflects both a problem of language, and of the aforementioned, ongoing, traditionally (if not geographically) Western, modern, Cartesian problem of materiality where putative objects are subdued and often treated as distinct from subjects. However, because Indigenous religious cosmologies are inclusive and non-dualistic, human and non-human entanglements do not need to suffer at the hands of a culturally cognitive disconnect.

As anyone who has read Harvey's *Animism: Respecting the Living World* (2005) can attest, language is one of animism's facilitating factors. Indeed, according to Maureen Matthews and Roger Roulette, in some cultures there is "an intriguing class of grammatically animate objects" (2018: 175). Matthews and Roulette are referring to the classic ethnographic conversation that took place between Irving Hallowell (an anthropologist) and Alec Keeper, Kiiwiich (a medicine man). In his fieldwork account, Hallowell said: "Since stones are grammatically animate, I once asked an old man: Are all the stones we see about us here alive? He reflected a long while and then replied, 'No! But some are'" (Hallowell, 1960: 24). Harvey, reflecting on this, writes:

> If not all stones are alive "but some are", how does someone encountering a stone tell the difference? It certainly makes a difference, not only grammatically and in other speech acts, but also in the way a stone is treated. People are spoken with and acted towards differently than objects (2005: 36).

In my own work on the material and performance cultures of religions, this is one of my most used and beloved Harvey quotes. Herein lies the seeds of the theory of relationality, a hint toward a proposed ethnographic practice toward a treatment of (seemingly inanimate) things, and a lens on Indigenous ontological perspectives that is capable of assisting in the decolonisation of the study of religions. To this effect, Andrew Jones and Nicole Boivin suggest that animism is a "participatory framework for understanding the place of human beings in the world (by participation is meant the close engagement between humans and other-than-human beings)" (2010: 343). A participatory framework is not only useful for conceptual considerations that move us away from *Scala Naturae*-like structures for understanding human and other-than-human relations; a participatory framework indicates action and "treatment", which includes addressing certain objects in ways that indicate both their personhood and their roles in the wider cosmological schema. The relational discourse of animism, therefore, helps conceptually understand (and practically treat, if appropriate) the persons who exist in, for example, Māori cosmologies. Here, and similar to (but not the same as) William Beren's account of stones, there are unique kinds of persons – some of whom are object-persons (or subjects) who have their own special place in the cosmic family tree.

Harvey, however, necessarily points out the fatigue that now accompanies many scholars as they feel obliged to repeatedly explain their post-Cartesian position. He writes:

> Many of us involved in what might be called the "New Animism," the "Material Turn," and/or the "New Materialism" are tired of having to explain that these are not curious belief systems but ways of behaving in a world that is, without question, thoroughly relational (Harvey, 2018: 35).

In other words, moderns have relationships with religious objects and material cultures too; it is just that researchers, particularly those living in Western European countries, are continuing to deal with the tensions associated with a long tail of modern and Protestant bias against materiality still found within our scholarship. The fatigue associated with repetitiously explaining "the problem of materiality" is, however, understandable. Yet as more established ways of thinking about things intersect and overlap with the growth indicated here, a paradigm shift is occurring that may simply require both endurance and patience. In other words, a slow burn is preferable to a quick fuse if real post-Cartesian change is to take hold. This is particularly true for traditionally Western countries whose cosmological and philosophical structural roots reach into the past as far as the ancient Greco-Roman world. The fact that there is a growing number of scholars experiencing the fatigue associated with having to explain the nondualist position of animism (myself included) is a good sign because it is indicative of an undeniable advance in scholarship where relationality is becoming normalised and used beyond a specific group of scholars. At some point, the drum will no longer require banging. This is yet another marker of Harvey's successful contribution to scholarship; indeed, it solidifies the unique place of his ideas in the network of kinship relations that now comprise our academic family tree, or *whakapapa*.

A Material Approach to Knowing

As scholars in the study of religions respond to world issues such as social and environmental (in)justice, climate change, gender and economic inequality, decolonisation, object repatriation (such as seen in the famous case of the Benin Bronzes among others) and cultural reparations, new approaches are required that are capable of (a) articulating problems, while (b) simultaneously offering solutions and revealing new opportunities for growth. This last section, therefore, builds on some of Harvey's ideas about animism and personhood to both inform a set of working guidelines, processes, and suggestions about how scholars might practically approach, participate with, and know (as best they can) the Indigenous religious material cultures they encounter in the field. As indicated, this is because animist personhood is dependent on relationships, e.g. some things (such as kūmara, *whakairo*, *pounamu* and wicker Goddess statues) are living, not in the same way that human-persons are alive, but because they have their own *whakapapa*, and are related with, understood, performed for, ritualised and treated in ways that tell us they are "more-than-human" persons.

This understanding (that bodies, actions and what are normally considered inanimate objects can be persons) may, however, make some scholars uneasy because the notion that things can be persons sits outside of their normal ontological frame of reference. In fact, Indigenous material cultures, because they are non-dualistic and capable of housing cosmologies as well as ontological perspectives, provide both a challenge and an opportunity from which to actively decolonise scholarly perspectives and know differently.

As a first suggestion for a material approach, then, it would be pertinent for researchers approaching the field of Indigenous religious material cultures to begin with the classic anthropological practice of cultural relativism. This may include a few moments of self-reflection about one's positionality regarding how a "subject" might be treated in relation to an "object". This exercise may also include reflecting on the study of religion's colonial legacy, and a further act of identifying the power relations associated with the term "religion" (see Smith, 1998: 269). Returning again briefly to the Māori notion of time where the past and the present are together in the same "space-time", the recognition of our scholarly past is significant because the peoples with whom we speak will often carry

> ...painful histories, many of which are within living memory, of their languages and traditional, religious practices being discouraged, made illegal, penalised, and reduced to being false, erroneous, or superstitious by missionaries and other proponents of colonialism (Whitehead, 2023).

Further, and significantly, many of the justifications for the abuses endured by Indigenous peoples were based on what missionaries and colonisers in a broad range of cultural contexts represented as superstitious, primitive, not true religion, and therefore dangerous. Therefore scholars who wish to carry out fieldwork or learn more about Indigenous, material religions should make themselves aware of these past abuses and their consequences, including how many precious *taonga* (not only in New Zealand, but all over the world), have been stolen, retained or put on display in museums. Luckily, however, changes toward more respectful curation and exercises in repatriation are increasingly common. This last gets to the heart of a material approach to Indigenous religions: it requires being prepared to engage with a series of difficult questions, negotiations and conversations with and about things, while understanding that the same things, when using animism and personhood as a participatory framework, offer renewed opportunities for helping us learn to decolonise our scholarly perspectives.

A further contribution to our academic *whakapapa*, Harvey's article "Guesthood as Ethical Decolonising Research Method" (2003), advances a method for research that can help buffer some of the difficulties found in approaching Indigenous (and other) religions. Harvey suggests that the dualism found in the method of participant observation facilitates an unnecessary distance between "researcher" and "researched". He writes:

> Guesthood arises as another relationship distinct from that between insiders and outsiders, or participants and observers. Guest-researchers recognise the powerful priority, sovereignty, and intellectual property rights of hosts, especially as they wait to know whether they will be made guest or enemy by hosts/locals. They recognise that knowledge is gained in relationships, performance, negotiation and that these require active presence and a fuller participation than that available even to those who deem themselves participant observers (2003: 142).

My own knowledge and experienced gained by working in Aotearoa-New Zealand dictates that if researchers are invited to spend time with Indigenous groups (which is not always guaranteed), no matter their status in their own culture, they will do so as students who are eager to learn ways of being in the world that are different to their own. In fact, researchers who would like to learn about Indigenous religions understand that Indigenous sovereignty over knowledge and processes for knowing must be placed front and centre, and that respectful, reciprocal relationships must be developed with a substantial amount of patience over time.

Having taken the time to enter into consultation to gain permissions, learn the history, correct etiquette, rituals and protocols of engagement *before* approaching a particular site of interest, an object-oriented approach that combines Harvey's animism and practice of guesthood can commence. A good guest-researcher might, for example, begin by asking: "Can you tell me about this thing?" This approach serves as an ethnographic buffer that can direct an outsider-observer's gaze by showing interest in a particular thing. Naturally, things will inspire and evoke feelings and interpretations in their own right; but significantly, things serve as excellent conversation starters. This can include the method of "object elicitation" whereby the researcher identifies an object such as the *pounamu* (green stone) worn by a participant and then asks the wearer questions that relate to, for example, the *pounamu*'s story, how the wearer came across the stone (which often needs to be gifted, not bought), how it is treated, and what the act of wearing it means for its bearer. I have proposed elsewhere that (Whitehead, 2020), if treated correctly, in some instances, objects can be used as participants in our research.

Researchers should be able, then, to ascertain how a thing (a) is understood (as an ancestor, kin or simply an object); (b) if it is forbidden to touch; (c) is addressed or spoken with; (d) is gendered; (e) is positioned, treated, cared for or displayed (whether next to, or not next to, other objects). Having paid attention, guest-researchers can then address objects in the same way as their hosts. They are not only open to treating Indigenous material cultures as persons; they realise that some things (think Hallowell's conversation with William Berens) can be teachers. From this they will be interested in learning the biographies, origin and creation stories that illustrate how the objects came into being, and what journeys they have endured (such as the kūmara). In other words, good guest-researchers realise that no object comes alone. Drawing a parallel with how Māori understand that they always carry their ancestors with them, guest-researchers never treat an object as a stand-alone, individual thing without connection to other persons and things. As established, in the cases of Indigenous material cultures, these things form part of a wider cosmological whole and should therefore be treated as such.

Returning to the examples of *Pou* carvings from the tōtara tree, willow Goddess figures, or *pounamu*, every *thing* has a story; and each story can be a lens on a particular ontological perspective. It is the job of the researcher to learn those stories prior to engagement, after which the details of the relationship between objects and their wearers or users can be explored.

Significantly, a material approach considers the whole artefact, as well as the "materials of the materiality" (see Ingold, 2007). As established, source materials (willow and tōtara trees, jade) are embedded within rich, genealogical cosmo-dynamics. More than an appreciation, the recognition of the personhood of raw materials found in the examples provided in this chapter illustrate further lines of potential inquiry. In some instances, a researcher may be invited to touch or handle particular things. This can be opportune. As Michel Serres suggests: "Pure touch gives access to information, a soft correlate of what was once called the intellect" (2008: 83). In other words: "To touch something is to gain knowledge of it, or to know it, and the knowledge gained through 'touch' can be referred to as 'full-bodied' knowledge. And 'touch-informed knowledge', as Serres suggests, is not oriented towards the mind exclusively; it requires the participation of the sum of all our parts" (Whitehead, 2018: 229). Using touch to move beyond "mind" and into "full-bodied" participation with Indigenous materialities (if appropriate and invited) is one building block in an overall decolonising strategy for the study of Indigenous and other religions that puts the notion of animism as a participatory framework into practice. It also reflects the significance of taking the parts of the whole, or the materials of Indigenous religious material cultures, seriously. It can be suggested that actions such as these illustrate a willingness to suspend bias and, if not to fully participate, then to at least experiment with being a non-anthropocentric, post-Cartesian, animist-researcher-person.

Last, in the beforementioned instances such as where painful memories about past abuses and ceremonial objects persist, respectful participation may mean doing nothing at all. Understanding that it may not be appropriate to have revealed some knowledges about certain things is also the sign of a good guest-researcher. Sometimes, it is simply not appropriate, or even ethical, to know. Eduardo Viveiros de Castro (2004: 483) writes:

> anthropology is practiced as if its paramount task were to explain how it comes to know (to represent) its object – an object also defined as knowledge (or representation). Is it possible to know it? Is it decent to know it? Do we really know it, or do we see it (and ourselves) through a glass, darkly?

In our positions as researchers, we must also know our limits. As if "seeing through a glass darkly", we cannot assume to know Indigenous material cultures with the same understandings as those who were born and raised alongside them in context. Materiality is, however, the meeting ground for Indigenous and non-Indigenous perspectives – all religions, traditions and cosmologies craft, create, utilise and engage with "things" as lived religious expressions. Contributing to our pursuit of more widely applicable cultural forms of relationality, Ingold suggests: "Knowing must be reconnected with being, epistemology with ontology, thought with life. Thus has our rethinking of indigenous animism led us to propose the re-animation of our own, so-called 'western' tradition of thought" (2006: 19). Indigenous religious material cultures, combined with the advances made by Harvey's new animism and guesthood methodology, are helping us to un-learn, re-learn and therefore re-animate our thinking about the world and to know better.

References

Astor-Aguilera, M. and Harvey, G. 2018. "Introduction: We have never been individuals", in Astor-Aguilera, M. and Harvey, G. (eds), *Rethinking Relations and Animism: Personhood and Materiality*. London: Routledge. pp. 1–12.
Bowman, M. 2022. "Folk Religion", in Chryssides, G.D. and Whitehead, A.R. (eds), *Contested Concepts in the Study of Religion: A Critical Exploration*. London: Bloomsbury. pp. 39–43.
Byrne, S., Clarke, A. and Harrison, R. (eds) 2013. *Reassembling the Collection: Ethnographic Museums and Indigenous Agency*. Santa Fe, NM: SAR Press.
Cajete, G. 2000. *Native Science: Natural Laws of Interdependence*. Santa Fe, NM: Clear Light Publishers.
Chryssides, G.D. and Whitehead, A.R. 2022. "Introduction: What is a contested concept?", in Chryssides, G.D. and Whitehead, A.R. (eds), *Contested Concepts in the Study of Religion: A Critical Exploration*. London: Bloomsbury. pp. 1–7.
Hallowell, A.I. 1960. "Ojibwa ontology, behaviour and world view", in S. Diamond (ed.), *Culture in History: Essays in Honour of Paul Radin*. New York: Columbia University Press.
Harvey, G. 2003. "Guesthood as ethical decolonising research method", *Numen* 50(2): 125–146.
Harvey, G. 2005. *Animism: Respecting the Living World*. London: Hurst & Company.
Harvey, G. 2017. "Performing indigeneity and performing guesthood", in Hartney, C. and Tower, D.J. (eds), *Religious Categories and the Construction of the Indigenous*. Leiden: E.L. Brill. pp. 74–91.
Harvey, G. 2018. "Adjusted styles of communication (ASCs) in the post-Cartesian world", in Astor-Aguilera, M. and Harvey, G. (eds), *Rethinking Relations and Animism: Personhood and Materiality*. London: Routledge. pp. 35–52.
Harvey, G. 2020. "Indigenizing movements in Europe", in Harvey, G. (ed.), *Indigenizing Movements in Europe*. Sheffield and Bristol, CT: Equinox. pp. 1–11.

Harvey, G. 2022. "Indigenous", in Chryssides, G.D. and Whitehead, A.R. (eds), *Contested Concepts in the Study of Religion: A Critical Exploration*. London: Bloomsbury. pp. 57–62.
Harvey, G. and Whitehead, A. 2018. *Indigenous Religions: Critical Explorations for the Study*, Vol I. London: Routledge.
Hazard, S. 2013. "The material turn in the study of religion", *Religion and Society: Advances in Research* 4: 58–78.
Ingold, T. 2006. "Rethinking the animate, re-animating thought", *Ethnos* 71(1): 9–20.
Ingold, T. 2007. "Materials against materiality", *Archaeological Dialogues* 14(1): 1–16.
Jones, A. and Boivin, N. 2010. "The malice of inanimate objects: material agency", in Hicks, D. and Beaudry, M.C. (eds), *The Oxford Handbook of Material Culture Studies*. Oxford and New York: Oxford University Press. pp. 333–351.
Keane, W. 2006. "Subjects and objects", in Tilley, C., Keane, W., Kuechler-Fogden, S., Rowlands, M. and Spyer, P. (eds), *Handbook of Material Culture*. Thousand Oaks, CA: Sage Publications. pp. 197–202.
Kraft, S.E., Tafjord, B.O., Longkumer, A., Alles, G.D. and Johnson, G. (eds) 2020. *Indigenous Religion(s): Local Grounds, Global Networks*. London: Routledge.
Latour, B. 2005. *Reassembling the Social: An Introduction to Actor-Network-Theory*. Oxford: Oxford University Press.
Neich, R. 2001. *Carved Histories: Rotorua Ngati Tarawhai Woodcarving*. Auckland: Auckland University Press.
Nye, M. 1999. "Religion is religioning? Anthropology and the cultural study of religion", *Scottish Journal of Religious Studies* 20(2): 193–234.
Primiano, L. 1995. "Vernacular religion and the search for method in religious folklife", *Western Folklore* 54(1): 37–56.
Reichel, E. 2012. "The landscape in the cosmoscape, and sacred sites and species among the Tanimuka and Yukuna Amerindian tribes (north-west Amazon) ", in Pungetti, G., Oviedo, G. and Hooke, D. (eds), *Sacred Species and Sites: Advances in Biocultural Conservation*. Cambridge: Cambridge University Press. pp. 127–151.
Roberts, M. 2013. "Ways of seeing: Whakapapa", *Sites* 10(1): 93–120.
Schmidt, B. 2022. "Syncretism", in Chryssides, G.D. and Whitehead, A.R. (eds), *Contested Concepts in the Study of Religion: A Critical Exploration*. London: Bloomsbury. pp. 129–133.
Serres, M. 2008. *The Five Senses: A Philosophy of Mingled Bodies*. London: Continuum.
Smith, J.Z. 1998. "Religion, religions, religious", in Taylor, M. (ed.), *Critical Terms for Religious Studies*. Chicago, IL and London: University of Chicago Press. pp. 269–284.
Taira, T. 2022. "World Religions", in Chryssides, G.D. and Whitehead, A.R. (eds), *Contested Concepts in the Study of Religion: A Critical Exploration*. London: Bloomsbury. pp. 141–145.
Viveiros de Castro, E. 2004. "Exchanging perspectives: The transformation of objects into subjects in Amerindian cosmologies", *Common Knowledge* 10(3): 463–484.
Weaver, J. 2015. "Misfit messengers: Indigenous religious traditions and climate change", *Journal of the American Academy of Religion* 83(2): 320–335.
Whitehead, A. 2013. *Religious Statues and Personhood: Testing the Role of Materiality*. London: Bloomsbury.

Whitehead, A. 2018. "Touching, crafting, knowing: Religious artefacts and the fetish within animism", *Body and Religion*. 2(2): 224–244.
Whitehead, A. 2019. "Indigenizing the goddess: Reclaiming territory, myth and devotion in Glastonbury", *International Journal for the Study of New Religions* 9(2): 215–234.
Whitehead, A. 2020. "A method of 'things': A relational theory of objects as persons in lived religious practice", *Journal of Contemporary Religion* 35: 231–250.
Whitehead, A. 2022. "Superstition", in Chryssides, G.D. and Whitehead, A.R. (eds), *Contested Concepts in the Study of Religion: A Critical Exploration*. London: Bloomsbury. pp. 123–128.
Whitehead, A. 2023. "Materiality and the study of Indigenous religions", *Oxford Research Encyclopaedia of Religion*. Available at: https://oxfordre.com/religion/.

About the Author

Amy R. Whitehead is Senior Lecturer in Social Anthropology at Massey University in Aotearoa New Zealand. An Anthropologist of Religion/Religious Studies scholar, her primary areas of research concern the material and performance cultures of religions, the "turn to things" in the Study of Religions, the development of new approaches to animism and "the fetish", ritual studies, Indigenous religions, and Earth Traditions (Paganisms, Goddess movements). She is the author of several journal articles and chapters for edited volumes, and co-editor of *Contested Concepts in the Study of Religions: A Critical Exploration* (Bloomsbury, 2022) with George Chryssides.

Index

Abbey, Edward 159
Aboriginal peoples of Australia 25–6, 30, 59–60, 75n
   human–plant relations 106, 109, 114
abortifacients 110, 113–15, 116
   poisonings 119
Abrahams, David 108
Abram, David 150
Achuar people 106
acorns 133, 134
action research 66–7, 68
Actor-Network Theory 7
Adjusted Styles of Communication (ASC) 8, 97–8, 100–1
   see also hallucinogenics; mediumship; spirit possession; trance
Aesop 81
Africa 30, 65, 120
   Benin 120, 181
   Kenya 66
   see also enslaved Africans
Aki dance (Mechoopda) 134, 135
Akins, Damon B. 133, 135
alder trees (t'at'am c'a) 130–1
Altered States of Consciousness 8, 97
   see also Adjusted Styles of Communication (ASC); hallucinogenics; mediumship; spirit possession; trance
Amah Mutsun Land Trust 140
Anderson, Alexander 115, 116–17, 118, 119
Anderson, M. Kat 133, 135, 137, 139, 141
Anglophone Caribbean 107, 110–11, 118, 123
   see also Caribbean
animals:
   as other-than-human persons 74, 86–7
   symbolism 74–5, 76, 87
   see also hares; other-than-human persons; rabbits
animism, as term 4, 5, 98, 147
   contested 2, 132
   distinct from relational ontology 95
   naturalistic 148, 149, 163
   see also other-than-human persons; Tylor, E.B.
anthropology 1, 2, 7, 92, 184
   methodological bias 91

ontological turn 94
   Victorian 4
   see also Tylor, E.B.
Aotearoa (New Zealand) see Māori people
appropriation see cultural appropriation
Arawak-speaking peoples 110
   see also Kalinago people (Caribs); Taíno people; Yukuana (Yukuna) people
Aristotle 77, 82
Aristotelian thought:
   procreation 77–8, 83
   plants 108
Arrernte-speaking groups 59–60
   see also Aboriginal peoples of Australia
asson (Vodôu) 121
Astor-Aguilera, Miguel 175
Atkinson, Lesley-Gail 114
Attala, Luci 112
Australia see Aboriginal peoples of Australia
'ava ceremony (Samoan) 16, 17, 17fig.
Ayuso, Avatâra 20, 21fig.
Azbill, Henry 134, 135

Bagel and Beans (coffeeshop chain) 157
Banahaw, Mount 3
basket-weaving 136, 137–8, 139, 140
BASR see British Association for the Study of Religions (BASR)
Bauer, William J. 133, 135
belief 4, 5, 64
   relationality and 65, 180
   see also animism
Bell, Emma 58–9, 61
Benin 120
   Benin Bronzes 181
Berens, William 180, 183
Berndt, Ronald 25
Bidwell, John 135
Bierwert, Crisca 154, 156
Billy, Susan 138
biosphere 148, 150, 163
Bird, Christopher 160
Bird-David, Nurit 132
Bixa orellana L. 115–16
#BlackLivesMatter 19
Blea, Chim (David Foreman) 161

see also Foreman, David
blood quantum 19, 22
Bohannon, Sarah 140–1
Boivin, Nicole 180
Borchers, Andrea T. 114
Border Crossings (multi-media theatre) 16, 20, 25, 30
Birmingham 22 Festival 20–2, 21fig.
Bowman, Marion 172–3
Brandon, George 121, 122, 123
Braun, Bruce 46
Brazil 93–4, 96–7, 98–102
  see also South America
British Association for the Study of Religions (BASR) 4, 6, 92
British Colombia see tourism
Bryman, Alan 58–9, 61
b.solomon//ELECTRIC MOOSE 20
Buddhism 150, 151, 159
Bullie's House (play) 25–6, 26fig., 27fig.
business studies 58, 70
Byrne, Sarah 171

caboclos 96–7, 101
California 130–2, 133, 134–7, 138, 140–2
  see also T.E.K. (Traditional Ecological Knowledge)
Calla, Linda 37
Camp Fire (2018) 139, 140, 141
Canada:
  history 36, 40–1, 43
  mass graves in 22
  Truth and Reconciliation Commission 15
  see also First Nations in Canada; tourism
Candomblé 93–4, 96–7, 98, 99–102
capitalism 29–30, 120, 149
  see also wealth
Cargo Cults 172
Caribbean 109, 172
  plant use in 106, 107, 109–10, 113–23
  see also St Vincent (island)
Caribs see Kalinago people (Caribs)
Carney, Judith A. 118
Carroll, Lewis 102–3
  see also Humpty Dumpty words
Cartesianism 178, 179, 80
  post-Cartesian position 184
cassava 119
cerebro-spinal fluid 77, 78, 82, 84
ceremony 23, 25
  compared to ritual 17–18
  opposition to materialist worldview 29–30
  potlatch 29–30, 40–1, 42

Changó (Orishá) 122
channeling 91, 153
  see also mediumship; spirit possession
Chico Traditional Ecological Stewardship Program 131
Chidester, David 147, 157n
Chief Seattle (Chief Stealth) 154–7
Chireau, Yvonne 118
Christianity 7, 40, 91, 135, 143, 154n
  Great Chain of Being 178, 178fig.
  Roman Catholicism 110, 119–20
Chryssides, George D. 171
Clandon Park House 56
Clark, Moe 16–17
cleft palette 80–1
climate change 28, 132, 136, 140
  see also environmentalism
Coates, Carrol F. 120
colonialism 16, 18–19, 24, 25, 109, 171, 181, 182
  "animism" as term and 147
  in California 131, 132, 134–5, 141, 142, 143
  in Canada 35, 40–1, 43–4, 45–6, 47–8, 50
  loss of ceremony and 20, 29
  research subjects and 33, 38
  Spanish 110, 114, 119, 123, 135
  tourism as 51
  see also cultural appropriation; decolonisation
Commonwealth 20
communication 95, 102, 150
  see also Adjusted Styles of Communication (ASC); human–plant relations
cosmology 173–6, 177–81
Council of All Beings 9, 149, 150–1, 156, 157–8
Covid-19 pandemic 28
Cuba see Regla de Ocá
cultural appropriation 18, 19, 20, 55
  see also colonialism
cultural relativism 181

dance:
  Aki dance (Mechoopda) 134, 135
  at Birmingham 22 Festival 20–1
  First Nations and 40–1
  haka (war dance) 57, 68
  at ORIGINS Festival 16–17
Daniel, Yvonne 122
Daoism 150, 159
Day, Frank 133
de Araújo Vilar, Daniela 115
death 30–1
decolonisation 7, 8, 50, 51, 55, 120, 124, 130n, 131, 132, 182

California wildfire zone 141–3
   Indigenous religions and 170, 171–2, 180, 181, 184
   landscapes 9
   research and 55, 57
   see also colonisation; post-colonial justice; reparations, cultural
deep ecology 150, 151
Deleuze, Gilles 7
Deloria, Vine 138
Derby, Lauren 114
Dhuibhne, Éilís Ní 83
diatopical hermeneutics 65
DiGenova, Raphael 136, 141–2
Dirks, Robert 116
Dominica 115
Druid Camp 8, 73
duppies (spirits of the dead) 118, 123

Earth Day 155
Earth First! 149–50, 151–4, 158, 159
   see also Foreman, David
Earth Liberation Front 152
Earth Maker (Mechoopda creation story) 133
Elcho Island mission station 25
electrons 70
Eliade, Mircea 98
Enlightenment, the 3, 24
enslaved Africans 109, 110, 113–15
   plant skills 116–18, 123, 124
environmentalism 1, 2, 149–51, 152, 154, 160
   see also climate change; Earth Day; Earth First!; Earth Liberation Front
Eostre/Ostara 82
ethical research:
   guesthood as 55
   protocols 38–9, 51
   see also guesthood; power, and researchers
ethnobotany 107, 114, 117
   see also plants
ethnomedicine 107
   see also abortifacients; human–plant relations; plants
Evans, George Ewart 78, 80, 81n, 83, 86
Evans-Pritchard, E. E. 91
Everson, Andy 34fig., 37, 40, 41, 42, 45, 49
evolution 151, 152
Ewe (Regla de Ochá term) 121
experiential knowledge 67

Favel, Floyd P. 15
Figueroa, Meleiza 131, 142
fire 23, 132, 135, 138, 139–41
   suppression 134
First Nations in Canada 16–17, 21–2, 39
   authenticity and 43–5, 48, 50, 51
   boundaries and 40, 41–2
   colonialism and 35, 40–1, 43–4, 45–6, 47–8, 50
   Indigenous researchers 33, 39
   Indigenous tourism 33, 34fig., 35–7, 48–9
   myth 81
   see also Canada; Native Americans
Flood, Gavin 60
folklore 1, 8, 75, 172, 173
   see also hares
Fon people (Benin) 120
Foreman, David 158–62
Foucault, Michel 3
Frazer, J.G. 76
GAFA Arts Collective 16
Gagliano, Monica 112
Gaia 9, 148–51, 152, 157, 158–60, 162–4
Geertz, Clifford 2
gender paradigms 84–5
   see also procreation
Gervase of Tilbury 80
Gilbert, Helen 18
Gilroy, Paul 108
Giraldus Cambrensis 82
Glastonbury Goddess movement 176, 177, 177fig., 184
Global History movement 7
Goetzinger, Alix 37, 40, 43, 44, 45, 50
Goode, Ron 140
Goodman, Marcio 101–2
Gough, Julie 20
gourds 121
Gramsci, Antonio 2
Great Chain of Being 178, 178fig.
Grimes, Ron 3
Guattari, Félix 7
guesthood 4, 9, 17–18, 55, 57, 170, 182–5
   alternative approaches 62–4
   Māori 33–4, 55–8, 92, 93
   as phenomenology 58, 61, 70–71
   as research approach 33, 34–5, 37–9, 49–51
   trust and 68, 70
   see also hosts; relationality

Habermas, Jürgen 66
Haiti see Vodôu
haka (war dance) 57, 68
Hallowell, Irving 92, 94–5, 96, 101, 102, 103, 132, 179, 183
hallucinogenics 107, 112–13

see also Altered States of Consciousness; human–plant relations
Han, Byung-Chul 30
Hankins, Don 135, 139, 141
hares 73, 74, 75–6
　cleft palette 80–1
　virility 76–7, 78–81, 82, 83–4, 85
　witches and 82–4, 85
Harvey, Graham 7, 9, 91–2, 93, 108, 132, 143, 147–8, 178
　on Adjusted Styles of Communication 8, 97–8, 101, 103
　appearance 77
　career 1–2, 6, 7
　at Druid Camp 73
　druidic attitude 87
　on guesthood 33, 34, 38, 49, 50, 51, 55–8, 61, 62, 68, 70, 71, 92, 170, 182–3, 185
　on Hallowell 95–5, 132
　on indigenising 176–7
　on Indigenous religions and 170–1, 172
　on interspecies relationality 75
　on language 47
　on material religion 3–4, 169, 173, 179, 180, 181
　on naturalistic animism 148, 149, 163
　and ORIGINS festival 7–8, 15, 16, 18, 20
　on "persons" 95, 102
　on plants 106–7, 111, 114, 120, 123–4, 160
　podcast with 4–5
　on research methods and colonisation 55
　at Riddu Riđđu festival 22–3
　on "things" 175–6
　Totem Latamat and 26–7, 28, 28fig., 29, 31
　writing style 39
Hazard, Sonia 179
Heaney, Seamus 23
Heisenberg, Werner 69
Héritier, François 84
hermeneutics 58–9
　diatopical 65
　of suspicion 3
　see also phenomenology
Hill, Dorothy M. 137
Hillman, Leaf 140
Hinemihi (whare) 56
hippies 158
Hippocrates 82
Hispaniola 114
　see also Vodôu
Hogan, Linda 98, 111
hosts 17–18, 57–8, 61, 68, 70
　see also guesthood

human–plant relations 106–7, 114–15, 123, 131, 133–4, 135, 136, 137, 138
　fire and 141
　through ingestion 112–13
　see also ethnobotany; plants
Humpty Dumpty words 92–3, 94, 102–3
Husserl, Edmund 60–1

imperialism 18, 19, 24
　see also colonialism
incorporation (mediumship) 100–1, 103
indigenising movements 19, 20, 176–7
"Indigenous", as term 170–1
Indigenous scholarship 33, 39
Indigenous Tourism see tourism
Indigenous Tourism Association 35
　see also tourism
Ingold, Tim 75, 96, 184, 185
interpolation 59, 60
"interpretivism" 58
　interpretive knowledge 68

jackalope 78, 78fig.
　sex change 85–6
Jamaica 110, 113–14, 118
Jewett, Donald 133
Jívaro (Shuar) people 106, 111–12
Johnson, Paul C. 4, 176
Jones, Andrew 180
Jotï people 107, 113

Kaiser, Rudolf 154, 155, 156–7
Kalinago people (Caribs) 110, 115–16, 123
Karuk tribe 140
　see also Native Americans
Keeper, Alec 179
Kelly, Éamon 23
Keneally, Thomas 25
Kenya 66
Kimmerer, Robin Wall 19, 138, 162
Kittredge, George Lyman 82
Konkow Maidu 130n, 133
　see also Native Americans
Korea 30
Kraft, Siv Ellen 170, 171
Krieger, David 65
Kristensen, W. Brede 60
Kwakwaka'wakw people 41
　see also Native Americans

Lacumí (Lucumí) 110, 172
Ladder of the Intellect 178, 178fig.
Lake, Frank K. 140

Landry, Timothy R. 120
land-tending 131, 132, 138-9, 142
  fire as 139-41
language 5, 18, 34, 35, 39, 47, 179
  groups 110, 171
  as problem in sprit possession 100-1
Latour, Bruno 3, 4, 5, 179
Law, John 3
Layard, John 80
LeDrew, Naulaq 20
Leopold, Aldo 149, 162
Lévi-Strauss, Claude 81
linguistic turn 2
Logue, Christopher 18
Lopez, Valentin 140
Lovelock, James 148-9, 150
Lucumí (Lacumí) 110, 172
lwa (Vodôu sprits) 121

Macy, Johanna 150-1, 152, 157
Madley, Benjamin 135
manioc 111-12, 121
Māori people 16, 18, 55-8, 132, 173, 178, 180, 182, 183
  guesthood (marae protocols) 33-4, 55-7, 92
  plant use in 106, 109
  Ratana religion 172
  Tāne (god of the forest) 174, 176
  whakapapa 169, 170, 173-4, 182
marae 33-4, 55-7, 92
Margulis, Lynn 148, 150
maritime customs 74, 75, 76, 84
Martin, Tsimka 37-8, 40, 44, 45, 46, 47, 48-9, 50
material religion 3-4, 169-70, 174, 179-80
  "animist materialism" 2
  knowing and 181-5
  material turn 172-3
  see also material religion
Mathisen, Stein R. 43
Matthews, Maureen 179
McKay, Mabel 134, 137-8
McLellan, Gordon 31
Meares Island 45, 46, 46fig.
Mechoopda tribe 130, 132-3, 134, 135, 136-7, 139
  see also Native Americans
Meders-Knight, Ali 130-1, 132, 133, 134, 136-7, 138-9, 140, 141, 142, 143
mediumship 98, 1002, 103
  see also channeling; spirit possession
Meine, Curt 162n
menstruation 76, 78, 82, 106

see also procreation
Mesoamerica:
  migration from 109, 110
  plant use in 106
  see also Caribbean; South America; Totonac culture
Middleton Manning, Beth Rose 142-13
mines 74, 76, 84
Minn, Pierre 121
Miwok people 134
  see also Native Americans
Moisseeff, Marika 84
"mola" (molar pregnancy) 81-2
more-than-human persons see other-than-human persons
more-than-human world 133
  aee also other-than-human persons
mortality 30-1
Morton, Nancy 160
mugwort (múnmuni) 136-7
Muliaumaseali'i, Sani 16, 17
Murdoch, Rupert 30

Native American Church 172
Native Americans 130-13, 154, 156
  at ORIGINS Festival 16
  Standing Rock 19
  Zuni ceremonials 159
  see also First Nations in Canada; Chief Seattle
Nelson, K'odi 37, 41
Nevins, M. Eleanor 132
New Age 153
New Zealand see Aotearoa (New Zealand)
Ngāti Porou 55
Ngāti Rānana 16, 55, 56
Nhat Hanh, Thich 151
Norgaard, Kari Marie 135, 140
North America 106, 109
  see also First Nations of Canada; Native Americans
Norway 22-3
Nuu-chah-nulth people 44, 46
  philosophy 39
  see also First Nations of Canada
Nuyumbalees Cultural Centre 41
Nye, Malory 4, 171, 177

oak trees 133-4
Obatalá (Orishá) 122
Obeah 107, 109, 110, 118-19, 123
objectification of research subjects 33
objectivity 55, 57, 63-4, 68, 70-1

O'Connor, Jim 149, 151–2
Ojibwe ontology 94–5
Omieros (Regla de Ochá ritual) 122–3
Onians, Richard B. 77, 78–9
ontology 3, 94, 101–2
Organicism 148, 149
    see also Gaia
ORIGINS Festival 7–8, 15–16, 18
    at COP-26 28
    Pocahontas 25
    political role 19
    Welcoming Ceremony 16, 17–18, 19–20
Orishás (orixás) 93, 95–6, 100–2, 120, 121–3
Ortiz, Bev 134, 137, 138
Osain (Orishá) 122
other-than-human persons 9, 19, 29, 92, 94–6, 102, 103, 108–9, 180, 181
    animals as 74, 86–7
    Council of all Beings and 151, 152, 153
    plants as 106, 1078, 111–12, 113, 118–19, 120, 121, 122, 123, 132–3, 136, 137, 138
    shamanic practices and 150
    spirits and gods as 91, 92
    see also wider-than human (w-t-h) persons
Ozains (Regla de Ochá ritual) 122

paganism 1, 2, 73, 76, 136
    David Foreman and 161
    Gaian movement and 158–9
    ORIGINS Festival and 19
Panikkar, Raimundo 65
pantheism 158, 160, 161
Papua New Guinea 172
Park, Peter 66, 67–8, 70
Patton, Laurie 62, 63, 64, 70
Peacock Flower 113, 116
Pena Branca (Candomblé) 97
Pentangelo, Joseph 80
Perdibon, Anna 28n
Perry, Edward 155, 156
Peru 111, 112
    see also Achuar people; Jívaro (Shuar) people
Peters, Josephine 137
phenomenology 55, 70, 96
    of religion 58–61, 71
    see also hermeneutics
Philippines 3
photons 69
plant-human relations see human–plant relations
plants 8–9
    abortifacients 110, 113–15, 116
    in Māori cosmology 174
    medicinal 111, 112, 114, 115–18, 120–1, 123, 124, 130–1, 136–7
    as people 106, 107–8, 111–12, 113, 118–19, 120, 121, 122, 123, 132–3, 136, 137, 138
    ritual and 107, 109, 118–19, 121–3, 124, 134, 142
    sentience 160
    as spirits 112–13, 120, 121
    uses 109–11
    see also human–plant relations
Plato 23–4
Pliny the Elder 82
Pocahontas 25
Pohatu, Maaka 16
politeness 87
Pomo people 134
possession see spirit possession
post-colonial justice 19
    see also decolonisation
Postlethwaite, Pete 15, 16
potlatch 29–30, 40–1, 42
Pou carvings 175, 175fig., 184
    see also whakairo (carving)
pounamu (greenstone) 174, 183, 184
power, and researchers 34
    see also ethical research; guesthood
practical knowledge 67
presentational knowing 67
Primiano, Leonard 172–3
procreation 83
    Aristotelian beliefs 77–8, 83
    analogous activities 74
    gender paradigms and 84–5
    hares and rabbits 76, 80, 81, 83–4, 85–6
    "molas" (molar pregnancy) 81–2
propositional knowing 67

quantum mechanics 55, 69–70
Queen Nanny 118

rabbits 74, 75, 76, 84
ranga (totems) 25–6, 27fig.
Ratana religion 172
Raymond, Rosanna (Sister Spacific) 15–16
Reason, Peter 66–7
REDO project 2
Regla de Ochá 107, 110, 118, 119–20, 121–3, 172
Reichel, Elizabeth 173
    see also guesthood
relationality 87, 169, 169–70, 185
    cosmologies and 173–6, 177–81
    distinct from animism 95

interspecies 75
guesthood and 70
relational research 55, 64, 65–71
relationships 98, 102, 182
    with fire 140, 141, 143
    human–plant 106-1, 114–15, 123, 131, 133–4, 135, 136, 137, 138
    with inanimate objects 94–5
    with land 142, 143
"religion", as term 171, 182
    "world religion" 172
"religioning" 171, 177
Religious Studies Project (RSP) 5, 6
reparations, cultural 181, 182
residential schools (Canada) 35, 47
Return to Earth Ceremony 27, 28, 28fig., 29, 31
Riddu Riđđu festival 22–3
Roberts, Mere 174
Rodríquez Vázquez, Emilio 99
Roman Catholicism 110, 119–20
Rose, Debbie 107, 114
Rossi, Carlo 71
Round River Rendezvous 149
Routlette, Roger 179
Rovelli, Carlo 8, 55, 68–70
Ryder, Sophie 85, 85fig.

Said, Edward 24
Salish nation 154, 156
    see also Chief Seattle
Samoa 15, 16
    'ava ceremony 16, 17, 17fig.
Santería 110, 121, 122
Sarris, Greg 134
Savin Juniper 114
Scala Naturae 178, 180
Schiebinger, Londa 111, 113, 114, 118
Scrivan, Marcia 76, 77fig.
Seed, John 150–1, 152, 157
Segal, Robert 62–4, 68, 70
Sellars, Peter 30–1
semen 77, 82, 83, 84
    see also procreation
Serres, Michel 184
sexual identity 84
shamans 92, 97, 98
    non-human personhood and 150
    plant shamans 112
    sacredness of nature and 159, 161
    see also spirit possession
Shepard, Paul 159
Shipino people 107, 112
Shuar (Jívaro) people 106, 111–12

Smith, Henry 154, 155–6
Smith, Linda Tuhiwai 33, 39, 47, 55
Smith, Wilfred Cantwell 60, 62
Social Science Medicine Africa Network (Soma-net) 66
songs 41, 59
Sørensen, Jesper 109
Soul Vine 1112
South America:
    Brazil 93–4, 96–7, 98–102
    plant use in 106, 109, 110, 111–12, 114
    see also Jotï people; Shipino people; Taíno people; Tanimuka people; Yukuana (Yukuna) people
Spanish colonialism:
    California 135
    Caribbean 110, 114, 119, 123
spirit possession 8, 91, 92, 93, 98
    in Candomblé 93–4
    as inadequate term 94, 97, 99, 100, 103
    see also channeling; mediumship; shamans
spirits 121
    azizà (forest spirits) 120
    of the dead 118, 123
    see also channeling; mediumship
spirituality 9, 24, 33, 39, 143
    nature 148, 149, 151, 156, 157, 158, 161, 163
St Vincent (island) 107, 110, 118
    Botanical Garden 110–11, 114, 115–16, 117, 123
Standing Rock 19
Starhawk 159
statues 179
"status and non-status Indians" 43
Stonehenge 2
Strehlow, T.G.H. 59–60
Strong, Pauline Turner 94, 98
suicide 119
superposition (quantum mechanics) 69
sweet potato (kumara) 174, 176

Taíno people 107, 110, 113, 114
Tajford, Bjørn Ola 19
Tāne (Māori god of the forest) 174, 176
Tanimuka people 173
taniwha (guardian) 174
Tann, Mambo C. 121
taonga (treasure) 182
Taves, Ann 103
Taylor, Douglas 115, 138
T.E.K. (Traditional Ecological Knowledge) 130, 131, 137, 138–9, 142
    basket-weaving 136, 137

Terrapolitan Earth Civilisation 164
textualism 2, 3
theatre 30–1
"things" 175–6, 184, 185
Thomas, Tana 37, 39, 41, 44, 45, 46, 47–4
Thomson, David 78, 80, 81n, 83, 86
Tiburcio, Jun 26
time, Māori concept 174, 182
Tla-o-qui-aht people 48–9
Tofino 49
Tompkins, Peter 160
Totonac culture 26, 29, 31
   see also Totem Latamat
tōtara tree 174, 175fig., 184
Totem Latamat 26–7, 28, 28fig., 29, 31
totem poles 34fig., 40, 41–2
touch 184
tourism 8, 33, 34fig., 35–7
   boundaries 40, 41–2
   guest-researchers and 37–9, 49–51
   guide motivation 47–9
   tourist expectations 43–7
trance 8, 93, 94, 98
   as inadequate term 94
   see also Altered States of Consciousness
translation 39, 47
Truth and Reconciliation Commission
   (Canada) 35
Tylor, E.B. 2, 4, 5, 98, 132, 147

U'mista Centre 41
Umbanda 96, 99, 101
uncertainty principle 69

Vancouver Island 41
Venezuelan Guayana 113
   see also Jotï people
Verbena Fields 130, 131, 132, 133, 134, 136–7, 138, 140–2
vernacular religion 172–3
   see also material religion
Verstehen 58, 59, 60, 61, 62

Vickers, Roy Henry 37, 39, 45
Viveiros de Castro, Eduardo 3, 184
Vodôu 107, 110, 118, 119–21, 123

wealth 41
   see also capitalism
Weaver, Jace 171–2
Weigel, Matthew James 21
welcoming ceremonies 29
   Birmingham 22 20–2, 21fig.
   ORIGINS Festival 16, 17–18, 19–20
whakairo (carving) 174, 175–6, 175fig.
whare nui 55
whare tipuna 55
white hegemony 156
Whyte, Kyle Powys 132
Wicca 159
wider-than human (w-t-h) persons 108–9, 118–19, 120, 121, 123, 124
   see also other-than-human persons
"wilderness" as construction 45–6
wildfires 9, 135, 139
   decolonising 141–1
willow (c'ipa) 130, 133, 134, 136
   Glastonbury Goddess movement 176, 184
witchcraft:
   Obeah seen as 109, 118
   witches 82–4, 85
World Fair 156, 157
"World Religions" as term 172

Yellowstone National Park 159
Yemayá (Orishá) 122
Yorùbá people 120
Young, George 115–16
Young, Tom 141
Yukuana (Yukuna) people 106, 173
   see also Arawak-speaking peoples

Zeilinger, Anton 69
Zent, Eglee 113
Zuni ceremonials 159

www.ingramcontent.com/pod-product-compliance
Lightning Source LLC
Chambersburg PA
CBHW062040220426
43662CB00010B/1586